TO SPEED ON ANGELS' WINGS

John Scally

To speed on angels' wings
THE STORY OF THE SISTERS OF ST JOHN OF GOD

the columba press

First edition published in 1995 by
the columba press
93 The Rise, Mount Merrion, Blackrock, Co Dublin, Ireland

Cover by Bill Bolger
Origination by The Columba Press
Printed in Ireland by Colour Books Ltd, Dublin

ISBN 1 85607 144 8

Contents

A Note to the Reader   9

1   Dates from the Diary   11

2   New Beginnings   20

3   A Divine Comedy?   39

4   A Passage to Australia   64

5   Changing Times   90

6   Finding Life in the Margins   121

7   Ripples in the Pool   143

8   Crossing the Channel   162

9   Out of Africa   163

10 The Winds of Change   205

11 Wandering between Two Worlds   223

Selected Bibliography   235

Acknowledgements

I would like to thank everybody, too many to mention individually, who has helped me directly or indirectly in the preparation of this book. In particular I would like to thank Helen Maher and Columba Howard for their consistent encouragement and practical support and friendship to me during my trips to Wexford. My thanks also to Stasia Clancy, the world's greatest cook, for her wonderful hospitality and to Teresa Finnegan for her practical assistance. I would also like to thank Brid Ryan and Mary Ryan for their work in co-ordinating my 'Irish tour'. During my visits to Pakistan and Australia I was overwhelmed by the welcome I received from the sisters. I would like to thank Corona, Verna and Michelle in particular for co-ordinating my travel arrangements and their many kindnesses. I am indebted to my good friend Dr Werner Jeanrond for directing me to this research project initially and his many helpful suggestions in improving the manuscript. I am grateful to Oliver Doyle and Fintan Morris for their assistance in my research.

Finally, my thanks to all the sisters who shared their stories with me so honestly and for their wonderful hospitality. The poem opposite is for them. I am grateful to Brendan Kennelly for permission to reprint it in full.

The Good

The good are vulnerable
As any bird in flight,
They do not think of safety,
Are blind to possible extinction
And when most vulnerable
Are most themselves.
The good are real as the sun,
Are best perceived through clouds
Of casual corruption
That cannot kill the luminous sufficiency
That shines on city, sea and wilderness,
Fastidiously revealing
One man to another,
Who yet will not accept
Responsibilities of light.
The good incline to praise,
To have the knack of seeing that
The best is not destroyed
Although forever threatened.
The good go naked in all weathers,
And by their nakedness rebuke
The small protective sanities
That hide men from themselves.
The good are difficult to see
Though open, rare, destructible;
Always, they retain a kind of youth,
The vulnerable grace
Of any bird in flight,
Content to be itself,
Accomplishing master and potential victim,
Accepting what the earth or sky intends.
I think that I know one or two
Among my friends.

A Note to the Reader

For many years, sisters have been saying, 'We should write our history.' When we have shared something of our John of God story with colleagues and friends, they too have been asking, 'Is this recorded?'

Following the Second Vatican Council, when we began to re-appreciate the charism of the Congregation and to get in touch again with its history and foundation, we came to a new aware-ness of the power of story to energise and inspire.

I believe that the publication of *To Speed on Angels' Wings, The Story of the Sisters of St John of God* is timely. Much has changed since Visitation Clancy and her companions came to Wexford at the invitation of Bishop Furlong, to begin the Congregation.

Social conditions are different, as is the understanding of religious life, and the role of women in church and society. Sisters of St John of God today must ask, and are asking, 'What does the call "to nurture the faith view of life" ask of us at this time?' Sisters will welcome this book with gratitude and find inspiration and consolation in the unfolding story that is still being written by their lives.

Another obvious and significant change that has occurred over the years is that today many lay people participate enthus-iastically and creatively in areas of ministry that were once con-fined to the sisters. For them, too, the book offers the opportunity, not just to learn about the factual history, but to capture some-thing of the spirit of the Congregation from early times.

I am very grateful to all who have encouraged and supported the writing of this history. It has been a joy to work with the author, John Scally. His enthusiasm for the project, and his obvious belief that this was a task well worth doing, made him the ideal choice as author. He carries his expertise in theology, and his accomplishments as writer, teacher and broadcaster, very lightly indeed, but his giftedness is evident in the book.

I would also like to express our indebtedness to Werner Jeanrond who not only acted as editor but encouraged us to undertake the task of writing our history and introduced us to the author.

Finally, our thanks are due to Seán O Boyle and the staff of The Columba Press who have been most helpful and courteous in bringing the book to publication.

May *To Speed on Angels' Wings* be enjoyed by all who read it.

Sr Helen M. Maher
Superior General
8 April 1995

CHAPTER ONE

Dates from the Diary

'Nothing matters but the quality of the affection – in the end – that has carved the trace in the mind.' (*Ezra Pound*)

24 April 1994

All seem soaked in a heavy despondency as if some totally melancholy spirit broods over the place. Flies feast on the sea of slurry, and the buzz of their relish produces a faint hum in the air. It might have been the Sahara desert rather than a *basti* (slum) in Lahore. Poverty is sucking the vitality out of it as a bee sucks honey out of a flower. The *basti*, foul-smelling and decrepit, is a monument to broken hearts and foiled aspirations, to innumerable tales of sadness and dawning shreds of hope. It is easy to imagine that the stinking stench would upset the stomach of a horse.

There are thousands of *basti*s like it throughout Pakistan, and every one tells the same story. Illness. Hunger. The death of hope. A person, it is held, can become accustomed, but poverty for these people is a recurring nightmare. In the *basti*, as in most places, money, or more precisely the lack of it, makes all the difference. It is difficult not to succumb to a great sense of the desolation of life which sweeps all round like a tidal wave, drowning all in its blackness.

She walks to the corner of the room, where the sick child lies tossing to and fro in the bed. Tasmin is now in the full grip of fever. She is two weeks old, a pale little thing with black eyes set in a small face. She is drenched in sweat and the blue towel near her head is quite wet. The baby's little hands jerk convulsively outside the tiny blanket. She looks pathetically small in the bed, a tiny martyr in the grip of illness. Instinctively the sister is terribly afraid.

As if by magic the baby falls asleep again; an uneasy fitful sleep, marked by pained little whimperings that cut like swords of sorrow into the sister's heart. Occasionally, the little body twitches convulsively as if it is going to break into little pieces. Every time it convulses, the sister leans forward anxiously as if beseeching God to allow her to bear the stabs of pain that needle through the little creature. Although her eyes are closed, the baby is sweating profusely.

From time to time her mother leans forward to wipe the baby's face and neck with the soft towel she keeps nearby. A few days earlier she had felt the cold of death spread through every limb and bone in the baby's twin sister until she was very cold and stiff. It was only then that the torture had left her face and a soft peacefulness set on it like a child on a Christmas card. That night the mother's screams tore like knives into the heart of silence, ripping it relentlessly asunder. There was an animal-like quality to her wailing, powered by notes of horrifying, intense pain and desperation. Her screams fell like a sentence on the room.

The sister's patience seems infinite. Time does not matter, for her it doesn't exist. For her the universe is centred in that child so small that she scarcely ruffles the blankets. She sits beside baby Tasmin, listening to her breathing, feeling her body twitch slightly as her restless mind flees through the corridors of her dreams. Occasionally she strokes her forehead. So delicately light is her touch, her fingers scarcely seem to fondle the baby's fingers. They are like frail fingers of gossamer brushing her tiny hands. Sr Michelle MacHale's vigil of love continues.

12 January 1911

The first rays of daylight flooded the Australian city of Broome. There had not been a drop of rain for weeks now, and the earth was parched. The fields were as hard as rock, and the grass was withered and burnt. Everyone longed for a cool, refreshing shower of rain, but the possibility was very limited. The locals had to endure the dual affliction of dust and heat. This was the busiest part of the day, when the carts rattled noisily through the streets and the high-voiced Japanese fishermen shouted salutations to each other in their amiable way. The sweat rolled from their faces and covered their straining bodies.

The heat was a mere inconvenience by comparison with the other problems in the community – the twin plagues of small-pox and typhoid. Moreover, in this community the number of people injured, often paralysed, in diving accidents was exceptionally high. As a response to this, a Japanese hospital was established. An immediate problem was to secure adequate nursing staff. An appeal was made to a predominantly nursing order from Ireland which had become the first Congregation of sisters to work with the Aboriginals.

They had begun in a bark-roofed hut, with flapping pieces of canvas for doors, and slits in the walls for windows. They slept on stretchers with no mattresses and their furniture was make-shift. In 1907 a missionary had reported to the aborigines department that the sisters 'maintained about sixty children, feeding and clothing them. They had sixteen half-caste children from Broome. The school was run by two sisters and had thirty-five children and about three hundred adult aborigines under the influence of the mission.'

Although they were seriously short-staffed, the sisters responded positively to the request from the Japanese. This was a gesture typical of a Congregation whose entire history had been a succession of fresh starts and new trials. It is the story of a group of women who live the philosophy: 'They only go forward by not standing still.' The sister chosen to answer the call of the Japanese was a young Irish woman.

She became swamped by heat and disease. The typhoid was like a worm gnawing her inner life, undermining and corroding it. She joined her hands together to still the trembling. Her heart, a heart of great passion, beat irregularly as if it belonged in some other body. Finally it beat no more.

All her life was a prayer, a recurring aspiration that soared into the heavens and came to rest at the feet of the almighty God. Now twenty-five-year-old Mary Immaculate Leahy would begin her eternal life.

Postscript

Such was the admiration of the Japanese people for her selfless-ness and heroism that they erected a Celtic cross in the Japanese cemetery in Broome in memory of the Irish sister who gave her life nursing victims of typhoid. Today this cross remains as a poignant, and appropriate, reminder of a woman who embodied the Christian virtue of loving without counting the cost, and who tragically paid the ultimate price.

This tombstone opens questions for the group of women who follow in her wake, about their history and identity, and goes even further to some secret compass points which steer them to somewhere they do not know – crossing boundaries where sadness and hope meet so dramatically. To walk in this graveyard one cannot but try to listen to the secrets of lives gained and lives lost, strange riches and sadness. It has a music of its own. The notes which enter one's consciousness are not as might be expected, notes of loneliness, poignant cries of quiet despair, but notes of inspiration and encouragement. Through this cross a woman long dead lives again, somehow speaking to years that belong to people not yet born.

Symbols give us our identity, self-image, our way of explaining ourselves to ourselves and to others. Symbols determine the kind of history we tell and retell. In the Christian tradition the cross is the ultimate symbol. The Celtic cross in Broome is perhaps the symbol *par excellence* of the Congregation of sisters which Sr Immaculate represented.

7 p.m. 13 November 1940

The battle of Britain is at its height. With the fall of France Britain stood alone and Hitler firmly believed that the war was almost over and that the British Prime Minister, Sir Winston Churchill, would be forced to make an ignominious peace. Churchill though had rallied his people with his stirring oratory: 'Upon that battle depends the survival of Christian civilisation. Upon it depends our own British life, and the long continuity of our institutions and our empire. The whole fury and might of the enemy must very soon be turned upon us … Let us, therefore, brace ourselves for our duties, and so bear ourselves that if the British Empire and its Commonwealth last for a thousand years, men will still say, "This was their finest hour."' Hitler had therefore decided to invade Britain 'to eliminate the English mother country as a base from which the war against Germany can be continued.' The battle, which began on 13 August 1940, would

ultimately depend upon the struggle for control of the air between the Luftwaffe and the Royal Air Force.

The British had made many preparations for the expected attack. The Local Defence Volunteers, also known as the Home
Guard, later affectionately known as 'Dad's Army', were
formed. Barbed wire, anti-tank devices and pillboxes were erected
along the coast. At first the Germans concentrated on daylight
raids on ports and airfields, using bombers protected by fight-
ers. However, this policy was not yielding the desired results as
the daylight raids were leading to heavy losses, so the Germans
changed tactics. Accordingly, they switched to night raids on
London and other large cities in an effort to break civilian
morale so that Churchill would have no option but to surrender.
On sixty-seven nights out of seventy-eight between 7 September
and 13 November, London was bombed in lengthy attacks.
During September and October alone there were over sixty
thousand casualties.

As darkness falls in the city of Bristol people brace themselves
for another air raid. Some had lost their homes and were searching for somewhere to lay their weary heads at night. They simply
carried their few belongings in a bag over their shoulders. The series
of human tragedies is evident in the tears, the heavily lined faces,
the letters to loved ones that can never be written and the aching
hearts for those gone to their eternal reward. The laughter is
gone from their eyes – not in the least surprising since those eyes
have seen many disturbing images because of the bombings: the
hideous outlines of charred human beings, empty eye-sockets,
teeth gritted with unbearable pain and flesh disintegrated into
mud-like form. Faces were bruised and swollen – young people
who look old. People who had joked and laughed and who were
full of the joys of life are suddenly transformed into creatures of
fear. It is impossible to describe the tension, the fear, the concern
people have for their families.

Some of the walls are covered with a horrible blackness.
Some of the buildings are now totally burned out – mere shells.
All their windows are gone. For those lucky ones whose homes
are untouched, there are many hardships to be endured.
Rationing of fuel, consumer goods and food is the order of the
day. Transport is problematic. It is difficult to keep up morale.

Sr Dolours McSweeney shivers in the frosty night air. Another hour left of her daily twelve hour shift of 'war duty', when she, with her colleague Sr Nativitas Power, are in charge of the air raid precaution station at Lodge Causeway in Bristol. Suddenly the siren goes off. The radar system has detected an enemy bomber. As she lies flat on the floor, Sr Dolours recites her rosary despite the handicap of wearing a gas mask. Anger rises within her because so many innocent lives are at risk. When the raid is over, she rushes out to put sand bags on a building catching fire from an incendiary bomb.

30 November, 1969

It is easy to feel overwhelmed. The equivalent of the population of an entire city is condensed into a makeshift camp, created overnight. This quiet, peaceful corner is home to tens of thousands of Biafrans who took flight from the civil war and genocidal slaughter that erupted when the Ibo leader, Colonel Odumegu Ojukwu announced the secession of the Eastern Region from Nigeria and proclaimed its independence as the Republic of Biafra on 30 May 1967.

The camp/city grows daily as people flee their native land each day to seek refuge. Only the lucky ones have the luxury of bringing with them whatever possessions they can carry. Their journey has been extremely traumatic and hazardous. Fleeing the slaughter, many have travelled by foot, through difficult terrain, for days upon days without any shelter and with insufficient food, arriving at the camp exhausted and in poor health. At the height of the crisis, so many corpses litter the roads and fields that the survivors no longer bother to move them – unless they are relatives or friends. People are left lying where they fall. More have died today than yesterday. Some had planned for it by climbing under their reed mats to die so that others could tie them up more easily. In this vision of hell, at night the living and dead lie together. It is as if the very ground is infected by the dying.

There are widespread epidemics due to poor sanitation and overcrowding. So far there has not been an outbreak of cholera, but measles and meningitis are rampant. A score of men, women and children sit in silent expectation around the food tent – a few have their hands out in supplication. They are destined for a disappointment. There will be no food until the morning. One of the children frantically seeks out a grain of spilled rice from the dust on the ground. Bliss would be biscuits and rehydration salts.

For miles around, the trees have been disappearing, fed into pitiful cooking fires. One corner of the camp is assigned for the dead. They lie in neat rows; some have their mouths ajar after what had been a painful end. When the weather hots up some of the corpses begin to bloat and burst. The children die the quickest in this latter-day slaughter of the innocents. It is always the weakest who lose out.

One little girl is getting special treatment. She was rescued from being buried alive when she was noticed moving amongst a pile of corpses tossed into the mass grave. Fear spreads like an eager germ through the camps that have doubled, then doubled again, in size.

The civil war has exposed the most profound shortcomings in the international preparedness and willingness to respond to such crises. The exodus has not taken the refugees to the promised land. The media are notable by their absence.

Dr Samuel Johnson once described marriage as 'the triumph of hope over experience'. Had he been in the aid camp, he would have extended the range of that maxim to include the work of the Sisters of Saint John of God with the refugees.

They are grossly understaffed, have inadequate equipment and medicines and are working in the worst possible circumstances, as part of a reactive relief-effort fighting to contain and then control the epidemics in this human tragedy. This illiterate, chiefly rural, population's most basic wish is a good meal for themselves and the surviving members of their families. Full bellies are nothing but a luxury for the survivors, frightened after living through three years of bloodbath in their country.

A round-the-clock service is provided lest disease and starvation exact a toll that even the most savage soldiers could not. Sr Carmel Dunphy bends over a young boy running a high fever and wipes flies from swollen eyes. He is dressed in torn rags, a shrapnel wound on the back of his leg reeks of infection. His eyes are empty, waterless like the rest of his body, and the sister cannot find a vein to insert the intravenous tube that could save him. The force of love, of unexpected and invigorating innocence, moves the woman. Only true love carries memorial weight, regenerates moments of tenderness, of unions of spirit. Such a love is never encountered in stony walls or architectural masterpieces rising to an impassive sky. The sister does not wish to build memorials to the dead but to give food to the living. The secret of life is that only in love for the living is the spirit praised forever.

25 October 1872

In the final scene of the medieval epic *La Chanson de Roland*, the great Christian hero Charlemagne sat exhausted in Aix, his battles with the Moors over. According to the poem, he was more than nine hundred years old. An angel wakened the old man from his sleep and told him to get up again and return to battle because the work would not be finished until the end of time. Charlemagne sighed, *'Dieu, si penuse est ma vie.* (O God how hard is my life). The work of the hero remains unfinished but who will do it if not he?'

It is highly unlikely that twenty-eight-year-old Visitation Clancy's reading material included *La Chanson de Roland*, but she certainly would have been able to identify with the sentiment. She sat in her new home, the little cottage at Sallyville in Wexford, which was the mother house, the only house, of the new Congregation she had established, the Infirmarian Sisters, later the Sisters of Saint John of God.

It was not an auspicious beginning for herself or the sisters in her care – they had no money and their furniture was entirely borrowed. The only thing they had going for them was the dedication of the sisters who had come to work in Wexford, moved by the terrible poverty and living conditions of so many Irish people. Heroism is often the bastard child of intense sorrow or need.

The sisters, prompted by love of God, had got involved in nursing the sick in their homes. This love would be a lamp for their steps and a light for their eyes. But in quiet moments like this, when Visitation sat before the Lord, she wondered what the future had in store for this fledgling Congregation for which she had responsibility. To herself the years ahead would bring many trials and sufferings. The utter poverty of the early years, her arduous work of organising, solidifying and extending the Congregation, the fatigues of travelling, and the failures of two early foundations, Carrick-on-Suir, and Kilmacthomas, almost broke her frail physical strength. But the most acutely painful sorrow of all would be the difficulties that would arise with three of the pioneer sisters. These, Sisters M. Aloysius Grey, M. Stanislaus Grey, and M. Joseph Costello, would eventually leave the Congregation in 1875.

Update

Over a hundred and twenty years later, the Congregation has grown and flourished. Visitation's legacy is apparent in missions in Pakistan, Australia, Africa, England and Rome, and in the life and work of women like Michelle MacHale, Dolours McSweeney, Immaculata Leahy and Carmel Dunphy. As we shall see in subsequent chapters the Congregation now faces difficult questions and challenges.

This is the extraordinary story of a group of women. The story is still being written and the end is uncertain. The beginning of the story, though, was fraught with difficulties – at a time when Ireland was in turmoil.

CHAPTER TWO

New Beginnings

This land, where every woman's son
Must carry his own coffin and believe,
In dread, all that the clergy teach the young
(*Austin Clarke*)

The Ireland of the 1840s was a vision of hell – the years of a tragedy beyond belief when over a million people on this tiny island died from famine. Nothing prepared people for it. Nothing could prepare anyone for the sight and smell of death on a massive scale – bundles of corpses where once there had been life. This traumatic time left many legacies, both positive and negative, in the Irish psyche. One of the most enduring is that it created an empathy on the part of Irish people to others who were subjected to great suffering. Many who lived through that time were moved to alleviate the pain of others. Among their number was the Bishop of Ferns, Thomas Furlong. Part of his response in the years which followed was to work for the establishment of a nursing Congregation in his diocese who would care for the poor in the workhouses and in their homes. Against this background, the Sisters of Saint John of God were born.

Stereotypes have done a great disservice to Irish history – none more so than that which depicts Ireland as a priest-run society. The clergy have never had it all their own way in Ireland. Towards the end of the eighteenth century, for example, a bishop in the West of Ireland was afraid to disclose the fact that Rome had suppressed a number of festivals in honour of Our Lady, lest the news should provoke a riot. The Irish have always been delighted to follow their clergy – provided they are leading where the Irish want to go!

Another stereotype is that of 'traditional Irish Catholicism' as if Irish Catholicism was a homogeneous entity. Historically there has been much more discontinuity and variety than unity in Irish Catholicism.

The story of the establishment of the Sisters of St John of God in 1871 cannot be told without reference to the context of the time. However, the Ireland of the period was a maze of inter-locking problems. It was also an era of upheaval on many fronts. To understand this turmoil it is necessary to look back briefly at its prequel, though it is impossible to do justice to the richness of historical development in a thumbnail sketch.

Celtic Christianity

Christianity had established itself as the predominant religion in Ireland by the middle of the sixth century. The legacy of this per-iod is still in evidence through pilgrimages to holy places. Although the stereotype of 'saints and scholars' is more than a little idealistic, the early centuries brought a great flowering of the religious imagination: a keen sensitivity to the link between faith and the environment, a strong emphasis on the local and largely autonomous Church (with a healthy scepticism towards Roman decrees), a thirst for learning of both the scriptures and secular knowledge, and a recognition that all (including women) had a role to play in the Church.

The Reformation shook continental Europe to its very found-ations, but Irish Catholics, like many of their European counter-parts, retained much from the medieval Church, keeping many practices that the reformers did away with, including their devotion to Our Lady and the saints and especially their Mass, celebrated in Latin by counter-reformation priests trained in continental seminaries.

As Patrick Corish has impressively documented in his study, *The Irish Catholic Experience*, (1982) the seventeenth century was a profoundly unhappy one for the majority of Irish people, be-cause many Catholics lost all their property and were subjected to great cruelty at the hands of the English forces in Ireland. Protestants suffered from many atrocities as their Catholic neighbours sought to exact revenge. The legacy of this century lingers maddeningly to this very day, particularly in Northern Ireland. Another damaging, perhaps the most damaging of all,

stereotype emerged: 'Popery' meant treason and the killing of
Protestants – 'Protestant' meant loyalty to the British crown and
hatred of Popery. Each took their identity from their opposition
to the other.

In the face of these waves of disasters, the institutional
Church was forced to be innovative with the result that pastoral
need rather than canonical adherence was the dominant force.
Baptism, matrimony, and the funeral rites were centred where
people were born, lived and died – in the home. This tradition
survives in certain parts of the country. New places of pilgrimage sprang up. On the down side, there was a worrying growth
in superstition.

In the eighteenth and nineteenth centuries, the institutional
Church began to pick up the pieces with a new emphasis on
obedience to Church authority and, as the century progressed,
to civil and ecclesiastical authority. The focus was on regular
sacramental practice, centred on the Sunday Mass and regular
rounds of prayers and devotions, especially to the Blessed
Virgin Mary. As anti-Catholic laws were gradually relaxed in
the nineteenth century, Catholics became more prosperous and
the laity were able to finance the building of new churches.

The Romanisation of Irish Catholicism

Where Catholicism was the established religion in continental
Europe, nationalistic forces tended to limit the influence of the
papacy. Nowhere was this tendency more apparent than in
France. The same situation did not pertain in Ireland as Rome
classed Ireland as 'missionary' territory. The Vatican favoured a
hands-on approach to these 'missionary' territories, and in 1622
had established the Congregation of Propaganda to keep a
paternalistic eye on them. Ireland remained under its direct
sphere of influence until 1908. Right through the eigthteenth
century, close links were maintained between Rome and the
Irish Church, through the internuncio in Brussels. This Roman
connection offset the fact that so many Irish clergy received their
education in France. Thus in the nineteenth century, Ireland had
a closer affiliation with Rome than any other country in northern
Europe.

As the special status of the institutional Catholic Church in parts of continental Europe came under threat in the wake of the Enlightenment and the French Revolution, Catholics felt threatened by the cold winds that were blowing around them and sought shelter from Rome. As a consequence, the spiritual authority and prestige of the papacy grew ever stronger.

In the Irish context, the man most responsible for this development was Paul Cardinal Cullen. Cullen was born in 1803 and had gone to a seminary in Rome at the age of seventeen, where he remained until his return to Ireland as Archbishop of Armagh in 1850. The most telling insight into his philosophy was his observation that to be absolutely loyal to the Pope was simply to be a good Catholic.

A National Synod, the first since the twelfth century, was held at Thurles in 1850. This was legally binding, with the full authority of Rome behind it. In the aftermath of the Synod, as everywhere in the Catholic Church, the number of priests was growing and they were more tightly disciplined. Cullen wrote to his colleague, Archbishop MacHale: 'We cannot avoid, I dare say, making some regulations for the clergy, secular and regular, and commencing to remove any abuses that may have sprung up in the times of persecution.'

In reality, there was nothing in Thurles that had not been laid down at Trent. Up to that point, the Tridentine reforms in their entirety had been difficult to enforce in Ireland. After Thurles, Ireland followed the path of Catholic Europe. The changes were most obvious in the life of the priest. From 1850 he was to be a man apart, clearly distinguished by his black dress and Roman collar, prayerful, devoted to a life centred on his Church and the focus of sacramental life for his people.

However, as late as 1880, Archbishop Croke reported that the Blessed Sacrament was not generally reserved in smaller churches. The older tradition of the administration of the sacraments of baptism, penance, and matrimony in private houses remained. Wherever there was a deeply rooted popular interest, the local priest was relatively powerless to counteract it, such as local customs at wakes and agrarian violence.

Freed from the shackles of the Penal Laws, the Catholic Church in Ireland went through a great period of institutional expansion in the nineteenth century. This century was a water-

shed in the history of the Church. Its legacy is still with us.
Centralisation was seen to be the one great guarantee of orthodoxy, indeed centralisation and orthodoxy were eventually
synonymous, not alone in the strong emphasis given to Papal
primacy, but throughout the entire fabric of the Church. This
was reflected in the neglect of the imaginative and aesthetic elements and an impatience with challenging questions and even
constructive criticism. Dissenting voices were anathema and
freedom was relegated to minor status.

The institution moved firmly to the centre stage with all the
strengths and limitations that this involved. Two generations
later, Patrick Kavanagh would react against an over-institutionalised religion which failed to see Christ outside the institutional
structures:

> Yet sometimes when the sun comes through a gap
> These men know God the Father in a tree:
> The Holy Spirit in the rising sap,
> and Christ will be the green leaves that come
> At Easter from the sealed and guarded tomb.

Pope Pius IX in his *Syllabus of Errors* (1864) condemned much
liberal thought, materialism, indifferentism (the belief that one
religion is as good as another), socialism, communism, Free-
masonry, natural science, secular education and the separation
of Church and State. Peadar MacSuibhne, Cullen's biographer,
claims that Cullen's appointment as bishop and primate was a
move on the part of Rome 'designed to strengthen the unity of
the Irish hierarchy'. It is a richly suggestive phrase, signifying
taking control and imposing his will. Cullen wanted to central-
ise all power in himself by having bishops, priests and lay people (even in politics) obedient to his will. A journalist later reported:

> There was to be no priest in politics – except bishops; no bish-
> op in politics – except archbishops; no archbishop in politics
> – except the Apostolic Delegate.

Cullen, and the bishops who shared his philosophy, lived by the
law. Religion was law. In the eleventh century Pope Gregory VII
had claimed that believers got to heaven by obeying the law.
Cullen would have been in perfect agreement with this idea. A

telling indication of Cullen's mindset was his first impression of 'his' cathedral in Armagh. He was really shocked to see that, in defiance of the liturgical laws, there was on the altar at Mass only one candle, of tallow, not beeswax. He wrote to a friend: 'Imagine what it must be elsewhere.'

The law was the mechanism by which Irish Catholicism was to be 'revived'. That mentality, where law had such importance in Irish Catholicism, would endure for over a century. While Cullen was successful in piloting the Church in the direction he hoped, there were dangers with this approach, for it tended to reinforce an image of God as lawmaker rather than as a loving presence. Little wonder that, almost a hundred years later, Brian Moore would begin one of his short stories: 'In the beginning was the word, and the word was NO!' This sentence cleverly sums up the experience of those who were brought up to see Catholicism, Irish-style, in a painfully negative way.

Last Among Equals

In the nineteenth century, the Catholic Church was an important agent of social change, establishing schools, hospitals, asylums, temperance agencies for the purpose of 'evangelising and civilising the poor'. Throughout this period Irish women entered convents in great numbers. Traditionally the life of the woman religious was one of contemplation and the cloister. This changed with the Counter-Reformation when congregations of women religious were established to participate in more active works of charity, chiefly in teaching and nursing. With the formation of the Daughters of Charity by St Vincent de Paul in 1633 a trail was blazed for subsequent orders of women religious dedicated to the active apostolate. In Ireland the pioneer in this respect was Nano Nagle, who was spurred on by the need to provide education for the poor.

Historical marginalisation was the fate of these women. One noteworthy feature of Irish historical records is that there is no central or even diocesan register of all the women who took religious vows in a particular period. In marked contrast, all the regular and secular clergy in the country are listed on a diocesan basis in the Catholic directories of the time. Nuns were relegated to peripheral status – their contribution was valued to the extent to which they were an assistance to the clergy.

In the 1870s, the famous Dominican preacher Thomas Burke undertook some publicity on behalf of the Catholic Church. He described the aspiring nun as 'the high-minded, the highly-educated, the noblest and the best of the children of the Church ... the young lady with all the prospects of the world glittering before her, with fortune and its enjoyments all around her.' It is most unlikely that the majority of women entering religious life were brought up with the silver spoon, whatever about being 'high-minded and good'.

Why did so many women enter religious life? A number of possible explanations present themselves. A desire to serve God and people in need was the main reason, but Catriona Clear, in her acclaimed study *Nuns in Nineteenth Century Ireland*, (1987) suggests a number of other possible reasons: a response to the evangelical 'crusade' of the time, the search for personal and spiritual fulfilment, a more attractive alternative than married life or an escape from particular problems and situations. A stereotype has developed of women fleeing the 'real world' for the sanctuary of the convent. While that may have been true in some cases, equally religious life was arguably the only possible career open to talented Irish women at the time.

Irish nuns had in some respects a privileged, even powerful, position in the nineteenth century by virtue of their prestige in society and freedom to work solely on their apostolate without obligations to family or husband. This respect was hard-earned, the fruit of unremitting work, undemanding service, and passive acceptance of second-class status in the institutional Church for both themselves and their ministry. In 1845 a contemporary observer described nuns as 'pious ladies who have forsaken all of the worldly pomp and grandeur for the sake of God'. While a religious sister renounced rights over property and had opted to exclude herself from 'social life', her social standing and her ministry in a socially-approved area of activity, were greater than that allowed to married women. However, in the Roman Catholic Church nuns were last among equals of those who took vows because they were denied any position of power in the institutional Church as a whole.

This should not provoke surprise, given the traditional prejudice of leading Church figures throughout history against women. Augustine claimed that although a woman's mind was equal to that of man, her spirit could equal his only when she denied her 'femaleness', i.e. abstained from sexual intercourse. Jerome stated that women were as different from men as body from soul, but that they could attain spiritual parity with men by serving Christ as virgins. Thomas Aquinas went further and declared that the female was essentially defective – a misbegotten male.

The women who were revered in the Roman Catholic Church's tradition transcended the 'limitations' of their sex, notably the Blessed Virgin Mary or prominent female celibates. Married women, like the overwhelming majority of married men, were deemed too close to carnal realities to be realistic candidates for holiness and sanctity. Nuns were the institutional embodiment *par excellence* of the caring, self-sacrificing and essentially subordinate celibate females. Male ecclesiastical attitudes to nuns oscillated between the extremes of misogyny and respect.

These nuns were remarkable women doing remarkable work in a difficult time. The tragedy is that their stories have never been told. So many heroic women's stories are woven almost anonymously in the tapestry of history, even though they deserve individual recognition. Most Irish nuns fit into this broader pattern.

It is instructive to consider the institutional Church's attitude to the newly-established Ladies' Land League, as an indication of its attitude to women at the time. The organisation was set up in January 1881 and by May had 321 branches. The women became responsible for a detailed register known as the 'Book of the Kells'. This was a record of every estate, the number of tenants, the rent paid, the official valuations, the name of the landlord or the agent, the number of evictions that had taken place and the number that were still pending. The register was compiled from weekly reports sent in by the country branches. The Ladies' League was also active in relief work – when notice of a pending eviction was received, a member travelled to the area with money for assistance.

The League quickly fell foul of the institutional Church. This was not perhaps surprising given that involvement of women in

such a political group was entirely new. Archbishop McCabe of
Dublin denounced the organisation and in the same breath re-
called the traditional modesty of Irish women and the splendid
purity of St Brigid. He went on to state that the proper place for
women was 'the seclusion of the home'. In a letter read at all
Masses in the Archdiocese of Dublin in March 1881, he continued:

> But all this is to be laid aside and the daughters of our
> Catholic people are called forth, under the flimsy pretext of
> charity, to take their stand in the noisy arena of public life.
> They are asked to forget the modesty of their sex and the high
> dignity of their womanhood by leaders who seem utterly
> reckless of consequences ...

Hard Times

If the nineteenth century was a watershed in the life of the Irish
Church, it was equally a milestone in socio-political life in
Ireland. The most traumatic event of all was the so-called 'Great
Famine' in 1847. The mid 1840s saw the plagues of Ireland –
hunger, disease and government neglect. Each plague com-
pounded the other like a battleground of contending dooms.
Fragile lifelines of aid reached only a minority of the population.
In the first year there were barely enough potatoes, in the next
only a trickle. Then nothing. Potato stalks withered and died.
There was nothing for seed. Many people had nothing to live on
and nothing to live for.

The death toll was seemingly unending in many districts.
Everything had to be rationed. It would have taken too much
land to bury the corpses individually so their relatives normally
buried them in mass graves. There were so many people dying it
was impossible to make coffins for them all, or even have a coffin for each family. Timber was very scarce. Sometimes villagers
decided to build one proper coffin with a sliding bottom. They
solemnly put the corpses into the coffin, carried them up to the
grave, slid back the bottom of the coffin and the body tumbled
into the grave. The coffin was brought back to the village and
passed on to the family of the next casualty.

Fear was the only real sign of life as people died slowly in agony. To the embattled, emotionally bankrupt and hopelessly disorganised, the ordinary joys and sorrows were an irrelevance. For many, death was a welcome escape from pain and heartache. The afterlife was the only dream they could still cherish. For the strong, life was a victory over death. Where possible the corpses were buried under hawthorn trees – because of their alleged special favour in the eyes of God. These trees were long palls in a parched place. They sang a lament to the angel of death. The memories were too sad ever to be healed.

Ireland was a country of extremes. It seemed simultaneously connected to the Garden of Eden in the landlords' palaces and, to some, a foretaste of doomsday destruction where the peasants lived to die. Nowhere were the gardens more luxuriant or a people more miserable. The tragedy was a moral test which those with power failed.

Deep in their psychic memory the famine was still a painful experience for Irish people right through the nineteenth century and beyond. People used the words 'I'm famished' whenever they were cold or hungry. The frequent usage of these words was just one symptom of the lasting effect of the famine. Often Irish people buried their thoughts of the famine deep in their subconscious. The story of the famine years was so horrific they just wanted to erase it from memory. There was great shame attached to failing to feed one's family. Parents blamed themselves for their children's death. Succeeding generations had inherited their shame. Even in the twentieth century, some people in rural Ireland would not travel anywhere without bringing a piece of bread in their pocket because the fear of hunger was so strong.

The term 'Great Famine' is itself a misnomer. It is more accurate to say there was a 'Great Starvation'. Famines are caused by natural disasters. There are no famines when there are large quantities of food in a country. There was plenty of food produced in Ireland during those years. That food was exported while people starved, in the country's greatest human tragedy, is an enduring monument to inhumanity, ineffectiveness and indifference.

There were two main options open to these people: emigration if they could afford it, or the poorhouse/workhouse. In many respects they thought they were safer in their own place. There was so much disease in the 'coffin ships' that chances of surviving a long journey in such a weak state were remote. People by and large did not trust the sea. They heard the story of the American sailing ship, *Stephen Whitney*. On a foggy December night in 1847 the ship, sailing on a voyage from America to Bristol, was wrecked off the Irish coast on Bolig Rinn na mBeann on the Western Calf Island. Within days ninety-four bodies were washed up on the beaches. Some people were desperate enough to try anything, but the majority preferred to meet their maker on their own land rather than on the other side of the Atlantic Ocean.

Nobody knows how many people went on the coffin ships. The one reliable statistic is about a group who went to Canada where they all died of typhoid fever in a place called Grosse Ile just outside Quebec City. Twelve thousand Irish people were buried in mass graves in Canada. They set out to make their mark in the world but the only mark they made was in a grave – a people with no name. It was their final indignity.

The workhouses had a huge stigma attached to them. Like the infamous coffin ships, there was so much disease in the workhouse that to sign into the place was often to sign one's death warrant. Generally the poorhouses postponed death for a short while, but no more. In the poorhouses and soup kitchens families were separated from each other. All the men were housed in one section, the women in another. There were separate places for babies, young children, young girls and boys. Once a family went in, they might never see each other again. There were strict rules about communication with another section. If one person broke the rules the whole family might be thrown out. Through speaking Irish in the workhouses, people could sometimes pass on messages without their masters knowing what was being said. In many ways the poorhouse was worse than jail. At least in jail you could get news from your family. It has often been claimed these places could have been called deathhouses.

In the years of their holocaust, the one ally ordinary people had was their faith. The Catholic faith was like a six-inch nail: the harder it was struck, the deeper it got embedded into the timber. There was a story told about the Virgin Mary walking by a house in the West of Ireland on a stormy night. She and the child Jesus had no coat to protect them from the elements. As they passed the house, the woman of the house called them inside and gave Mary a bowl of nettle soup and an old sack to give extra cover to the Child. Mary's final blessing was that the family line would always remain intact. They were one of the few families who survived the Great Hunger. A sign that God's favour rested on them was that their rooster did not crow 'cockadoodledoo' but rather *'Mac na hóighe slán'*, 'the Virgin's Son is risen'.

Irish people had the strength and resilience to outlast the Vikings, Cromwell the cursed, and the Great Starvation. Hardship and degradation were often their second homes, but somehow they always pulled through. God was as close to these people and their joys and sorrows as any other member of their family.

The shadow of an Empire

Ireland had been governed from Westminster since the Act of Union in 1800. In the House of Commons there were about a hundred members who represented Irish constituencies. The Viceregal Lodge in Dublin's Phoenix Park was home to the Queen's representative. The Chief Secretary and his staff administered the daily routine of government from Dublin Castle.

One of the main problems faced by administrators in Ireland in the nineteenth century was to reconcile democratic principle with the continuation of ascendancy privilege. County grand juries were non-elective bodies drawn from the largest landholders in the county. Local government was in the hands of the grand juries. The British army had an important and visible presence throughout the country. The Royal Irish Constabulary was an armed body, though the Dublin Metropolitan Police was not.

The close connection between Britain and Ireland made it seem natural to judge by English standards and, in comparison with England, Ireland was still a poor country. In the conventional portrait, the most familiar figures are the greedy and tyrannical landlords squeezing every last penny of rent out of hungry peasants to finance their life of debauchery. While there were a number of such landlords, they were not all like that. The evil was not all on one side. Southern Protestants were slow to forget the stories they had been told of the fanatical fury waged against Protestants during the 1798 Wexford rising and the social intimidation of Protestants which had persisted for years afterwards.

The second half of the nineteenth century saw the gradual extension of voting rights in both Britain and Ireland. For the first time, the demand for votes for women was being made with conviction. In the Irish context an important milestone was the introduction of the secret ballot after 1872 since it relieved voters from pressure by landlords to vote according to their dictates.

The education system was imperialist rather than Irish, with the prescribed reading books filled with Victorian values and designed to inculcate British loyalties. However, there were a number of counterbalancing forces at work, particularly the press. By 1860 national papers were available cheaply following the repeal of heavy taxes on the newspapers. *The Nation*, founded by Thomas Davis, carried on its national tradition in the 1860s. Songs formed an important agent of political evangelisation, notably 'God Save Ireland' which became virtually a national anthem in 1867.

The Irish national pulse was strengthening perceptibly. The demand for self-government was being made with more vigour. Political structures were not as secure as they had been. The old establishment was being challenged in various ways. In the country the stirrings could be seen among the tenant farmers.

Throughout rural Ireland, agrarian unrest accelerated with increasing demands for tenant rights reforms. Landlords were seen as a privileged minority, alienated from the majority of their tenants by differences in both religion and politics. Tenants normally held their holdings from year to year, thus having no security. In times of bad harvests, many could not afford to pay the rent. A high number of landlords were absentees, living outside the country and leaving the management of their estates to agents. The great disaster of the famine was followed by mass evictions of tenants. The need for reform of the system was becoming more obvious in the years that followed.

In 1870, a formal demand for Home Rule began when Isaac Butt, a lawyer and member of parliament, founded an association to campaign for a separate Irish parliament. However, the movement really only began in earnest when Butt was replaced as leader by Charles Stewart Parnell, a charismatic figure whose tactics brought increasing success to nationalist members of the House of Commons and eventually succeeded in making the 'Irish question' the central issue in British politics.

Mary Eugenia Brennan, SJG, in her 1989 study of *The ecclesiology surrounding the foundation of Saint John of God Sisters*, perceptively and colourfully observed:

> Looking at the history of Ireland in the twenty years between 1860 and 1880 is like looking at the patch visible under a magnifying glass placed on a Galway shawl. The mesh of fibres all have their origin and conclusion beyond the frame of the glass. There are dominant fibres. The dominant fibres and 'knobs' of colour are more sharply evident than the background mesh of holding fibres. The dominant fibres would include: 'The land question', poverty, 'Home Rule', Education, Church – Catholic and Protestant, and the Fenians. 'Knobs' of colour would include Archbishop Paul Cullen, Archbishop John MacHale, Charles Stewart Parnell, Michael Davitt, Jeremiah O'Donovan Rossa, William Gladstone, Benjamin Disraeli, James Stephens, Terrence Bellew MacManus, Fr Patrick Lavelle, The Manchester Martyrs, and Clarkenwell.

The barrel of a gun?

For a long time people who talked about the origins of the Irish State did so in very simple terms. Nationhood was won through the barrel of a gun in a David (virginal/pure) and Goliath (dark/demonic) struggle. The 1919-21 War of Independence was the final episode in a whole series of attempts including Grattan's volunteers in 1782, the 1798 rebellion, the bold Robert Emmet 'the darling of Eireann' in 1803, the Young Ireland rising in 1848, the militant revolution of the Fenians in 1867, the 1916 Rising ('A terrible beauty is born'), and the War of Independence. In this perspective there was only one problem in Ireland – the British presence. The way to get rid of this presence was by violence.

As Brian Farrell incisively demonstrated in his groundbreaking work, *The Irish Parliamentary Tradition*, (1977) the reality is much more complex than the illusion. As the experience of many countries, established in the wake of the collapse of the great colonial empires after World War II, demonstrated, to start a nation-state from scratch is very difficult. A number of things need to be in place before nationhood can be sustained, such as literacy, a civil service, civil administration, roads, schools etc. Farrell identifies three essential prerequisites for nationhood: religious freedom, ownership of wealth and participation in the electoral process. Ireland had achieved these conditions in advance of the War of Independence.

Under the Penal Laws, Irish Catholics were denied religious freedom because of the prevalent belief at the time throughout Europe that in Church-State relations you proved your loyalty to the king by being part of the established religion. In 1829, following Daniel O'Connell's election in a by-election in Co Clare, Catholic Emancipation was won.

1832 was the year of the Great Reform Bill, which was a very minor bill in itself. It increased the number of people who could vote to two and a half per cent of the adult male population. Its importance was more for what it promised in the future than what it delivered in the present. Although it was to take almost a hundred years for women to get the vote, the bill began a process which eventually brought universal adult suffrage. The 1918 British Representation of the People Act was a crucial milestone along the way, as it removed the property qualification on the right to vote.

As John B. Keane's wonderfully evocative play, *The Field*, demonstrated, land is crucial to Irish people not just in economic terms but in terms of identity. Irish people waited for centuries to own their land. The Land Acts of 1870 and 1881 began the process by which Ireland was transformed from a nation of peasants to a nation of landowners.

By a supreme irony, the Act of Union, which so many Irish people considered anathema and fought so long and hard to abolish, was step-by-step turning Ireland into a modern state. Each of these important advances was achieved by an Act of parliament. Thus in the second half of the nineteenth century, on many different levels, change was driving Irish life like a great engine. When Thomas Furlong was made Bishop of Ferns he had to face many challenges.

A man for all seasons

Thomas Furlong became Bishop of Ferns in 1857 (the diocese of Ferns was founded in 633 by St Aidan), and held that position until his death in November 1875. Born the only son of James Furlong and Biddy Bent, probably in 1802, Thomas Furlong was a native of Mayglass, Co Wexford, where it was said his parents had 'occupied a good position as landowners'. This seems a remarkable fact given that so few Catholics were landowners at the time. One of the problems with checking out anything about Furlong's life is the lack of source material, a difficulty compounded by the fact that much of the diocesan archives of the period were lost, largely because of a lack of a permanent home for them. They were frequently moved from place to place.

Left motherless at a very early age, Furlong was reared by relatives. In 1814 he entered the seminary at Wexford and remained there until his departure in 1819 for St Patrick's College, Maynooth. One of his teachers was Dr MacHale, subsequently to become Archbishop of Tuam and the greatest thorn in the side of Archbishop Paul Cullen. Although he was ordained as a priest for the Diocese of Ferns in 1826, Furlong remained at Maynooth until 1857 where he served variously as professor of three different faculties, humanities, rhetoric and theology, until his appointment as bishop.

Little is known of his early life. He would have made a fascinating subject as a psychological profile because he spent so much of his life without any significant contact with women – motherless so early in his life and spending so many years in all-male institutions. Perhaps the loneliness he must have felt did give him both a sympathy and an empathy for those who suffered – qualities that were to lead to practical action when he became bishop. On the positive side, he did have a lifelong friendship with his cousins, the Whittys, where at least he had some contact with women.

In the light of controversies about the appointment of bishops in Ireland without the consultation of clergy or laity, it seems astonishing to read, that 140 years ago, Irish priests had such freedom. At a gathering of the priests of the diocese of Ferns, in Enniscorthy, to vote for the bishop of their choice in September 1856, Thomas Furlong received 21 out of 36 votes. Archbishop Cullen appeared less than enthusiastic about his selection. Writing to Monsignor Kirby at Rome, Cullen remarks 'his (Furlong's) ideas are not easily known'.

Furlong felt that the laity were lax in their religious duties and much given to drunkenness and disorder, especially on fair days. He sought to encourage greater participation by the laity in the life of the Church and to improve the educational, religious and social facilities of the diocese. In one important respect, Furlong shared Cullen's vision – he believed that the continued existence and development of the faith in Ireland depended on a system of education which was essentially Catholic. As a result of his time in Maynooth, Furlong, like Cullen, was keenly interested in the extension of a Catholic system of education and, on becoming bishop, he immediately set about taking action.

Drunkenness was, in his view, the most serious social ill of the day and so he set in motion a number of reforms which would limit the number of occasions on which drink could be purchased. Patterns, fairs and market days were deemed unworthy of all God-fearing Catholics as they were the chief occasions on which drink was taken.

He had a great interest in the clergy of his diocese. It is believed that his concern for clergy stricken with illness was one of his main reasons for introducing a nursing Congregation into his diocese. His first aim on becoming bishop was to provide churches so that the faithful could give due worship to their God. During his time as bishop the number of churches in the diocese rose from forty to ninety.

The Church in Ireland in the later nineteenth century was a Church which became more institutionalised, more clericalised, and more tightly under the control of Rome. However, Furlong did not passively row in with the forceful stance of Cardinal Cullen in this respect, and accordingly was labelled as 'smacking of Gallicanism'. In 1873 he defined his own understanding of infallibility:

> I prefer to say for myself that bishops who are placed over their flocks by the Holy Ghost to govern the Church of God,

are the divinely authorised interpreters, each for his own flock, of the divine law, and that the mandate of the bishop, resting on the authority of the word of God and its ablest and wisest expounders, is the only rule by which all directors of conscience can be guided.

Although Furlong attended the first Vatican Council in 1870, he was not willing to cast a vote in favour of papal infallibility, nor was he prepared to vote against it. Accordingly, he was one of a number of delegates who came home early.

In the many pastoral letters Furlong published between 1857 and 1875, the importance of the sacraments and their accessibility to the people is repeatedly emphasised. The priest's mission centred increasingly on his church, with the church becoming the centre of the parish for the dispensing of the sacraments. In this respect Ferns fitted into a nationwide pattern of a more institutionalised Church. Furlong is a fascinating man because he was at once a man of his time and ahead of his time, anticipating in thought and action some of the principal emphases of Vatican II.

Furlong would leave a big impression on his diocese. In 1871 he was also to change irrevocably the lives of a group of Dublin-based nuns. In the best Irish tradition, the circumstances of this event were bizarre, to say the least.

Mother Visitation Clancy

Bishop Thomas Furlong

CHAPTER THREE

A Divine Comedy?

In the beginning was the dentist!

Although one might expect all human life to be found in a dentist's waiting room, it still comes as a surprise to find that in such a setting the Sisters of Saint John of God reached an important stage of their development! A chance meeting in the summer of 1871 in a dentist's waiting room between Bishop Furlong and two members of the Congregation of Bon Secours, based in Mount Street in Dublin, Brigid (later Visitation) Clancy and Margaret Byrne, was a milestone in the establishment of this new Congregation – though the vital first contact had been made earlier.

Brigid Clancy had previously met the bishop at the residence of a Mr Doyle of Maudlintown, Wexford, where she had been sent to nurse the old gentleman. Furlong was a frequent visitor to his residence and was impressed by the young nun's dedication. They tentatively explored the possibility of a 'Foundation of Nursing Sisters' in the Diocese of Ferns. Between the Wexford and Dublin meetings, Brigid had discussed this with other Irish women in the Bon Secours convent. Other women had shared Brigid's dissatisfaction about the French nature of the living arrangements in the convent and the exclusiveness of the Bon Secours' mission to the wealthier classes. In the dentist's surgery, Bishop Furlong was told of five Irish sisters of Bon Secours who would volunteer for the new Congregation. Both parties had different agendas. These women were unhappy with the restrictions of the Bon Secours' rule. The bishop was seeking assistance for the sick and needy in his diocese.

For his part, Bishop Furlong did not let the grass grow under his feet and visited Paul Cardinal Cullen with a view to obtaining 'his approbation for the foundation of a new Congregation in his diocese'. Furlong felt obliged to approach Cullen because the Bon Secours Sisters were based in his diocese. By another coincidence, two of the sisters in question had just nursed one of the Cardinal's nephews, also a priest, which had given the Cardinal both a prior knowledge of the disquiet among the Irish sisters in Mount Street and a profound admiration for their commitment to their ministry. This hastened the granting of approval for the founding of the Congregation. Both bishops had something to gain from this development – Cardinal Cullen had removed a thorn from his side in the sense of an unhappy community in his own diocese, while Furlong obtained the services of a group of women committed to the task of serving the sick in the diocese of Ferns.

However, all did not run smoothly. The Bon Secours posted Brigid to Paris for a short time and some of the others were transferred to different convents. Of the two remaining, one got necessary money for the train fare to Wexford from, according to the Annals, a 'Mrs Moloney while out on the marketing business for the convent'.

A tale of two cities

The Bon Secours Sisters were founded in Paris by Josephine Potel and eleven companions in 1824 and by the Bishop of Paris, Monsignor de Quelon, with a special concern for the more prosperous section of the population. In due course they were invited to Ireland and established themselves in Mount Street in Dublin. Dublin was a handsome, well-laid out city with wide streets, elegant squares and many fine buildings. Situated as it was between the mountains and the sea, a pleasant and comfortable life-style was the reality for the upper and middle classes.

In the back streets the picture was very different. Grinding poverty was the lot of many, due largely to chronic unemployment. Just a stone's throw from Georgian elegance, the multitudes lived in dreadful conditions with much over-crowding and poor sanitation. Upward social mobility was virtually non-existent, with the poorest groups having the least hope of improving their position. Within the city and its suburbs, people were deeply divided by both religion and social class. Although in the second half of the nineteenth-century Catholics were getting a tiny foothold in the professions, Protestants were over-

represented in these circles and in the more prosperous commercial arenas. The chronic unemployment was largely due to
the high numbers of unskilled workers. Casual work was all that
was generally available to them. Lacking secure employment, at
best they lived on the edge of acute poverty.

Their distress was regularly exacerbated by bad weather. The
chief medical officer of Dublin Corporation described the public
house as the 'poor man's club'. The Poor Law system was the official relief agency. Charitable organisations prominent in the
city included the Society of St Vincent de Paul and the Sick and
the Indigent Room Keeper's Society. A trip to Sandymount
Strand or to the Phoenix Park was a major outing for the poor.
Families were large; it was common to have ten children though
infant mortality was high. In the 1860s, there was a dramatic increase in the number of pawnshops, indicating the dependence
of the poor on this expensive form of credit.

Although some Irish sisters had entered before the Bon
Secours came to Ireland, they quickly attracted Irish sisters to
their convent in Dublin – but all were not destined to live happily
ever after.

Professor Patrick Corish, in his booklet to mark the centenary
of the Sisters of St John Of God in 1971, observed: 'As was only
to be expected, there were some problems in adapting a French
community to Irish conditions, problems sufficiently severe to
disturb and even to some extent divide the community.'

This is at best a massive understatement. The community
was divided to a considerable extent, leaving a long legacy of
bitterness. The split generated a wave of correspondence, most
of which has been preserved, particularly that to Cardinal
Cullen. There is no mistaking the depth of feeling and pain on
both 'sides'. It was clearly a traumatic and bruising experience
for all concerned and one from which it would take a long time
for the pain to be exorcised.

If anybody ever doubted that historiography is about interpretation, it is illuminating to read the contrasting accounts of
the circumstances of the establishment of the new Congregation,
known initially as the Infirmarian Sisters. While the Annals of
the Sisters of St John of God depict the four founding sisters
(who remained) as virtual saints, the history of the Bon Secours

Congregation describes them as 'dissidents'. Similarly, while the St John of God Sisters celebrate October 7, 1871 as their date of foundation, the Bon Secours note that on the same day in Mount Street 'many *Te Deums* were sung' – with relief that they were finally free of these 'troublemakers'.

Sister M.Visitation Clancy was then twenty-eight years of age. She was born in Fermoyle, Ballyouskill, Co Laois in 1842, and had entered the Bon Secours Sisters in 1863. Visitation had no hesitation in agreeing to the bishop's request to form a new Congregation, and was confident that more of the Irish sisters in Mount Street would willingly follow in her footsteps. Her superiors were, to put it at its kindest, understandably less than enchanted about this development but the bishop and Visitation were not to be dissuaded. On 7 October 1871 the first sisters arrived in Wexford.

There was no fanfare to mark the founding. The sisters had one shilling and sixpence between them. The bishop arranged temporary accommodation for them at the Convent of Mercy and on 25 October they moved to a little cottage at Sallyville which the bishop had obtained for them. The Sisters of Mercy provided them with beds and chairs and the community of Reparation Sisters presented them with a table. Apart from Brigid Clancy, the pioneer sisters of the future Congregation of St John of God, were sisters M. Philip Barron, M. Kevin Byrne, M. Angeline Renehan, M. Joseph Costello, and M. Aloysius Grey and M. Stanislaus Grey, who were siblings.

The first Constitutions of the fledgling Congregation were approved by Bishop Thomas Furlong on 5 November, 1873. The document reflects the spirituality of the time:

> Abnegation of self comprises humility, self denial, and perfect disinterestedness, makes us accept without trouble all the humiliations and fatigues of our state, teaching us to regard as a precious treasure the coldness and rebukes with which we are often repaid. That which is lowest and most disgusting to nature should be looked upon as the most desirable part of our duty, nothing being more essential to the humble servant of Jesus Christ crucified than forgetfulness of self. (art 17)

Sallyville Cottage

There is also a definite note of pragmatism:

> If purity of soul and all that regards it are of such importance, cleanliness of person should be regarded and practised as an emblem of it. Therefore it is obligatory that the sisters should have the invalid kept perfectly clean, and the sick room ventilated and kept in order. The more the air they breathe is contagious the more they must use precautions against catching the infection or bringing it to the Community. For this the best and most necessary precaution is extreme cleanliness. (art 18.)

The Pomegranate

It was Bishop Furlong who provided the name of the Congregation. According to the Annals it came to him in a dream. John Ciudad was born in Montemor-o-novo, Portugal, in 1495. He spent almost all of his life in Spain from the time he left his home in Portugal at the age of eight. Drawn by the prospect of travel and adventure, he joined the army. He found the adventure he craved but not in the circumstances he would have wished. He narrowly escaped death by hanging, as punishment for the theft of the army's booty that occurred while he was the sentry on duty. The noose was already about his neck when a superior revoked the death penalty and ordered that John be released.

When he completed his stint in the army, he went to north Africa where he worked as a servant to a noble family. On his return to Spain, as he walked through the streets virtually penniless a child gave him a pomegranate. That piece of fruit led to a curious decision – he went to Granada, the city that has the pomegranate as its emblem. There he became a bookseller of Christian books even though he was not especially religious. Then came a watershed in his life when he heard a sermon by John of Avila, an itinerant preacher. After listening to the homily John became a man possessed. He roamed around the city decrying the many injustices he saw around him and gave away his belongings, including the contents of his shop. As a consequence, he was imprisoned in the Royal hospital where he was given the 'best' psychiatric care of the time – he was whipped. When he was finally released, he began taking care of sick people in a rented house, financed by gathering and selling firewood and by seeking alms from wealthy patrons. Later he set up a hospital which introduced new standards of hygiene.

Before he died, he received the title 'John of God' from the local bishop and with it the garment that became his habit. The bishop stipulated that John should wear it constantly. This brought an abrupt end to his habitual practice of exchanging his clothes with anyone he met whose clothes were in a worse state of repair than his own. Simplicity of lifestyle was an integral part of his life. A typical meal for him was a boiled onion.

John of God is a name synonymous with care for the poor and sick. However, there was much more to his activities than bandaging the wounds of society. He set up a hospital in competition to the one provided by the State – stirring the conscience of the people of Granada. He turned the highly stratified social structure of the day on its head by seeking an egalitarian social order, calling everyone 'brother', even the king. John himself was a frail human being who had his own crises, through which he gained a richer insight into his own self, God and others. Apart from his hospitality, his special gift was to bring out the best in others. His belief in the incarnation caused him to adopt as his motto: 'Through the body into the soul'. Pius XI urged the

Brothers of St John of God to use 'the same charity with modern means'. Apart from giving the fledgling Congregation of Irish sisters its name in 1871, John of God also gave it its symbol – the pomegranate. The crest of the Congregation shows a pomegranate set between two branches with a surmounting cross. The pomegranate is a symbol of charity because when the fruit is ripe the skin bursts open. It is unable to contain the seeds. The cross is a reminder that to love is to suffer as well as to give, while the branches are a sign of victory to those who persevere in doing good.

Last Will and Testament

If in life people could not live in dignity, then Furlong believed that in their last hours on this earth they could be treated with respect and care. Apart from human concern for the sick, he had a very strong sense that the faith of people was in danger in the workhouses because they would not be treated with dignity nor with Christ-inspired compassion.

The bishop also sought to shape the ethos of the Congregation. He believed that true poverty was the absence of the awareness of Christ present in the world and in the human person:

> For if our hearts be not moved, in vain shall we hope to move the hearts of others... Nothing is lost, nothing is little in God's sight. It is in the giving that we bring Christ to others; it is through going out to others that we open their hearts so that Christ may enter and be present to them.

He went on to add that they must welcome all 'the humiliations and fatigues of our state ...' True service implies emancipation from 'pride, selfishness and all other interior faults'. Christian service 'depends not so much on doing extraordinary actions, as on performing the ordinary exercises of each day extraordinarily well'.

The paternalism which would have been a feature of his time was also part of Furlong's dealings with the St John of God Sisters. The Annals note: 'Bishop Furlong ... addressed all the sisters with just a little advice in an informal, homely manner, a heart to heart talk of a father to his children.' Subsequently he

told the sisters: 'The Church has a right to expect Sisters grounded in solid faith and loyalty, fitted in every way to undertake the
responsibilities of their calling, and to uphold the traditions of
the Congregation.'

Furlong had the distinction of founding three religious
Congregations. In order of foundation, they are:

1. The Missionaries of the Blessed Sacrament – a Congregation
of diocesan priests devoted to the provision of missions and
retreats for the people of the diocese.

2. The Sisters of Perpetual Adoration – a single community devoted to contemplative prayer for the faithful of the diocese.

3. The Sisters of St John of God – in the 1990s, an international
Congregation devoted to the care of the sick, to education
and to other apostolic works.

Furlong performed his last act of charity just before he was
taken ill. When driving home one very wet evening, a little girl,
barefooted and poorly clad, came along. The bishop instructed
the driver to take the girl into the carriage and bring her home.
When the bishop returned to his home he went into his room
and sat in his chair. When he tried to get up and walk over to the
window he collapsed from an acute heart attack. Two sisters of
St John of God came to nurse him but they could not prevent the
inevitable.

At the time of his death, on 12 November 1875, the local
newspaper, *The People*, observed: 'Throughout his long episco-
pate he swayed every heart by his benignity ... Some of the evils
he wrestled with were of long standing, and even seemed to
have the sanction of the laws of the land ... he boldly entered on
a crusade against Intemperance.'

Bishop Furlong was not long dead when people began to
refer to him as the Bishop of the Eucharist. In 1870 he founded a
Community of Reparation Sisters in Wexford which developed
into the convent of Perpetual Adoration. This tradition of perpetual adoration of the Blessed Sacrament remains to this day.
He called the body of missionaries he founded in the diocese to
give parochial missions the 'Missionaries of the Blessed
Sacrament'. In his sermons and Pastorals, he exhorted the faithful to partake frequently of the Bread of Life 'that they might

have strength to avoid sin, fortitude to bear their severe trials and favour to advance in the love of God'. To encourage frequent communion among children, Bishop Furlong arranged to have translated and circulated through the schools of the diocese, Monsignor De Segur's devout little book, *Practical Counsels for Holy Communion*. He wrote an introduction for the book which indicates his own understanding of the importance of the Eucharist:

> I desire that you should catch from this little book the spirit which breathes in every line of fervent love to your dear Jesus in the adorable sacrament of the altar. You know how, when here on earth, He would have the little children come to Him, and how he embraced them; laying His hands on them He blessed them.

> Dear children, your Jesus, unseen in the Blessed Sacrament, loves each one of you as tenderly now, and he would have you too, to come frequently to Him in the sacrament of His love, that he may embrace you, and bestow His choicest blessings on you.

Back to the future?

As we head towards the third millenium, the Spirit in all its diversity is drawing the Sisters of St John of God to uncharted waters, with all the excitement and uncertainty that such change brings. The fact that this Spirit is blowing throughout the Congregation is the most conclusive evidence that the Congregtion is still vibrant. However, as more and more sisters are called to particular ministries, questions about identity inevitably arise. The ministry of Tom Furlong may have a key insight to offer at this point.

All share the Gospel call: 'Seek ye first the kingdom of God'. As sisters are increasingly involved in different apostolates, the Eucharist provides a common basis for the different approaches to their search for the kingdom, nurturing a sense of community and solidarity. From its earliest days, the Christian community has gathered and celebrated the Eucharist. There are two crucial dimensions to the Eucharist, thanksgiving and remembrance. In the Eucharistic celebration, Christians have always found their identity – thanking God and remembering how God revealed the divine plan for our salvation in the life, death and resurrection of Jesus. The Eucharist is the primary occasion of Christian self-understanding.

In the New Testament there were a number of different Christian communities, with particular cultural, linguistic and geographic traditions. However, despite this diversity, all the Christian communities celebrated the Eucharist to tell the good news of God's revelation in the life, death and resurrection of Jesus Christ. Thus the Eucharist offers a common identity even if, in the complex world of the 1990s, many people are taken on different paths in their ministries. Moreover, it unites by calling all together to confront, in the words of the German theologian J.B. Metz, the 'dangerous and subversive memory of Jesus Christ', reminding all that Jesus Christ gave himself as a sacrifice of love for our sake and calling all to do the same.[1] Sharing the bread and wine symbolises the bond of love which unites us all in God's spirit and in that way creates an authentic community.

Another important quality about the Eucharist is that while it forges a bond of unity within a group it is never an exclusive celebration. Jesus sat down to have meals with a number of different people, and it is noteworthy in the contemporary context that many of them, like the tax-collector, were on the margins of society. To be true to the example of Jesus, Eucharistic communities are compelled to share their most precious experience with all people of goodwill. It may be that the most important legacy of Furlong to the Sisters of Saint John of God is to be an enduring reminder of the centrality of the Eucharist in their lives. This is an important insight because of the danger of sisters becoming too preoccupied with the apostolate. Should they limit themselves to finding Christ's image in their sisters and brothers, they will be limiting themselves to contemplating the works of the Lord without being able to contemplate the Lord himself.

In a lecture to the members of the General Chapter of the Sisters of St John Of God, in August 1983, Reverend Oliver Doyle, SPC, Wexford, offered a penetrating insight about Furlong's legacy to the Congregation:

Taking the words of St John of God as his motto, 'Labour without intermission to do all the good works in your power'

Furlong inspired the first group of sisters to be active 'co-workers with Christ in bringing about his kingdom'. Activity, however, was only an expression of the sisters' relationship with Christ. We find this idea expressed in the first draft of the constitutions of the Congregation, drawn up by Furlong and Visitation. Every sister must 'keep herself' in the holy presence of God and so, when dealing with the dying or sick, bring them to Christ. In Furlong's overall plan for the diocese we can see the resolution of the Martha-Mary tension of the Gospel: action-service-doing, flowing from a relationship of being – being in the Presence of Christ.

It has been remarked that if normal procedures for a canonised saint had been followed, and had Bishop Furlong been an Italian, he would certainly be a saint by now, particularly because of his role in founding three religious Congregations. However, if you hope to become a saint, you do not pass up the opportunity to vote for papal infallibility.

The Mission
The first postulant, Hannah O'Leary from Clonakilty, was accepted at Sallyville on 8 December 1871. After a probationary period, she received the habit and with it the name Sr M. Conception. Just over a year later, the sisters took a bold step forward in their ministry to the sick and the dying when, at the insistence of Tom Furlong, Visitation applied for the post of Head Nurse in the Wexford workhouse hospital on behalf of her community. The application was successful, and two sisters were sent to take up nursing duties in the workhouse.

The workhouse, as we saw in the previous chapter, retained strong connotations of the Famine. In the years of the Great Hunger, it held out a last-resort prospect of survival, but at an enormous cost in terms of human dignity and self-respect. The stigma attached to admission to the workhouses has no direct parallel in contemporary society. The legacy of the workhouses is that there remains to this very day a reluctance on the part of some old people, particularly in rural Ireland, to be admitted into a hospital.

In 1873 two sisters packed their bags and headed for New Ross following a request for nurses from the parish priest there.

This request was made on behalf of the Governors of the Houghton Hospital. This was a private hospital, founded and endowed by Mr Houghton, a wealthy convert, for fever patients who could afford to pay for their care and did not wish to attend the workhouse hospitals – which had been the only place up till then where such cases were treated.

The sisters' first task had been to nurse the sick in their homes. From there they went to the workhouses. Some sisters also worked in Wexford Infirmary, an early nineteenth-century building which later became Dr S. Furlong's Nursing Home. The Congregation's apostolate continued there right up to the 1950s.

Another new departure was the provision of a home for poor and homeless women who would otherwise have to face the workhouse. Having the idea was one thing, financing it was another. An appeal to the Wexford people produced £400 to supplement a bequest left specifically for this purpose, and St Joseph's Home was opened in a house in Hill Street on 21 November 1874. As one set of problems was resolved another set began. The new house had no regular income and quickly found itself in debt. The sisters coped by moving first to a house in a garden attached to Sallyville and then, in 1887, to Rockfield House, which they purchased in that year when the Sisters of Perpetual Adoration moved from it to their new convent at Bride Street Church. Most of the women were moved from St Joseph's to Rockfield, but some women remained there until the 1940s. In 1924, Rockfield was selected as the Congregation's general novitiate.

1875 was a significant year for the Congregation. Firstly, three sisters took up service at the workhouse hospital in Enniscorthy and lived in a little convent built for them by the Poor Law Guardians. The Congregation opened New Street Convent in Enniscorthy in 1897. Sisters worked there until the 1960s. From their earliest days in the town, the sisters were involved in home nursing, a ministry they continued in Enniscorthy until the 1960s. Secondly, they got seriously involved in the education apostolate for the first time. A wealthy Catholic benefactor, Mr Richard Devereux, had built a school in the Faythe area of Wexford town for the Christian Brothers. Such was the demand for admission that the school could not possibly deal with all the pupils who wanted to attend and Devereux built another school and house for the brothers. The sisters sought and received permission to take over the building and set up a school in the Faythe. Also in 1875, four sisters began ministering in another new frontier in the workhouse hospital in New Ross. We shall return to these foundations in Chapter Seven.

Obstacles were occasionally put in the sisters' way. As early as 1884 the Catholic members of Gorey Board of Guardians had wished the sisters to take charge of the workhouse there, but the proposal was not favoured by the non-Catholic majority. Not until 1902 did four sisters arrive in Gorey workhouse.

The impact of the sisters is described in the local newspaper, *The People*, on March 23, 1872:

> They seek by every effort which religious love can prompt, to procure for the dying that crowning blessing – a happy death. And how consoling it must be to the poorer classes of society to know that the ministrations of those devoted sisters are not confined to those possessed of ample means. No distinction is made by them between the rich and the poor, the titled or the humble. They are ever ready when necessity knocks at their door; for their only watchword is 'duty' – duty to God, duty to their neighbour, and 'neighbour' with them means every class and sect in society.

Amongst heroic women

The Congregation was founded at a time when other Congregations were well established, so they cannot have been expected to be as widely-distributed throughout the country as other institutes like the Mercy Sisters. Like the Brigidines, who were founded in the diocese of Kildare and Leighlin in the nineteenth-century, the Sisters of St John of God went against conventional practice among active, female Congregations by choosing to work in a 'rural' diocese rather than in cities. Nonetheless, the work of the Sisters of St John of God also spread to other dioceses. Their very first venture outside Ferns was appropriately in the diocese of Ossory, the native diocese of Brigid Clancy. Two sisters were sent to Castlecomer workhouse hospital in 1875 to care for the poor, homeless people in the area. When the matron died the following year, the sisters assumed full charge of the hospital.

In 1886 the sisters were invited to the City Fever Hospital in Kilkenny by the Board of Guardians. In that year also the Bishop of Ossory requested a foundation for his diocese. Eight sisters moved to Kilkenny. Although they were living in the 'Marble City', their residence was a very humble one, the 'Ark House'. Their ministry was in the City Fever Hospital in Kilkenny and two years later they took over the responsibility of the work-house hospital in Thomastown.

It was from the Kilkenny community that five sisters went on the first national pilgrimage to Lourdes in 1913. It was unheard of at the time for sisters to go away on such a venture. Sisters worked in the Kilkenny City Infirmary, later replaced by the General Hospital, from 1914 until 1942. The early part of the century saw a lot of amalgamations of small, unviable hospitals and institutions. The sisters, for example, worked in Urlingford Infirmary from 1917 until 1920 when it was amalgmated with other hospitals in the vicinity.

Following a request for a foundation from Dr Sheehan, Bishop of Waterford and Lismore, in 1893 four sisters moved to John's Hill in Waterford to dedicate themselves to nursing the sick in their own homes. This private nursing continued up to the time of the opening of Maypark Nursing Home in 1926. Between 1893 and 1907, Waterford was ravaged by recurrent outbreaks of fever, and in 1894 the first two sisters took up duty in the Fever Hospital. This was where the true heroism of those brave women who joined the Sisters of St John of God was most dramatically illustrated when they literally put their lives on the line in the interests of their patients. Although they saved many lives themselves, five sisters – Benignus Brennan and Benedict Kenny (both from the diocese of Ossory), Ita Tynan and Assumpta Mochler (both from Tipperary) and Margaret Mary Hogan (a native of Cashel and Emly) – lost their own lives because of the fever.

A happier apostolate for the sisters in the city began in 1897 when two houses in St Alphonsus' Road were temporarily rented for use as a school. Nearly one hundred pupils attended on the opening day. A new school was completed and ready for use in 1900. In 1910 a fire broke out in one of the school rooms and much damage was done to woodwork and furniture. While the repairs were in progress, the classes had to be accommodated in the convent parlours and grounds.

Also in 1900 the sisters took charge of the Holy Ghost hospital in Waterford city, again at the request of the local bishop. It was founded under two charters, one being that of King Henry VIII and the other of Queen Elizabeth I. These two sovereigns were prayed for by the patients, in the daily rosary recited in the Institution. The hospital was run as an endowed home for people in reduced circumstances in the city and suburbs. Great improvements were made in the hospital to bring it up to the sisters' standards of cleanliness and neatness.

1920 saw one of the most dramatic episodes in the sisters' history in the area, at a time when the War of Independence was raging. Two of the sisters were attending Mass in the local church when a group of Black and Tans came marching up the chapel and arrested them. They had been treating an alcoholic patient at the time who was profoundly unhappy with their exacting standards. He had informed the Black and Tans that the two sisters were the ringleaders in the local unit of the IRA. Common sense prevailed and the sisters were released when they established their innocence.

Visitation

Tragedy had afflicted the Congregation, even before the sisters died in Waterford, with Visitation's death in 1889 at the age of forty-six. It was a devastating setback to a Congregation still grappling with its establishment. The dreadful decade in which she was born was the time of the 'famine' in which her native townland lost more than half of its population. The impression of the suffering may have given her the desire to help alleviate the suffering of people in need.

According to the Annals, 'her own convictions reflected from her into her community, like a stone thrown into a pool of water – one good action set off another.'

Her deep spirituality is well documented: 'The secret of her success was prayer. She spent most of her time in front of the

Blessed Sacrament in the church, her prayers were almost always for the strength of her sisters and their work. She knew that the stronger her sisters were the better and more lasting their work would be. Many times she spoke to them of how they should behave in public, always appearing to be strong, never displaying negative feelings and at all times being an example of God's love for all men, rich and poor.' In the period 1878-86, Visitation was herself in charge of the workhouse in Wexford. During the final three years of her life, she was novice mistress. According to the Annals, 'hers was a culture and fineness of feeling that belongs to the cloistered life – a leader of hearts and souls through hidden paths of toil and sacrifice.' She claimed, 'Whatever a sister does should be well done and this should be our motto.' She encouraged the young sisters to 'develop a business-like manner in attending the sick as this gave both the patients and their friends confidence, and they would consider the sisters competent in fulfillment of their duties.'

There is a wealth of adjectives used to describe the foundress but a poverty of specific details about her life, especially the early stages. One of the few stories told about her concerns her role in the conversion of a hardened criminal facing execution in Wexford jail. The chaplain had repeatedly failed to get him to repent. On hearing this story, Visitation asked to be allowed to speak to him. She immediately struck up a rapport with the man. Eventually she gave him a Scapular of the Sacred Heart and asked him to wear it. He stood looking at it for a few minutes and eventually said, 'God rest my poor mother's soul, she often gave me such things'. He pulled out a scapular from his coat pocket. Another prodigal son had returned to the fold. The extent of his conversion is evident in his response to the question, would he like some breakfast the morning of his execution? 'No. I have God in my heart. That is sufficient.' The Annals deduce that he went to his execution 'in an edifying manner'.

After a long period of trial and suffering, Visitation died in the convent at Wexford on 29 October 1889. For years she had suffered from delicate lungs and had haemorrhaged several times. Her deep bond with her sisters is indicated by this passage from the Annals:

The day of her death and exactly at the hour she passed

away, two sisters were talking about the business of the hospital where they were located, when one of them said to the other, 'Somehow I feel that M. M. Visitation is dead, but I suppose if she were we would get a wire.' After a short time she said the same thing and added: 'If I were far from the convent, nothing would persuade me but that she has gone to her reward.' Again after a short time she said 'A great lonely feeling is over me'. She had hardly uttered these words when a telegram arrived announcing her death.

Perhaps Visitation's most enduring legacy was her humanity. One of the most striking things about talking to Sisters of St John of God today is the recurring message that so many of them were attracted to the Congregation because of the influence of an older sister from the Congregation who was 'human' and 'normal'.

In the footsteps of Visitation

Despite the trauma of Visitation's death, the Congregation continued to flourish. In 1898 they were invited to found a convent in Kilmore, Co Wexford, their first convent in the area having been established in Ballyhearty. The first community of sisters were engaged in training girls in domestic work, including lace-making. They were given charge of a nearby school in Kilturk, and they drove there by pony and trap daily. In 1905 the foundation stone of the new convent was laid. Soon after, a technical school was started in Kilmore convent, under control of the county council. Scholarships were awarded by the county council, and pupils from Wexford and Carlow attended. In 1912 Chapel Garden school, which had been built in 1898 as a one-roomed school, was taken over by the sisters. The convent became a popular destination for sisters from other convents of the Institute for holidays, because of its proximity to the sea.

Sisters in Kildare

In 1902 the sisters once more answered the call of the local bishop to run the County Infirmary in Kildare. Such was the high standard of patient care that the sisters provided, that the infirmary was selected as the principal hospital for the county. In many respects, the challenge facing the sisters in the Kildare hospital was a microcosm of the sisters' problems throughout the country. The old workhouse hospitals were changing rapidly. The developments of medical science and the growth of social conscience led to a vast programme of consolidation and modernisation, which remains ongoing. New buildings and equipment were constantly needed to serve the new techniques of medicine. For the sisters, all this has meant a constant striving to keep up with the new developments, and to maintain a high quality service in those places where they had begun in grimmer surroundings many years before.

In 1924, at the request of the local bishop, the sisters accepted responsibility for the provision of nursing services at Naas hospital, which was then the Naas Union. Subsequently, in the mid 1920s, the hospital was designated as the county medical hospital for Kildare county and it continued as a county hospital until 1941 when it reverted to the status of a district hospital.

Where the Mountains of Mourne sweep down to the sea

In 1904 the sisters responded to the request of the Bishop of Dromore and the local Board of Guardians to take charge of Daisy Hill Infirmary and Workhouse in the historic town of Newry, after the infirmary had been relinquished by the Sisters of Mercy. In the nineteenth century, the workhouse had a reputation for draconian punishments: one inmate was transported for seven years for 'stealing a number of books and other articles from the establishment'; a second was 'whipped for picking the putty when soft off the windows newly glazed'; another was 'whipped for attempting to leave the workhouse by scaling the walls at the graveyard, having on the Union clothes.' The sisters brought many improvements, the destitute were transferred to welfare homes and patients got special quarters and care. One practice they changed immediately was the custom of burying paupers who died in the workhouse without any religious rite whatever. Up to that time the thinking was:

Rattle his bones over the stones
He's only a pauper whom nobody knows.

The three pioneers were paid yearly salaries of £40 (for the matron) and £28 (for the two nurses), plus rations.

Fanfare for the Uncommon Sisters

In 1898 the Bishop of Kildare and Leighlin requested the sisters to found a house in Edenderry, Co Offaly to oversee the local workhouse hospital. Crowds of people, expecting the arrival of the sisters, congregated near the station in Edenderry to await their arrival. At the first sight of the train, the sisters were greeted by a band. A wagonette was in readiness to convey them to the parochial house. A procession was formed and marched through the town to the parish priest's residence. Later in the evening, the sisters were taken to the hospital and shown to their apartments which had been transformed into a miniature convent.

At the invitation of the Board of Guardians, the sisters took charge of the Workhouse hospital. In 1899 two additional sisters came from Wexford, one for night duty and the other succeeded the matron who had retired. The sisters continued in their ministry in the workhouse, living in the little convent attached to it, until 1921 when the workhouse hospital was amalgamated into the district hospital.

A further chapter in the sisters' history in Edenderry began in 1904 when they were asked by the local priest, Fr Kinsella, to take charge of the school. At that juncture there was no girls' school in the town, and boys and girls were being taught in the one building. Fr Kinsella died in 1905 and in his will he left sites for a convent, church and schools. His assets were left, half to the convent and the other half towards the building of the new church. As numbers increased, a new school was needed to relieve the congestion. A new school, vested in local trustees and capable of accommodating nearly 400 pupils, was built, two thirds of the cost being defrayed by the government and one third by the sisters. The school was completed and opened in 1911 and the new convent blessed and opened in 1919. One of the people who taught in the boys' school was Sinéad Bean de Valera, wife of one of Ireland's foremost statesmen, Eamon de Valera. Soon the numbers in school increased so rapidly that a junior school was completed and opened in 1929.

A crafty cleric

In 1904 the sisters were invited to take charge of the girls' school in Rathdowney, Co Laois, by the local parish priest, Canon Brennan. There was no building suitable for a convent. In fact the only vacant house of any size was the Freemason Lodge, and there was little chance of that ever passing into Catholic hands. Rathdowney was a veritable stronghold of Protestant ascendancy and Masonic influence. Nevertheless, the parish priest decided to acquire this building if possible, but he calculated that its purchase would require delicate handling, so he watched his chance. One Sunday morning when the Catholic and Protestant congregations were at Divine Service, he got admittance, unseen, through a back door, and having satisfied himself that the house would serve his purpose, he deputed a wealthy man of the town to obtain, on lease for ninety-nine years at a fixed yearly rent, the house which became the convent of St John of God. When all the legalities were completed and it emerged that the lodge was being converted into a 'papist' convent, consternation prevailed for a time amongst the Protestant community.

The sisters came to Rathdowney on 30 November 1904 to teach in the primary school. In 1912, as the old school was unable to accommodate the number of children attending, a new school, vested in local trustees and capable of accommodating three hundred pupils, was built near the convent. The deeds of the original title stipulated: 'No religious objects are to be displayed nor no religious title may be used.' The yearly rent for the plot of ground was 'one penny if demanded'. Ireland at the time was still under British rule and schools were multidenominational though the school in Rathdowney was officially registered as a convent, which suggests that 'convent' was not perceived as a religious title at the time. The number on the rolls when the sisters took over the school was ninety, but over the years it reached three hundred.

A new partnership

The educational apostolate of the Sisters of St John of God took them to the secluded, scenic village of Owning, Pilltown, Co Kilkenny in 1909. As in other places, the school was in a deplorable condition, but repair and extension work was soon commenced and the scholastic standards improved accordingly. As in their other schools, the sisters did not limit themselves to 'talk and chalk' but educated the whole person and engaged in extra-curricular and extra-apostolic activities, like the Legion of Mary, Church Music Society and the Pioneer society. The school also had a great reputation for Gregorian chant.

Kilkenny is arguably the hurling (Ireland's national game) capital of the country. Four-year-old boys came to the school in Owning on their first day, as on every day of their school life, with three items: in ascending importance they were their schoolbooks, lunch and hurley stick. From the first day, they developed the skill of eating their lunch discreetly during class so that they would not lose a minute of hurling during lunch time.

Bite the hand that feeds?

As we have seen, the Sisters of St John of God worked with oppressed, outcast and marginalised social groups. One aspect of their work which strikes the present-day observer is the degree to which the sisters reacted to the effects of poverty without apparently showing any concern for the system which caused people to be so poor – their total absence of demands for social reform. This was a reality in all female Congregations at the time. There was a variety of factors which came together to achieve this result. Firstly, sisters were simply too busy with their apostolic work to engage in social analysis. Secondly, their position on the bottom rung of the Church's hierarchical ladder did not encourage them to be a critical, even a confident, voice. Thirdly, they were in part dependent on the social system for their position and property – it would not have served their short-term interests to be seen to be critical of the rich. A jocose comment from Mother Mary Aikenhead to an aspiring Sister of Charity in the 1830s, 'We are ignorant women, and do nothing but spin and obey', may have had a much deeper truth (except for the 'ignorant') than she intended. By entering convents, sisters were indirectly identifying with a patriarchal power structure which severely limited their capacity to side with the poor to campaign for social changes.

Poverty was a big issue within religious institutes at the time. In 1840, in a letter to the Bishop of Birmingham, Catherine McAuley, founder of the Sisters of Mercy, outlined her ideas on the ideal environment for the practice of poverty. The building should be 'in the plainest style without any cornice'. Twenty-five years later her Congregation stated: 'In the parlours all that savours of worldliness should be carefully avoided, but neither should ostentatious poverty be displayed. The parlours are the parts of the convent most liable to secular criticism. Great neatness, with simple convent furnishing, will be most calculated to edify.' Excessive display of wealth provoked scandal. In 1873, when Presentation Sisters from Limerick settled near Melbourne, Australia, neighbouring sisters claimed that the house provided for them was 'too grand'.

Another issue for Irish Congregations was expansion into new areas of ministry. Religious sisters initially gained a strong foothold in education, but their apostolate gradually moved to include more nursing after 1865. For example, in 1882 only ten per cent of convents were attached to hospitals. By 1900 that figure had grown to 22.4 per cent. As a norm, nursing sisters worked for the local authority in workhouse hospitals and city infirmaries. By 1898 there were seventy-three workhouse hospitals under the care of sisters and a further eleven five years later. None of these Congregations were established simply as nursing Congregations. The Sisters of St John of God fitted into this pattern with their mandate from Dr Furlong to 'teach school, visit the sick and poor and, where possible, nurse in the workhouses.' This highlights the prevalence of the 'multiple-project' convent – 63 per cent of convents in Ireland ran more than one concern in 1900.

In the early days, there was occasionally a very cavalier approach to training on the part of some of the institutes. In the 1890s a sister of St John of God was quoted as saying, 'Sisters require no special preparation except the instructions they receive from their Reverend Mother on nursing.' However, as religious sisters gained a more prominent role in local authority hospitals, convents started to provide a more professional approach to training. For example, a local doctor gave instruction to the Wexford branch of the Sisters of St John of God. Today all sisters embarking on a ministry in nursing get a relevant professional education.

In the Name of the Son

In the early years it would never have occurred to the founding sisters to speak of a 'Sisters of St John of God spirituality'. It would appear that, like many Irish institutes of the time, they followed an eclectic spirituality, taking influences from a variety of sources, like 'the French school' and Ignatian spirituality. What is certain is that they had a very strong spiritual commitment. From the very beginning, Sisters of St John of God were women who thought, spoke and acted, not in their own name, but in the name of the Lord. Jesus called the disciples to live in his name, to pray in his name (Jn 15: 10), to meet in his name (Mt 18: 20), to welcome little children in his name (Mt 18: 5), to cast out devils in his name (Mk 9: 38), to work miracles in his name (Mk 9: 39), and to preach repentance to all nations in his name (Lk 24: 47). To live in the name of the Lord is to partake in an intimately personal relationship. To think, speak and act in the name of the Lord means that the divine name is the sacred space in which a sister can hear with her own ears, see with her own eyes and touch with her own hands the Word who is life and the subject of her witness (1 Jn 1). The name is a dwelling place, the ideal retreat to listen to Christ and receive the Word which is to be spoken. The name is the setting where the future meets the present. Only when the name is the true centre can sisters be free to heal the sick because it is only then that it is possible to understand that the love of God and the love of neighbour cannot be separated.

The first Constitution showed a great tenderness and an explicit recognition that the sisters were part of a healing ministry. Jesus Christ was to be encountered in the suffering of the sick and the institute was founded for the poor and the rich. However, the apostolate was never an end in itself. A sister of St John of God was one who lived in communion with Jesus, and through him, in the Trinitarian God. Visitation and the founding sisters were clearly alert to the danger of sisters being in touch with numerous people, but out of touch with the Lord – involved in a commendable and worthy apostolate but divorced from divine 'affairs'. To be true to the Gospel vision, it is necessary to keep one's eyes on the Lord, to remain attentive to his will and to listen with care to his voice (Lk 10: 42). Only with, in and through Jesus Christ can the apostolate bear fruit. Consequently the first, indeed in a sense the only, concern must be to live in ongoing communion with the one who calls sisters out to witness in his name.

From this starting point, it was inevitable that the founding sisters would recognise that prayer was the basis and centre of all ministry. The sister of St John of God must be, first and fore-most, a woman of prayer. Without prayer, religious life easily descends to a mere busy life in which a person's need for respect or affection dominates actions, and being busy becomes a badge of honour, an end in itself. It is not necessarily true that absence makes the heart grow fonder. As many a ruined romance has demonstrated, absence may cause the heart to wander. The parallel for prayer life does not need to be laboured.

While the founding sisters in many cases heroically gave all of themselves to the apostolate, they never deluded themselves that their work was their prayer. This is as crucial an insight for religious life now as it was then, because it is when a sister prays by herself that she keeps in a special way the divine flame burning within her. Equally, in prayer she experiences the Presence to whom she is called. Prayer is inclusive, helping all in need to open themselves to the healing presence of the Lord.

Today the question is posed: 'Who ministers to the minister?' Visitation recognised that healthy ministry was impossible unless her sisters first of all ministered to each other. Like everybody else, sisters are broken and fragile people. They can only care for the wounds of others if they allow their own wounds to be healed by those who live with them in community.

Heaven knows no frontiers

In the Bible, the question of where and how we can serve the Lord has an unambiguous answer. We find him in the hungry, the thirsty, the stranger and the naked, we see him wherever people are in need and cry out for help. The Christian God, revealed to humankind in a definitive way in the bruised and broken body of the suffering Jesus, continues to reveal himself wherever human suffering is to be found. From the beginning, Sisters of St John of God were women who recognised God in the course of their daily care to others. The heart of their ministry was the ongoing discovery of God's presence in the midst of the human struggle.

Although, as we have seen, their genesis came out of pain and division, their faith insulated them from the danger of being totally overwhelmed by their problems and ensured that the disappointments and disillusionments of their apostolate did not narrow their vision nor blind them to anything beyond their own problems. Although their apostolate brought them, in a very concrete and immediate way, in contact with great misery, they were able to see the face of a loving God even when nothing but darkness seemed present. In their practical 'hands-on' approach to people in need, they came in touch with a larger presence. Their care for the sick and the poor revealed the deep connections of their individual lives with the saving life of Jesus Christ. As they entered into the struggles and pains of the people they served in Wexford and beyond, they reached out to these people to reveal to them God's presence in their lives.

Their recognition of the importance of prayer was prophetic and particularly relevant to the 1990s. 'That's only a contemplative order' is a phrase one sometimes hears today when people are talking about religious life. Apart from what it betrays about our understanding of religious life, it also says something about our attitude to prayer. It is as if prayer is on the periphery of the Christian life, instead of at the very centre. In the hustle and bustle of our everyday lives, it is often difficult to find the inner stillness to make space for God to speak to us. Much of prayer is the struggle to overcome our many distractions, to concentrate on the presence of God. The founding sisters knew the importance of spending time alone with God.

It is not surprising that such God-centred women were very much in demand in the Church. In 1895 the Sisters of St John of God would answer the call for assistance from half way across the world. A new and exciting chapter in the story of this group of women was about to unfold. In the mingled garden of weeds and flowers which is life, this chapter too would provide a lot of challenges and call for many more acts of heroism.

Notes:

1. J.B. Metz, *Faith in History and Society*, Burns and Oates, London, 1980.

CHAPTER 4

A Passage to Australia

The people of the dream watched the people of the clock come out of the sea and plant their flagstaff firmly into the sand. They assumed that the pale-skinned mariners were the spirits of their ancestors returned from the islands of the dead and that they would act in accordance with ancient international etiquette ... The strangers, for their part, secure in the certain values of an expanding empire, had no doubt that the simple but apparently intelligent primitives would soon appreciate the blessings of civilisation and gladly abandon their godless and feckless ways for those of a superior culture ... Both people were mistaken ... Neither could appreciate the other's logic, but whereas the Aborigines learned to anticipate the whiteman's conduct with reasonable accuracy, they themselves were seldom, if ever, to behave as was expected.
(*Mary Durack*[1])

The history of the Catholic Church in Australia can be traced back to the arrival of the first fleet in January 1788. Three-quarters of the one thousand passengers on board were convicts, many of them Catholics. By 1828 one-quarter of the Australian population was Catholic. The identification between Catholic and Irish was encouraged by the Australian bishops. Preaching a St Patrick's Day sermon in 1924, Archbishop Mannix asserted that wherever there were Irishmen, Catholicism was strong. The more deeply the Congregation breathed the Irish atmosphere, the stronger would be the Catholic faith in Australia.

Notwithstanding that Ireland and Australia were literally half a world apart, when Cavan-born Bishop Gibney of Perth appealed to the Sisters of Saint John of God for personnel, in

1895, his request found a willing response. He was greatly concerned for the people of Perth and its out-lying gold-fields because, over the previous summer, a typhoid epidemic had taken many lives. In his letter to the sisters, he stated that a combination of hospitals overcrowded with typhoid patients and the shortage of qualified, caring nurses was 'why so many of them succumbed'.

Eight sisters, Mothers M. Cecilia Dunne and M. Antonio O'Brien and Sisters M. Magdalen Kenny, M. John Gleeson, M. Ita Gleeson, M. Angela Brennan, M. Assumpta Hanly and M.Veronica O'Hanlon were selected from the volunteers. On 16 October 1895 they sailed on the *Orizaba* and arrived in Albany on 23 November. The pioneers left Ireland travelling, according to a Penal Law of that time, in the large cloak, bonnet and gossamer veil which took the place of their religious habit, as no religious was allowed to wear a habit in public. There is a profound irony in the historical fact that the 1890s saw Irish Catholic sisters come into a predominantly British Protestant colony to start hospitals and schools for all.

A group of Sisters outside the first convent in Subiaco in 1900:
Back row, left to right: Srs M. Ita Gleeson, Assumpta Hanly, Ignatius Lynagh, Patrick Mulally, Kevin Doyle, Martha Devlin, Joseph Codd.
Front row: Srs M. John Gleeson, Cecilia Dunne, Antonio OBrien, Patricia Baggott, Angela Brennan.

A painting of Sisters nursing in the goldmines.
Kalgoorlie, 1896

A voice in the wilderness

There was a major material and educational vacuum in Western
Australia at the time, notably in terms of an acute shortage of
schools and hospitals. For a long period in the boom days of the
gold rush of the 1890s, there was only a sprinkling of females in
the gold towns, and the need for nursing care was particularly
acute. Bad housing, unhealthy water and tainted food brought a
train of illnesses that were beyond the capacity of doctors and
hospital nurses. Then came fever epidemics. Another appeal
from Bishop Gibney in March 1896 saw three Sisters of Saint
John of God from Perth taking service at the gold mines in
Coolgardie, where the living conditions of the miners were atrocious. These sisters were warned that they might be committing
themselves to a premature and terrible death. Typhoid fever
was rampant, chiefly because of scarcity of water. The sisters immediately made nonsense of the description of women as the
'weaker sex' by living in canvas huts like those of the miners.
Before long, one of the sisters died of typhoid fever, but the survivors showed the courage that characterised the Sisters of Saint
John of God in Waterford where, as we saw in Chapter Three,
five of them lost their lives whilst treating the same disease. But
the sisters persevered, making collections from mine to mine to
provide more permanent accommodation for the sick.

Two years later the Great Gold Strike in Kalgoorlie saw the

sisters following the miners across the open desert 'in a two-horse buggy, driven by a Mr Gibbons of Perth'. They had travelled more than 300 miles over bush tracks and parched desert wastes, under a blistering sun. The ravages of typhoid and other complaints were then causing heavy mortality among the diggers and there was little hospital nursing and medical attention available. Kalgoorlie welcomed them with the ceaseless thud of stampers, with clouds of white dust, and with a heavy sickening odour, a symbol of the dread disease raging in the canvas town of two thousand miners.

Securing a tent as their headquarters, the sisters began their work, attending to the sick miners as they found them – in their tents, in hotel rooms or even lying under trees. The two sisters could not cope by themselves and four sisters left almost immediately from Perth to assist them. Soon a hospital, which was opened on 21 March, 1897, a school and a convent were to provide outward evidence that the young Congregation from Ireland had definitely made its mark. In Australia as in Ireland, there was a determined response to needs such as the typhoid epidemic. The sisters had a preference for the poor over the rich, the uneducated over the educated.

In the more sedate setting of Perth, the sisters followed the pattern set in Ireland, establishing a school, and a small hospital after an initial involvement in home nursing. Reinforcements were sent from Wexford. Initially four sisters and two postulants departed on 11 November 1896, followed by further groups in 1898 and in 1903. At that juncture, the sisters had established a secure foundation. At Perth, the sisters took charge of a large and growing hospital and as we shall see in the following chapter, gradually extended their influence throughout Australia by founding hospitals at Ballarat (1915), Goulbourn (1925), Rivervale (1934), Geraldton (1936), Warrnambool (1938), Bunbury (1939), Northam (1948) and Brighton Psychiatric Hospital, Melbourne (1949). We shall return to these missions in the following chapter.

'The finger of God is here'

One mission which underlines the courage of the pioneer Australian missionaries is their work in the remote northwest region of Dampier Land (after William Dampier, the Dutch explorer who came to the region in 1688). Dampier Land, today a vast Aboriginal reserve of over a million acres, is washed on the west by the Indian Ocean and on the north by the placid green waters of King Sound. Inside King Sound is Disaster Bay – a name which suggests its own story.

Disaster Bay was the scene of the first Catholic Mission settlement in the North West, made by the Trappist Monks in 1890. Later they changed to Beagle Bay, the spot specially chosen by Dr Gibney, the Bishop of Perth. In 1889 Bishop Gibney had gone up to Derby, on King Sound, and from there rode across the country towards the site of what would subsequently become the Beagle Bay Mission. He worked with his own hands day and night clearing the bush, erecting the cottages and planting bananas, sugar cane and other tropical plants.

The Pallotine Fathers had taken responsibility from the Trappist Monks for the spiritual welfare of the local people in the 1890s. They requested Bishop Gibney to arrange for nuns to take charge of the women and girls. The bishop was initially unsuccessful in his efforts to attract nuns because most religious communities were already overstretched. At that time the Sisters of Saint John of God had only two communities – in Subiaco and Kalgoorlie. In 1906 Mother Antonio O'Brien was sent home to Ireland with a sick sister. She brought back another group of postulants with her. The bishop requested that she would found a convent in Beagle Bay. The problem with this request was that it meant that she had to separate herself entirely from her community. Nonetheless Antonio accepted his invitation. Again following a request from the bishop, two sisters, Bernardine Greene, Benedict Courtney, and six novices, Patrick O'Neill, Margaret Carmody, Michael Power, John Walker, Joseph McCafferty and Bridget Greene, volunteered to join her.

The nine sisters, eight Irish and one Australian, arrived at the remote mission of Beagle Bay in 1907. These women were the first sisters to minister among the Aboriginals. It was difficult work on many levels: the living conditions were, at its kindest, primitive; the climate was extremely taxing because of the tropical heat and rain. And, above all, there was major difficulty in developing any kind of rapport with the Aboriginals, particularly as the sisters were culturally conditioned to think of various aspects of Aboriginal life, like nakedness as a natural state, as lacking in 'civilisation'.

Meeting the locals

The sisters arrival at Beagle Bay was watched with interest. The half-caste boys waded out to meet them with low bows and words of welcome, while the full-blooded people looked on furtively from behind the sand dunes. One boy described Mother Antonio as she waded ashore and went down on her knees and kissed the hot sand as being 'like a big, white gull'. The Aborigines initially thought it was a sign of her relief at reaching dry land but with the benefit of hindsight they understood it as a symbol of her dedication to this country and its people.

The next part of the journey was a comedy of errors as they were being driven to the mission using poorly broken bullocks to take them to their destination. The bullocks frequently broke their harness, went bush and had to be brought back again. The sisters were on the point of collapse because of fatigue and hunger when they reached the mission. However, they were forced to wait outside the gates until the community was ready to greet them. Half an hour later the Aboriginals returned, chanting 'Hail Queen of Heaven' above a peal of bells, and led the sisters in a procession to their new residence.

The convent which the sisters had been promised had not been built because of lack of money. The sisters' new home was a bark-roofed building that had been vacated for them by the Pallotine Brothers. The doors were covered with nothing but pieces of canvas while the windows had no covering at all. Their furniture amounted to nothing but a few boxes while they had no mattresses or pillows on the stretchers which served as their beds. Mother Antonio's reaction offers a wonderful insight into her resilience and character: 'Heaven be praised. We'll not be tempted to be sleeping in.'

In Beagle Bay the words of the Magnificat were patently untrue: 'He has filled the hungry with good things. The rich he has sent empty away.' The sisters resolved to do all they could to reach out to the poor and quickly turned their attention to a long-running problem, the neglect of half-caste children. Many of these children were unacknowledged by their white fathers in a land where white women were almost non-existent, but others felt a sense of responsibility to their part-Aboriginal progeny, and were quite prepared to pay for their care and education at the mission. As a result of the care they received from the sisters, many of these children went on to become the parents of well-adjusted families.

Reading the sisters' own accounts of the hazards they confronted in the Kimberley, one thing stands out – they experienced all kinds of hardship, physical, material and emotional, but no matter how bad things were they were happy whenever they were able to attend Mass.

In the history of the Kimberley mission the dominant personality was Mother Antonio.

It's a long, long way from Clare to here

Bridget O'Brien was born in Ennistymon, Co Clare. A daughter of a merchant, little is known of her early childhood though the business acumen she acquired from her father would stand her in good stead in the years ahead. In her daily life she saw at first hand the wretchedness of the poor, the deprived, and the downtrodden in post-famine Ireland. This was a key formative influence on her future orientation in life. Her grim determination to alleviate some of the suffering of her own people and to devote her life to God's work, led her as a young woman of nineteen years to join the recently-formed Congregation of Infirmarians. As a member of a community of women living in sparse conditions, Antonio experienced the value of discipline, the endurance, the limitations of obedience and the dynamics of inter-personal relationships. It was here that she became imbued in the philosophy, 'through the body to the soul'.

Physically, Antonio had an iron constitution, unusual strength and inexhaustible energy. She could and would undertake the almost impossible. Her companions found it impossible to keep pace with her. In personality terms she was an enigma. She was capable of being very gentle and affectionate, while her generosity extended to all parts of human life. On the other hand, her independent, determined manner, blunt speech, forthrightness and her inflexible attitude, at times, caused problems for her friends. Although she did not make friends easily, when she did she always had total loyalty.

She was professed in 1880 and completed her nursing training shortly afterwards. For fifteen years, she nursed in the workhouses and private homes of Ireland. She was instrumental in shaping the development of Visitation Clancy's reforms on the health care needs of the workhouse poor when institutional care was just beginning in south-east Ireland.

In 1895 she volunteered for mission work in Australia and was based in Subiaco. Australia must have been a severe cultural shock for Antonio and the other sisters from Ireland. In 1896 she began nursing in the gold fields of Coolgardie and Kalgoorlie. Antonio attended the miners and their families, sick and dying, as they lay on the bush tracks, in tents, shanties and in the sweltering hotels. Her stay in the goldfields lasted for nine years, interspersed with visits to Perth. Eventually, over a number of years, a fine hospital was built, co-founded by Mother Antonio and Mother Baptist Kissane, in Kalgoorlie.

Antonio faced two major obstacles even before she set off to work with the Aboriginals. Firstly, public opinion was against the project, as these were women and the first nursing and teaching sisters to go to the Kimberley region. Secondly, her colleagues in the Congregation were deeply opposed to the establishment of a major new commitment in the north-west. As the Australian mission was still in its infancy, they did not feel capable of releasing sisters for work in a new apostolate. Antonio's decision to go ahead despite these objections fuelled a lot of acrimony and led to strained relations between sisters in the northwest and the other sisters in the Congregation throughout Australia. Subiaco did not believe it was in a position to undertake the task and regarded the withdrawal of members, already too few, as a betrayal of their work. In 1916 an attempt at amalgamation failed. In 1924, when the Congregation amalgamated, Subiaco offered to 'take back' the Broome Sisters provided they would give up their mission. As we shall see in the following chapter, these wounds festered for decades and were not resolved until after the Second Vatican Council.

New problems awaited the sisters when they arrived at Beagle Bay. They found that they were dependent on the

Pallotine Fathers for everything – shelter, food, clothing, postage, medicine and transport. It is probable that Antonio was spurred on to action, despite all her problems, by the similarities she saw between the Irish peasant and the Australian Aborigines – both browbeaten, maltreated, oppressed and dispossessed of their lands by the British Administration of the times.

The sisters themselves became adept in the cooking of 'bush tucker'. In those days a bath was a luxury, for beer was more plentiful than water. There was no milk except tinned milk and one paid ten shillings for an egg. They kept no private stores because Antonio's attitude was that they should not live any better than those they were pledged to serve. The few luxuries they had, like eggs or fruit, were saved for the expectant mothers and the sick. She would never speak of the sisters' kindness to the Aboriginals but of the Aboriginals' goodness to the missionaries. She often reminded her colleagues: 'Remember the Aboriginals did not ask us to come. We are here of our own choice and we can remain only by their goodwill and the grace of God.'

One particular area of concern was to provide 'proper' clothing for the Aboriginals. She concluded that, as far as the women and children were concerned, any type of old clothes would be adequate but that one good, clean dress must be worn on Sundays. She quickly learned that making rules for the people was one thing but implementing them was an altogether different proposition. Initially when she gave people clothes, they were passed on to other people. Antonio's solution to this problem was to keep the better garments under lock and key, to be handed out on Sunday mornings and returned immediately after Mass. Before dawn one Sunday, she was abruptly awakened by the sound of a score of naked women waving lighted fire sticks and shouting at the top of their voices. She shouted a word of warning to her colleagues, closed her eyes and braced herself to meet her maker. Moments later the penny dropped – the women had simply arrived to gather their Sunday clothes.

Antonio and her sisters faced a big challenge adjusting to the culture of the Aboriginals. Two examples illustrate this. One day she was working in the laundry with some of the Aboriginal women when a child began pulling at his mother's skirts, demanding that she play with him. His mother told him she must first finish her work. This prompted the child to throw himself screaming on the ground and kick mud over the newly-washed clothes. Antonio intervened by slapping the boy. His mother picked up a plank of wood and rushed at the Irish woman with demonic fervour. Antonio simply said, 'Go on. Hit me if you must.' The mother was taken aback and fled the scene. Subsequently the woman returned with a gift of a lizard and some wild berries which she gave to Antonio with tears of remorse.

The sisters learned that the Aboriginals considered it inappropriate for anyone but a parent to discipline a child, and that the parents themselves were prepared to tolerate almost any behaviour from their children. Their belief was that life would quickly impose its own harsh disciplines, for girls in the responsibilities of early marriage and for boys through the hazards of initiation.

Another problem was the restrictive taboos which influenced the association of people within certain degrees of tribal relationship. When a marriage was celebrated shortly after their arrival, they had prepared a 'wedding breakfast' of bread, jam and tea and had ushered the women to one side of a long table and invited the men to sit opposite. All of a sudden the blissful scene was shattered by howls of dismay as everybody fled in apparent panic.

The priest on hand persuaded them to return and seated the men and the women back to back. The food was then passed around and everyone seemed content. The priest explained that, within the intricate system of tribal relationships, men belonging to one tribal classification were forbidden to speak to or even look at another. This applied above all to the mother-in-law son-in-law group, including boys and girls born within these classes of tribal relationship to each other. The sisters could not fathom the rationale behind this custom but had no choice but to observe this taboo, even in the classroom.

In 1908, a year after the beginning in Beagle Bay, Antonio and Mother M. Benedict sailed to Broome, by lugger. They walked ashore in the early morning and went into the first house they saw. The owner was a Tipperary woman! She brought the sisters in for a hearty Irish breakfast. Although there was no resident priest, there was a church. There was a hut, one room of corrugated iron, near the church; it had been the home of a Filipino, but he vacated it and it was handed over to the sisters. Some gifts from the Aboriginals enabled the sisters to buy household goods and beds and by night they had set up home in their new 'convent'. They removed the scores of bottles left by their predecessor, but retained a skull which was in residence. Within days the sisters had collected children for a school. A piano was purchased and music lessons were given in the convent. While in Broome, Antonio set out to secure some kind of financial assistance for her mission. Her appeals to the generosity of the people of Broome yielded a rich harvest and succeeded in securing independence for her group and their work, as well as making friendships which would endure the test of time.

A priest who visited Beagle Bay gave his impressions of the work of the sisters in the *West Australian Record* in 1911. It makes for interesting reading on many levels, from the admiration of the work of the sisters to the patronising attitude it reveals towards the Aboriginals:

It is a delightful place; from both a material and a spiritual point of view it may be truly called 'an oasis in the desert'. It is reached by lugger after a journey of one hundred miles, which may take any period of time from a day to a week, according to the inconsistent Nor'-West breezes. To a visitor, and more particularly to a priest, it is a complete surprise; for, here in the heart of the Australian forest, there is a world of genuine Catholicity. The Aboriginals, both young and old, would do credit to any Catholic community in Australia. They have, under the careful training of the St John of God nuns, made progress both spiritually and intellectually. The theory that the Australian savage cannot be educated is undoubtedly exploded at Beagle Bay. I saw the Aboriginals in all their varied occupations, following the avocations of experienced tradesmen; some working at the sawman's bench, others forging and repairing farm implements, and all carrying out their duties with marked success.

The School is conducted by the St John Of God nuns, and you

would be surprised to see the handwriting of these dusky denizens of the Australian Bush. There are about one hundred Aboriginal children attending the school, some of them fine types of growing manhood and womanhood. In fact one is struck by the absence of the rather repulsive features of the blacks we are accustomed to meet in other parts of West Australia. They can be trained to almost anything, and this is remarkably evidenced in their beautiful well-trained choir which is under the direction of Brother Mathias. Before my departure they tendered me a farewell concert and I was astonished to hear some of the items rendered in four languages – English, German, French, and their own beautiful Aboriginal dialect. The first portion of the programme closed with the 'Watch by the Rhine' and the Grand Finale was none other than the well-known 'God Save Ireland'.

With her sisters, Antonio extended the mission from the work with lepers, to the care of orphans, visiting Aboriginals in their camps in the remotest areas, and nursing the young, old and sick through the establishment of new missions in Lombadina (1913) and Derby (1937). Later they branched out into clinics, hospitals, dormitories, hostels and schools. Instruction was given in numeracy, literacy and the Christian faith. However, this brought problems of its own.

As has been well documented in many quarters, while the motives of missionaries were laudable, they did unwittingly contribute to cultural and Christian imperialism. It would be unfair to apportion blame to these people because they were culturally conditioned to think in no other way. The consequences of this imperialism was that people were made to feel dependent, and their beliefs, customs and traditions were adversely affected. However, some commentators point out that only for the intervention of the nuns and priests in the Kimberley, the Aboriginal communities would now be extinct; they provided the tools of survival.

As Mother Superior, Antonio carried a heavy burden and years of hardship, uncertainty and poor diet finally took their toll. Sometimes she fainted because of the intense heat and would reluctantly rest until evening. She then returned to work expecting the sisters who had continued working all day to keep

Mother Antonio O'Brien

up with her. One of the most original tributes in praise of her efficiency was the comment: 'She'd manage to take a brood of
geese through a city centre in peak traffic!' She suffered from
Bright's disease and anaemia, and in 1918 she retired from
superiorship. She died in 1923, sitting fully attired, in starched
head-dress and the heavy serge habit, on the verandah of the
Broome mission.

A new Broome

The sisters faced varying difficulties in the Kimberley at different stages. For a few years after the outbreak of war in the
Pacific, the Australian Northwest became embroiled in the heat of
battle as the Japanese occupied the East Indian archipelago and
threatened Australia. Broome itself was bombed and machine-
gunned.

The sisters were faithful to the pioneering spirit, which is such

Sr Ignatius surrounded by Derby school-children

a central part of their heritage, by introducing a whole series of measures to improve the quality of life for the indigenous people. In 1924 they founded the first kindergarten. In 1961 they started the first permanent infant health clinic in Broome. In 1973 the first public health sister, Damian Brannigan, was appointed. Tragically she was killed in a car accident while on duty. Shortly after Damian's death the first pre-primary and Aboriginal teaching assistant programme was established. In the 1980s the sisters continued on their innovatory ways with the training of the first Aboriginal catechist and pastoral associate, helping to staff the Catholic education regional office, and setting up a hearing impairment programme and a spirituality centre.

Teacher training in the Kimberley began in Derby at Holy Rosary School, as a result of a request for this service made by an Aboriginal woman, then working as a teaching assistant at the school. In Broome itself a counselling service began in the same way at the request of two local men who asked for training to help them begin the service. In both cases, whilst the sisters saw the needs, they would not act until the request was voiced by the people. In the early years, the people were not asked to make such decisions. The Church provided the personnel. However, today the sisters are no longer comfortable with the role of being the voice of the voiceless. Instead their primary concern is to help the voiceless find their own voices.

Today, one of the most visible signs of the sisters' contribution to Broome is the Sr Germanus Kent hostel for senior Aborigines called after a sister who has become an institution because of her lobbying campaigns to the commissioner of health, premiers, federal leaders, local leaders and to representatives of both the upper and lower houses of parliament. Her legacy is a series of practical measures which have improved the quality of life for the Aboriginal community.

The Big Sick

A new mission initiative began in 1937 when the sisters took charge of the leprosarium at King Sound in Derby, about 150 miles from Broome. The carers were exposed to risk of infection (leprosy is highly contagious) and moreover faced the prospect of isolation from their own community. The public health department accordingly had great difficulty in attracting nursing staff. They turned to the Sisters of St John of God and found a ready response. They voluntarily lived and worked amongst the afflicted. From day one they established a deep bond with their patients. Hitherto the lepers had been seen as the 'untouch- ables'. Male and female patients had been trained as orderlies and nursing aids. The sisters bathed the patients and made the beds – wearing gloves when it was necessary to touch the patients doing dressings, smears and other treatments. They did not touch or handle anything the patients touched or handled. All doors had two knobs – one for the patients and one for the sisters. One Sunday morning at Mass they had a new priest and he had his lengthy sermon written out on several pieces of paper. A gust of wind caught them and they dispersed all around the Church. Not one patient moved to pick them up – the patients knew why, the sisters knew why but the priest could not under- stand it. The sisters were not allowed to sit in the church with the patients.

Long before the concept of 'holistic care' had been articulated in medical journals, these women were living that approach to people in pain or distress. Their literal 'hands-on' approach won them the hearts of those vulnerable and needy patients. Their power as agents of evangelisation came from the way they lived their life.

For the sisters it required a radical change of heart and working approach. One young sister faced a baptism of fire when she was sent down to deal with a troublesome patient. The patient was wearing nothing but a leather belt and was writhing in agony because of the effects of a tummy bug. When asked what was wrong with him he replied, 'I have guts ache from government soup and I'm buggered up!' After that encounter she could cope with anything.

The Sisters of St John of God were responsible for changing many of the strict rules regarding the isolation of leprosy patients, giving them a freedom not experienced for many years. They insisted that coffins be used for burial rather than blanket wrappings. Occupational and music therapy was introduced and flourished.

In the western world, since biblical times, to be a leper is to be an outcast. However, leprosy has no stigma attached to it for the Aboriginals. This was very much a mixed blessing because they aided the spread of the disease by not isolating those affected in their communities. They described the disease as 'the big sick'. The term was appropriate because many victims were forced to spend all their adult lives in the leprosarium – cursed with the inability to live a normal life. One of the last four residents, Teresa Puertollano, had entered the leprosarium when she was thirteen. The introduction of multidrug therapy for leprosy patients in 1970, and a follow-up system of surveillance out in the field, led to the closing of the leprosarium in 1986.

An article in a local newspaper, *The Record*, on August 28, 1986 written about the closure of the leprosarium observed:

> The closure of the Derby Leprosarium testifies to the success of arresting, if not eliminating, a disease which has proven a scourge. The agonising, flesh-destroying, humiliating and disfiguring disease can at last be controlled. Conditions for lepers in the north were shocking. Pathetic services, insufficient knowledge or suitable arresting drugs and limited care meant misery and a futureless outlook in the early part of the century. But the birth of the Derby's Leprosarium changed all that. In fact to such an extent the whole enterprise since its

inception in 1937 has been an outstanding success to the huge credit of the experts and the dedicated.

In 1952 the sisters had taken responsibility in Derby for an Aboriginal general hospital where rudimentary conditions prevailed. Two years later they opened a school there. In 1966 they supplied five sisters, one who acted as assistant matron to the new hospital at Derby which catered for both Aboriginals and other Australians.

Now the potential mass killer for the Aboriginal community is AIDS and the sisters are at the heart of the campaign to prevent an epidemic by gathering all the baseline data on disease in the area. They are also involved in meals-on-wheels, counselling and family ministry.

One of the interesting things about the sisters' work in Derby, and indeed in the Kimberley mission in general, is that they were less affected in some ways by the new patterns of religious life in the aftermath of Vatican II than other sisters. By the nature of their work and their simple lifestyle, they had already created many changes from the traditional convent style of life and work.

The sister who is most closely associated with the Derby mission is Sr M. Alphonsus Daly. She joined the Congregation in 1912 and was transferred to the Derby Leprosarium in 1944. For her work she was honoured with the M.B.E. in 1957 and received an honorary Fellowship of the College of Nursing in Australia in 1962. She was one of many sisters to win honours and distinctions for their services to the needy. Her memoirs make for fascinating reading and provide an invaluable insight to life in the Kimberley mission:

> As one of the six postulants, I joined the St John of God community who were residing in the Broome convent, which consisted of two galvanised iron rooms surrounded by a high iron fence to 'keep out the world'. In this limited area, sharing the problems of food shortage, trying heat, sandflies and fierce mosquitoes, we lived out our every-dayness convinced that we were there to do God's work – to be His eyes, His ears, His hands, His feet.

With modern technology now making life in the Kimberleys

more liveable – we fondly look back on the era when in company with the early pioneers in that area, we shared the local problems of heat, isolation and lack of facilities. 'If only we could get a net or two – we could use them in turns to get a good night's sleep.' Instead we made do with cans of smoking sticks placed in every nook and corner. Manure fires lit for the same purpose left an odorous smoke and although they were very effective, we had to endure the aftermath of many stings. The invariable order was 'don't scratch' and we didn't, for fear of getting the maladies associated with the bites.

For recreation we walked to the jetty and elsewhere, gradually becoming accustomed to our surroundings. During one of these excursions we were shocked to be faced with an Aboriginal with leprosy. The distasteful sight made us re-think our vocation – we each wondered whether we had the stamina and goodwill to care lovingly for these victims. In those days, little was known about this disease, so the people were not isolated as they were to be when science caught up on them. On Sunday mornings we went to the local church and prayed with the people – in keeping with the times, the full habit was always worn – starched guimps certainly added to the discomfort of living in an extremely hot climate. The prayers were long and frequently interrupted by someone knocking on the door for assistance.

For the most part the cosmopolitan community of Broome got on well enough together but in 1920 resentment, due to the Koepangers undercutting the Japanese on the labour market, flared up between these two groups. The result was one of the most serious civil disturbances of that time. The Japanese, brandishing torches and clubs, led an attack on the Koepangers, chasing them to the beach where fierce fighting continued on and off for three days. The Koepangers were vastly outnumbered, many of them sustaining head injuries from the efficiently plied Japanese clubs. All the sisters were called upon to assist at the two hospitals as one after another fractured and bleeding head was proffered for treatment. Despite the fact that there were no blood transfusions in those days only one Koepanger died as a result of his wounds.

Ex-students have found ready employment in offices and shops, and many are now following careers as fully qualified nurses or hospital aides. Boys too have qualified for a variety of occupations and become skilled tradesmen. I smile when I look back to the time when the grandfather of one of those trained workers was assisting a Trappist Missionary brother with some building repairs. From high up the ladder the Brother called to his helper to tell him how much cement was left in the barrel. The reply came back: 'Little bit, plenty, full up, not much!' The Trappist gave up trying to calculate this sum and descended to look for himself.

Concerts were a popular form of entertainment and many revealed unsuspected talents. When one of the sisters came up with the idea of staging Gilbert and Sullivan's 'H.M.S. Pinafore', everyone entered enthusiastically into the spirit of producing this delightful musical. One of the German priests undertook to make naval caps which he ingeniously constructed of cardboard and flour paste. The chorus, mostly Aboriginal, was excellent and the captain, a fine singer, proved himself a true artist. On the night of the performance the hall, decorated with coloured streamers and brightly lit with hurricane lanterns, was packed to the doors with an excited audience. Sisters and German priests and brothers were given seats beside a representative of His Majesty's government, who occupied the place of honour centrefront. He joined the rest of the audience in cheers and hearty expressions of congratulation. It was indeed a night to remember and the sisters went to bed with the feeling of having co-operated in a real triumph.

Leprosy became endemic throughout the north. The Aborigines reaction to pain was deep silence.

The story of our work with the lepers of the Kimberleys would be incomplete without some reference to the orchestral band that was established at the leprosarium during the war when the incidence of the dread disease was at its highest level. The project started in a modest way after five violins were made available to us and five patients began learning to play them. As more and more patients expressed interest, so the orchestra grew until, over a period of years, there were no fewer than forty violins, six banjos, one cello and a cornet – all played by full or part Aborigines. It might be found hard to believe that the members of that Aboriginal leper band played excerpts from Beethoven, Mozart, Wagner and even Handel, and that they played not only with considerable skill and feeling, but also with genuine appreciation of the works of these great masters. In lighter vein, they also enjoyed playing dance music and beating out the rhythm of honky tonky.

The Flying Doctors

In 1956 the sisters established a food-centre and hospital at Balgo, on the edge of the Northern Territory where they cared for the children in dormitories and for the adult Aboriginals in camps. One sister, in her memoirs, offers an eyewitness account from her time in Balgo in the 1950s:

> The people lived in tribal groups. They had no houses or shelters and moved camp every two or three months for hygiene reasons. The children lived in two dormitories and I did the cooking for them in the dining room, with the help of two or three women. All the bread was made by three women. The men killed their own beef. The women could not have their babies in the camp, so when the baby was due, the mother went bush with other women. The baby's cord was sealed with ant-bed mud, many babies did not survive. The mothers were reluctant to come to our little hospital, as they were afraid of being sent into Derby hospital on the Flying Doctors' plane. The plane came once a month. There was always a doctor who attended to any sick people and, if necessary, took them into Derby on the plane. They also brought our mail and a few perishables. We called plane day, 'Christmas Day', as we were happy to receive our mail, and hear news from our sisters and home.

For over thirty years, the sisters willingly accepted the isolation of the region before reluctantly the decision was made to close the mission and pass on the torch to others. The closure of the mission was a sharp reminder of the rapidly dwindling numbers of active sisters in the Congregation.

Nature's wondrous liturgy

The sisters play an important collaborative role in the Catholic mission in La Grange (now known as Bidyadanga) where Catholicism is still young. The mission was founded in 1956. In the past, one of the big impediments to progress on many levels has been the 'grog', alcohol. Although the locals have shaken off the yoke of subservience, western culture has brought many new problems. Inability to control drinking has created a range of social problems including domestic violence. There has been a domino effect to the alcohol problems with large sections of the white community labelling Aboriginals as 'lazy-good-for-nothings' and arguing that money handed to them in welfare payments is wasted. In turn, Aboriginal rights have become something of a political football in mainstream Australian politics. However, in recent years in La Grange the local community has started to take more control of their lives and has managed to eliminate many of the problems of the abuse of alcohol by issuing an ultimatum – stay sober or else clear out.

Since becoming involved in the area, the small community of sisters, sometimes only one sister, has been at the forefront of self and community development programmes, though always in collaboration with the local people. They have been greatly helped by the innate spirituality of the people they have come to serve.

Aboriginal spirituality has some striking similarities with Celtic spirituality, notably a shared emphasis on the sacredness of the land and nature. Here, in this marvellous world of sheer rock walls, deep gorges, high ridges and spellbinding beaches, it is easy to really pray the words of the creed, 'I believe in God, the creator of heaven and earth.' The vast acres of beauty, prisms of light and fertility, hint clearer than candlelight at the face of God. The divine in the ordinary, the ordinary in the divine, represents a mutual movement of love in nature's wondrous liturgy. The locals can discern the voice of the transcendent in the near silence of the whispery breeze. In this environment, the sisters have been challenged by the locals to reassess their own faith and priorities, and have come to a much heightened appreciation of what is really important in life.

The best tribute to the sisters' work in the area comes from one of the Aboriginals, Madelene Jadai, a teaching assistant in the local school about to embark on a degree course in the Broome campus of Notre Dame University, where the sisters are at the forefront of the campaign to ensure Aboriginals have access to third level education:

> When the St John of God Sisters came to work at La Grange they were taken in to be part of our Aboriginal family. We were able to share with them our culture and way of life. They were then able to help us learn about God more easily. Because of the sisters being with us, I have learned that we are all important and special to God. The sisters have really made me feel I belong to the Church. And that I have the right to do things in Church to encourage others to be involved in the life of the Church.

> We are beginning to feel that the Church is the people of God and that we are in charge and can be responsible for our life in God. Now we are beginning to know that Aboriginal culture and the Catholic way go together. Many people have come to help us over the years – but most also go away again. The sisters have stayed with us and shared everything with us – our happy times and sad times.

Producing tomorrow's leaders is seen as a priority in facilitating the Aboriginals to take control of their destiny. The sisters have responded to the increasingly obvious need to provide higher education for Aboriginals in remote communities by establishing the Broome campus of Notre Dame University and the Kimberley Centre. The Centre offers Aboriginals the opportunity to receive the formal training necessary to fill leadership positions, while not requiring total dislocation from their communities. It is important for their autonomy to have the opportunities to work within their communities as teachers, nurses and in other service and leadership positions.

Emerging from the shadows

In considering the sisters' dealings with Aboriginal people, it is easy to say with the benefit of hindsight that things could and should have been handled differently. Children, occasionally described as 'pagans', were taken from the families and raised in a way which was 'right and fitting' for children who were Catholic and white – thus contributing to the decimation of aboriginal culture. This was government policy and was not initiated by the sisters. However, it must also be borne in mind that the sisters were putting their own lives at risk in the leprosarium in North West Australia.

Verbum Caro Factum Est, the Word was made flesh. The Latin tag is still inscribed on the tabernacle of the church used by the Aboriginal community at Balgo. It serves as an ironic reminder of past attitudes to the Church's mission work and of how much things have changed. The sisters who work with indigenous people are most interested in encouraging them to express Christian faith in terms of their own culture, rather than through the European culture brought by the first missionaries. A St John of God sister was the first non-cleric to be appointed as a director of the Pontifical Mission Societies in an Australian diocese, and from that position of leadership changed the focus towards drawing out of the people what is within them, rather than imposing ideas from the outside.

This process is reflected in new forms of Aboriginal Christian art, music, liturgy and story telling. A prime mover in this development was Sr Alice Dempsey who began working at Balgo to encourage the practice of ceremonies and painting among older people who had asked to be baptised later in life and were making connections between being Aboriginal and being Christian. What emerged is a now world-renowned group of artists painting religious, traditional, and dreaming stories in new forms, using canvases, paint and a new range of colours.

Another key objective is the gathering of oral histories so that the life stories of the old people, who were the foundation of the Church in the Kimberley, will not be lost. It is a process of assessing the past, the arrival of the missions and the impact upon traditional culture, both good and bad. This is complemented by paintings which tell the story.

The local women have taken leadership roles as group leaders, teachers of the faith, and song leaders. The women are more confident, less self-conscious about getting up in a religious setting, and religious ceremony sits more comfortably with them. In contrast, the lives of the Aboriginal men have been tragically eroded by the impact of 'white culture', chiefly alcohol and legal systems, so even among the young people the women are more present in leadership.

A respect for Aboriginal customs means grappling with sensitivities which would not emerge in the 'white' world. A good example is the way they exhibit their respect for the dead. When a Balgo person dies his or her name may not be mentioned and the word *Kumunytayi* is substituted. Many fear that the spirit of the dead person will trouble you if you mention the name. But because of the mission background, many people use biblical names, which poses difficulties with scripture readings and preaching.

Some Aboriginals consider themselves as Old Testament people, particularly as 'Old Testament-like' things happen to them. For example, at Warmun, they chant a song about how one year they were travelling to the Pentecost celebrations at a distant community. A cloud travelled with them, which they saw as an indication that they were being led. When they got there the cloud stopped and they knew that the Spirit of the Holy One was going to come to them.

Christian ceremonies, such as healings, anointings and blessings, resonate deeply with the Aboriginal psyche. The difficulty is in deciphering to what extent rituals are understood in a Christian way and how much in a traditional way.

Aboriginal people have, with justification, in recent times been critical of the way in which, in the past, Christian missions have suppressed the Aboriginal culture. However, some Aboriginals readily admit that at dangerous times the Church provided essential buffers – against the miners during the Northern Territory and Kimberley gold rushes late last century and, in recent times, against the destructive side of tourism. Some of the old people recall times when the police went out to shoot Aboriginal groups and appreciate that many of the Kimberley people would not even have survived without the protection of the Church.

These problems are compounded in every location where there is a displaced Aboriginal population. Such people are continually changed and changing as they respond to overwhelming numbers of people and the impact of modern technology. In many respects they are at a crossroads in their history. There is no realistic proposal to return to their past. Their challenge is to take the advantages of modern life, whilst retaining the most valuable elements of their culture which are deeply ingrained in them. Changes need to be integrated in a way which maintains their identity, their sense of community and their belief in the value of their own society.

History has taught them that it is not safe to rely on the consistency of favour of 'whitefellas'. Their experience serves as a powerful reminder that it is risky to let anyone have too much power over other people. It simply is not safe. The Sisters of St John of God are at the forefront of the movement to redress the injustices which have been perpetrated against the Aboriginals and to help them build up their self-image. A key principle for the sisters is that all the education and training programmes they undertake will have some form of accreditation so that the trainees will leave with a certificate in their hands. Such measures help to overcome the problems of low self-esteem. A crucial factor in the sisters' work in this area has been continuity. Sisters have given a major commitment to the indigenous people rather than working for just a few years and then returning to other parts of Australia. This has given the Sisters of St John of God tremendous credibility in the Aboriginal community.

The work of Antonio and the sisters who followed in her footsteps is keenly appreciated by the indigenous people. One local woman, Elizabeth Puertollano, wrote of the sisters' work in Lombadina:

> The John of God Sisters came with a mission. They were nurses and teachers, seamstresses, musicians, carers and helpers. The centre of the mission was to form us into God's way. In my time I have seen many sisters come and go. Some have gone because of accident or sickness, which may have been in God's plan, but it was sad for us. We have so many lovely memories of the sisters. With their care and discipline the sisters left a mark in my life of a firm foundation in the Christian tradition. When I go back to what I know of the Aboriginal way, I know that it is in God's dreaming.

> The sisters made us feel that we are all the same; we belonged to the one God. They accepted us and our way. We

felt part of them and hid nothing from them. The sisters went through hardships. They left their homes to come to us. Some of them never went back. What better way is there to show their love for the Aboriginal people. They prepared us to face the challenge of the world in God's way. They proved to be mothers to us – in times of joy, times of sorrow and times of pain. Real mothers! The John of God Sisters came 100 years ago and we want to thank them. I would ask the sisters to look around the whole of Australia and feel proud of what they have accomplished in this big country.

Today the sisters' evolving understanding of their mission with the Aboriginals can be summed up in the following way: 'We used to walk before them. Now we walk beside them to get ready to walk behind them.'

Notes:
1. Mary Durack, The Rock and the Sand, Corgi, 1969, p 21.

CHAPTER FIVE

Changing Times

One of the largest private hospitals in the southern hemisphere is the St John of God hospital in Subiaco, an inner suburb of Perth. Nearby is the administrative centre of the province of St Thérèse, which today governs all the sisters' projects in Australia and Pakistan. Things could have been very different. After the surrender of the Japanese military and navy in World War Two in 1945, plans were discovered on which the hospital was marked as the Japanese Headquarters!

Subiaco Hospital grew by a process of organic growth. In 1895 Bishop Gibney made two cottages available to the sisters in Adelaide Terrace in the city of Perth, one for their accommodation and one for the care of sick people. It could only accommodate three patients, hence the need for the sisters to care for patients in their own homes. Home nursing was quite common in those days. In 1897 the sisters moved from Adelaide Terrace to Subiaco which became, and remains, the mother house of the Australian Province. There the first single-floor hospital was constructed, with beds for thirty-five patients. A double-storey convent was also built. Both buildings were made of wood. The hospital grew as the needs emerged though one development was aborted. An open-air T.B. ward, as tuberculosis was rampant at the time, was constructed. However, because of the fears of other patients, it had to be closed.

The sisters opened the first school in 1897 in Subiaco and two sisters also established a 'Select School', a secondary school enabling pupils to prepare for tertiary education or nursing exams. A loan from the bank allowed the sisters to extend the hospital and rebuild the convent in brick. A new wing was added to the hospital during the first world war. In 1924 a large block to house forty postulants was erected behind the convent. Over the

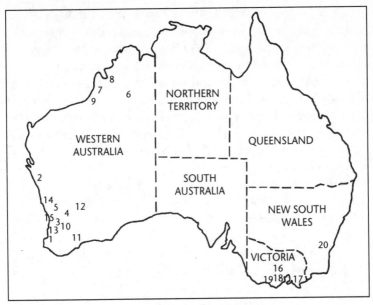

Sisters of St John of God
Australian Province 1995

Western Australia		Victoria	New South Wales
1 Bunbury	8 Derby	16 Ballarat	20 Goulburn
2 Geraldton	9 La Grange	17 Brighton	
3 Murdoch	10 Armadale	18 Geelong	
4 Rivervale	11 Lake Grace	19 Warrnambool	
5 Subiaco	12 Northam		
6 Balgo	13 Safety Bay		
7 Broome	14 Wembley		
	15 Fremantle		

next six years, one hundred and twelve novices were trained at Subiaco. Plans for a new hospital were halted temporarily because of the Great Depression. The finance was eventually raised and a new building, with four floors and a basement with X-ray and pathology departments, was completed. The third floor, 3A, became known as the 'Maternity' and the first baby was born there in 1937. In 1963 a new three-storey midwifery section was constructed. In the same year a radiotherapy clinic was added. In 1965 a nurses' home was opened though shortly after it became redundant when the Nursing Board changed its requirement that trainee nurses 'live in'. The building was subsequently converted to medical suites for various practitioners.

Throughout the sixties and seventies, the sisters faced many changes, including the growing economic equality and independence of women, the economic pressures of a credit-based social economy, changing social attitudes, changing demands on hospital care, and a sharp decline in religious vocations. All these changes had a cumulative effect on their work in the hospital. Hospital function and staffing had to be considered in a new light. The sisters decided that, if they were to maintain their reputation for excellence and, more importantly, their commitment to the optimum level of health care for their patients, the only course of action open to them was to build a new hospital. Accordingly, a seven-level ward block was constructed between 1977 and 1981. A new wing was added in 1990 at the cost of 31 million dollars. With 360 licensed beds and ten operating theatres, the hospital caters for 20,000 patients each year and delivers more than 2,400 babies annually. A 'twinning' arrangement has been established between the hospital and some of the Catholic hospitals in Indonesia to assist them with nursing and medical training and development.

As the population grew and spread out over the vast area in the latter part of the nineteenth century and early years of the twentieth, the call came from other areas. In Western Australia, this led to the establishment of the School of the Sacred Heart in Greenbushes (which ran under the auspices of the sisters from 1907 to 1915), and St Aloysius school in Rosalie in 1909 (which the sisters ran until 1912). As they established a reputation for high quality service, the sisters increasingly became in demand in other states of Australia, beginning in Ballarat, Victoria.

King Arthur and Bailey's Ghost

The site of the St John of God convent and hospital in Ballarat has a colourful history. In the 1880s Ballarat was a bustling town because of gold mining. Only a handful of people made much money as a consequence of working in these mines. One of the exceptions was Somerset-born William Bailey. In 1883 he built the family house destined to become known as 'Bailey's Mansion'. One night, when his senses were dimmed, he mistook a statue of King Arthur, which stood poised on top of the newel at the foot of the stairway, for a burglar. He whipped out a pistol in defence of his property and fired a shot, as he kept a large sum of money in a strong room built into the thickness of a wall. King Arthur was wounded in the back and the resultant bullet hole was used by staff in the early years of the hospital as a repository for used cigarettes until one caused a small fire.

Despite having cost Bailey £14,000 in the 1880s, his derelict mansion was bought by the Roman Catholic Church in 1914 for only £4000, with a view to establishing a Catholic hospital. The house had been empty due to a local belief that it was haunted by Bailey's ghost. The local bishop invited the Sisters of St John of God to take charge of the new hospital and the following year they were ready for business. The sisters took seriously the reports that the house was haunted. The first night they had a reception committee waiting, including a candle and holy water but the ghost did not show up. The ghost was never seen or heard again!

A more serious problem facing the sisters was that the style of building was too ornate for their purpose. They were compelled to remove the magnificent ceiling which cost them an extra thousand pounds. Every pound of that cement was thrown out the window by the two sisters in charge. They had to clean and polish the floors and then buy lino from a firm who was kind enough to give them credit.

Although the hospital was renovated to the most exacting standards, for the first three months there were no patients. The sisters were advised by many priests and others to return to Western Australia. The bishop was ill and was in no position to help. One Sunday, the Superior suggested that the sisters offer the fifteen decades of the rosary to Our Lady that she might send patients. They began and got as far as the second mystery when they heard a ring at the hall door. It was their first patient – a postulant from the Loreto convent, suffering from peritonitis. Two sisters took charge, when the doctors examined her and decided that an operation was useless because she would be dead within a few hours. Eventually they decided to operate, although claiming she had no chance of pulling through. Their diagnosis was proved incorrect because the patient went on to make a full recovery. Over the following weeks the patients started to flood in.

In 1927 a wing in the same style was added. The sisters carried out all the nursing duties in addition to laundry, cleaning and cooking. In keeping with the commitment to have self-supporting institutions, the sisters also had responsibility for a dairy and large vegetable garden. 1948 was a significant date for the sisters in Ballarat when the foundation stone of the new hospital was laid. A combination of a deep economic recession and the Second World War had delayed progress on the site. It took six more years for the hospital to be completed. Four years later a school of nursing was opened. In 1977 a medical services block was begun and completed four years later. In 1984 the hospital was re-developed despite the fire which destroyed part of the on-going project. It was completed in 1986. A feature of the new hospital is an excellent diagnostic unit. This high-tech world has required a major cultural shift for the sisters working in the hospital. Up to the end of the 1950s their filing system was nothing but a sugar bag! Now there is a sea of files and sophisticated computer systems.

The one constant, throughout all the changes, is the sisters' high reputation for their holistic care. One patient penned this tribute entitled, 'For the St John Of God Nuns', following a lengthy stay in Ballarat:

> Prop me on the pillow nurse
> My journey is almost done
> I'll see the dawn for that is near
> But not the setting sun.
>
> I knew this day for me would come
> all die who have been born.
> And as my time is drawing near
> I do not feel forlorn.
>
> Instead I feel the gentle hands
> are reaching out for me
> but these are hands no earthly being
> except in death will see.

For they are hands whose touch was love
throughout my lifetime's length
and that same love will now uphold
weakness in its strength.

The sun is climbing higher
there are people in the street
where shoulders bear the worries
in a world without retreat.

Don't grieve for me, I'm happy
but spare your tears for them
for those who live must suffer
this is the creed of men.

The sun is almost overhead
my body weaker grows
and now an inner strength appears
from where, no mortal knows.

Now someone stands beside me
extends a welcome hand
a voice so soft and gentle,
is this the promised land?

Suddenly I see it all
so simple, nothing grand
the miracle I now behold
a babe could understand.

Incredible why no-one's guessed
and let the whole world know
the mysteries of life and death
why people come and go.

The nurse bent down, no uttered word
the span of life had passed
and still the secrets of the soul
were locked in heaven's grasp.

In the 1990s a number of new programmes were introduced, for example, 'Living with Cancer', a support course with meditation and relaxation classes which allows the relatives of the patients a better understanding of what their loved ones are going through. Oncology is the subject of on-going development. In 1993 a helipad was constructed to assist with emergency cases. In the same year the Bridget Clancy Women's Health Centre was established with a range of new services for women, including a body image course. The hospital caters for two hundred and twenty-four patients.

Strong links exist between the hospital and the local community. There are regular exchanges with tertiary educational institutions such as the Aquinas campus of the Australian Catholic University, to develop the level of medical research and expertise in the region. An emergency medicine department has been established, providing a 7-days-a-week, 24-hour service to meet the needs of acutely and critically ill patients. The hospital has a 'twinning' programme with the Vaiola hospital in Tonga, to assist them in meeting their medical, educational and resource needs. The project involves educational exchanges between the two hospitals and assistance in areas such as staff development and training, clinical and management expertise and community health education.

The odd one out

Goulburn, Australia's oldest inland city, is unique among the hospitals in the St John of God Health Care System in four respects. Firstly, the original hospital, when the sisters came to the area in 1925, is still in use though obviously it has been updated through the years. Secondly, it is the only community which has continued to use the exact same building as its convent throughout its history – allowing that the building was extended in 1968. Thirdly, it is a public hospital run and financed by the State. Fourthly, like an increasing number of hospitals in Australia, it employs the more cost-efficient 'cook and chill' system of providing meals to patients, that is, meals are cooked outside the hospital by a company, delivered to the hospital days in advance, stored in the hospital, re-heated and served to the patients at the appropriate times.

As in all the other John of God hospitals, staff training and development is an important focus, as is pastoral care. Sustaining and nurturing the care-givers is seen as 'a must'. Today the hospital is a modern 55 bed unit with its own hydrotherapy pool providing essential aged care, palliative care and rehabilitation service to the local community. Two major developments have been introduced in recent years. Firstly, 'Giles Court', called at the staff's request after Sr Annunciata Giles as a tribute to her sterling service in the hospital down through the years, is a specialised residential unit for the confused and disturbed elderly, consisting of two eight-bed units. The units are purpose-built to provide an uncomplicated, secure, home-like atmosphere where dementia sufferers can easily become familiar and comfortable with their surroundings. The design enables the resident to wander around, if they so desire, in relatively secure surroundings. It offers 24-hour care for elderly confused people with behaviour disturbances, who are still ambulant. The staff do not wear uniforms, a factor which is in keeping with the policy of creating a home-like atmosphere, instead of the clinical atmosphere often found in hospitals and nursing homes.

Secondly, there is 'Carrawarra', which is a purpose made transitional-living unit. It provides a home-like environment where, following traumatic brain injury, adults can re-learn the skills necessary for them to return to the community as independent as possible. It is designed to facilitate a smooth transition from hospital care to living in the community. Each resident has an individual programme and participates in everyday activities such as shopping, preparing meals, washing, personal hygiene, work skills etc. Residential carers provide 24-hour support and guidance, assisting residents in daily living skills. Residents attend therapy sessions at the hospital on the same basis as other outpatients, with access to services such as occupational therapy.

One woman and her horse

In September, 1927 the sisters took up residence in Bunbury, overlooking the vast Indian ocean. The administrator of the cathedral opposite the building, who was slightly eccentric, went to the country the day the sisters arrived rather than meet them. A massive tidy-up was required before the building would make a suitable hospital. While the tidy-up was in progress, the sisters slept out on the side verandah, and in the morning their slippers were covered with snails. The night before the hospital opened on 11 December, there was a most violent electrical storm – the lightning was running all along the walls. The sisters were still sleeping on the verandah and took refuge in the oratory. The workmen were still working and they too took shelter claiming, 'It is just like shrapnel at the war. It is the work of the devil, so mad that the sisters had arrived.'

In 1935 the hospital received its most unusual patient ever. A big horse-race was taking place in the vicinity. Shortly before the race the favourite sustained an injury. Nonetheless the trainer wanted to run him in the race. The authorities would only let the horse run in the race provided the owner could furnish evidence of a clear bill of health. He asked the sister in charge at Bunbury if she would X-ray the horse. The sister agreed – on condition that if the horse won, the hospital would get a share of his winnings. The horse had to be put on the elevator because the X-ray unit was on the second floor. Although the sisters had never learned the logistics of X-raying a horse from the nursing manual, they rose to the occasion. The X-ray was clear and the horse went on to win the race. With their winnings the sisters bought a grandfather clock which today sits proudly and in perfect working order in the St John of God house in Rivervale.

Apart from its unusual patient, Bunbury was also blessed with extraordinary sisters. Among their number was Mother Alacoque. She has a hallowed place in the folklore of the Congregation. In the pre-Vatican II days it was common for the sisters to maintain silence during meal times as they listened to spiritual reading, usually the life of a saint. An exception was normally made on feastdays when the sisters were allowed to converse freely. On one feastday when Mother Alacoque was away from the community she sent a telegram to her sisters but the message lost something in the translation. She intended the message to read, 'No talk for breakfast. M Alacoque.' However, the message the community received was, 'No talk for breakfast. All cuckoo'!

The hospital serves the South West region of Western Australia, which has the largest population outside the metropolitan area of Perth. Major refurbishments were carried out in the hospital during 1952, 1972 and 1986 to meet the increasing demand for quality health care in the region. The hospital has 125 beds and provides medical/surgical/paediatric and urgent care for patients. One of the problems facing the John of

God Health Care System as a whole, and the Bunbury hospital in particular, is the difficulty of planning for the future because of the frequency of changes in government health policy, especially with regard to the location of public hospitals. If a new public hospital is situated beside a St John of God hospital, it is clearly not advisable to spend millions of dollars on a new private hospital at precisely the same time. In the short term the hospital will examine possible working opportunities with the government's health department in extending health care services to public patients.

The migraine sister

In the 1930s, because of the great growth of population on the Eastern side of the River Swan, the sisters decided to build a hospital there in Rivervale. An elegant domestic dwelling named 'Hill 60', which was built in 1888, was purchased by the sisters in 1932 and they converted it into a hospital. It was quickly found to be too small but continued as a hospital until 1936 when it was adapted as a convent and a new hospital constructed. The orders given to the architect were, 'Build the best and equip with the very latest.' Over the years a number of extensions were added, for example, in 1969 a new wing of the hospital was opened with beds for 36 patients. On Easter Sunday night 1970 a near disaster occurred when a cyclone blew the roof off the convent, shattered windows and caused a lot of damage to what was left of the building.

For a variety of reasons, part of the old hospital and convent were modernised and converted into a hospital for the care of the chronically ill and frail aged. In 1984 that part of the building was vacated and the patients placed in nursing homes. In 1989 the building was redesigned as Fatima Medicentre, with a number of doctors renting rooms. In the light of shifting health care needs in the area it no longer made sense to keep the new hospital open and the decision was made to close it in 1994.

Although Rivervale was not one of the bigger hospitals, it had a number of claims to fame. The first brain surgery done in Western Australia was performed in the hospital. For some years it served as the only bone bank in Western Australia and supplied all hospitals in the State. One sister who gained an international reputation was Philomena Earle. She pioneered a cure for migraine by dietetic treatment. Her discovery attracted so much media attention and correspondence from the public that a special secretary had to be engaged to deal with it. To this day her notes are regularly sought by research students in this area. She also developed insulin treatment for diabetes, in tablet form, and an autogenous vaccine for leprosy. During 1985, the urology department was upgraded to accommodate ultrasonic renal stone disintegration. This speciality increased the occupancy of the hospital, and gave the unit the title of 'centre of excellence'.

A hospital with a view

As was the case with so many of their foundations, the Sisters of Saint John of God came to Geraldton, in 1935, at the request of the local bishop. A site had been donated by a local man for a hospital to serve the sick of the town and its environs. Like Subiaco, the hospital initially seemed very remote, being in the bushland, about a mile and a half from the town. Again as in Subiaco, the sisters' foresight was rewarded and the hospital quickly attracted patients from the locality. It had the advantage of a picturesque view of the Indian Ocean from the balconies on three sides.

Although the plans for the hospital were drawn up by the acclaimed architect Dean Hawes, it quickly emerged that there were deficiencies in the design – the rooms were small while the corridors were excessively wide. However, the double-storeyed building had the benefit of wide verandahs which afforded the patients an opportunity to convalesce in pleasant surroundings. The facilities included a men's ward on the ground floor with adjoining rooms, with an operating theatre and a doctor's room, a tiny office and reception room. The plan was substantially repeated on the second floor with a ward for women. As supplies of electricity at the time were unreliable, no lift was installed which meant that patients for surgery from the second floor, had to be carried on a stretcher to the theatre by orderlies, and sometimes, the sisters, and then back again when the operation was completed.

Initially the sisters were accommodated in the hospital. After four years a convent became essential as the hospital needed the beds. In 1960 the existing convent was extended and remodelled to cater for a larger community staffing the hospital, which in its turn, in 1968, was re-designed to meet the new demands of surgery, X-rays and nursing. The district had grown considerably and the port was playing an important part for the hinterland discoveries of iron ore which rapidly became a major export. Further north the State also grew, with new industrial complexes meaning more road, air and sea transport, and Geraldton became a growing residential centre for these activities.

The hospital was re-built at a cost of $10 million and officially opened during 1992, to continue to meet the increasing health care needs of the Geraldton community. A lack of space meant that the convent had to be demolished. The sisters lived in rented accommodation initially but then four residential units were built to accommodate two people in each. Such units would be easier to sell should the sisters contemplate withdrawing their personnel. The following year a new medical clinic, complete with doctors' consulting suites, diagnostic services as well as education and meeting facilities, was added to further involve the hospital in community activities. The hospital delivers 40% of babies born in the surrounding region, and each month caters for more than 200 patients who require emergency treatment through the urgent care unit.

Borromeo's Kingdom

When 23-year-old Margaret Mahoney became the first patient of the new St John of God hospital in Warrnambool in 1940 with ear trouble, nobody, least of all herself, could have foreseen that she would enter the Congregation two years later, and after more than twenty-five years she would return, as Sr Borromeo, to serve in the hospital. Today she is still buzzing like a bee in the community.

The sisters came to Warrnambool at the request of the local bishop. This town, west of Melbourne, is in an area which has a large Irish colony. It is believed that so many Irish congregated in the region because it is the area in Australia which is best suited for the growing of potatoes! The Irish influence is evident in some of the place-names, such as 'Killarney' and 'Belfast'.

The original plans for the hospital had to be scaled down dramatically because of the confluence of the outbreak of war and depression, and there was insufficient money as well as a shortage of building materials. The hospital accommodated 29 patients and had well-equipped surgical, X-ray, midwifery, and catering departments. An extension was added in 1961 and in 1965 a new convent was opened. A second extension was completed in 1971. Additional extensions were made in 1985.

However, that was something of a holding operation. If the sisters were to have a long-term future in the area they would need to build a new hospital. Accordingly, plans were put in place for a new single-storey sixty-bed hospital adjacent to the old one. The development was designed with a view to extending the range of speciality services provided by the hospital.

The new hospital features two fully equipped operating theatres, a home-like birthing suite, a high-dependency unit, day surgery, outpatients clinic and diagnostic services such as radiology and pathology, as well as the highest standard patient accommodation with ensuite facilities. The highest point of the $11 million redevelopment is a cross, symbolising the hospital's commitment to care. The cross stands over a glazed turret which is floodlit at night. The purpose of the glass around the turret is to allow light into the hall.

The army hut convent

In 1948 the sisters answered the needs of the women of the wheat belt of West Australia who needed specialised treatment and care for their babies, without having to resort to the long road to the city. Northam was chosen as the most central for the surrounding districts. At that time there was still no convent for the sisters. An army hut of asbestos, with rooms for five sisters, an oratory, parlour, community room and bathroom, was transferred complete from the army camp at Northam and set up beside the brick hospital.

For years, this venture prospered and medical facilities were excellent. However, in 1970 the government built a large regional hospital for both general/surgical and maternity care. Increasingly sophisticated techniques were having a dramatic effect on the intake of patients in Northam. The tiny hospital was no longer viable.

For a short period it carried on as a 'C' class hospital for the aged with accommodation for sixteen. There were never more than ten beds occupied at one time. However, the sisters were hamstrung by the fact that the hospital badly needed repairs and restoration. In such circumstances the hospital could not be maintained. The curtain came down in 1973.

The impact of the hospital was considerable. In its twenty-five years of existence, seven thousand babies were born.

The sisters received a nice tribute when news of the closure became known. The deputy mayor observed, 'The greatest hospital in the world could not replace the human kindness and patience of the sisters'.

Music is the food of healing

In 1949, at the request of Archbishop Mannix, the sisters went to Brighton to staff a psychiatric hospital in close proximity to the centre of Melbourne, and a short walk from Brighton Beach. In addition to transforming the premises into a proper hospital suitable for the care of patients, the sisters were also required to gain the acceptance by the local community of a hospital devoted entirely to the care and treatment of psychiatric patients. This was a serious problem as an attitude of prejudice against mentally ill patients prevailed. Sadly this problem has never been fully eradicated and at various times the sisters have been greatly pained by the attitudes with which they have been confronted from a significant minority of the local population.

A more immediate problem facing the pioneer sisters in Brighton was that they had no training in psychiatric nursing. The problem was considerably exacerbated by the fact that there was not the range of drugs available then that there is now, particularly for dealing with violent patients. The patients, all men, were difficult for the sisters to manage, and there were many chases after absconding patients. Once the sisters had undertaken psychiatric nursing courses, they were more readily accepted and became more adept at the rehabilitation of those for whom they had to care. On the plus side, the hospital is set in a beautiful garden environment which provides tranquil scenes and a place to sit in peace.

When a successful application was made to take female patients, the upper floor was reserved for men and the lower for women. In 1959 a convent and chapel was built at the upper end of the hospital. Extensions to the hospital in 1960s and1970s raised the bed occupancy to forty-three.

The community has one of only seventy-five music therapists (1994 figures) in the world. Music therapy is the planned use of music to assist people with special needs such as people who are aged, affected by strokes, heart attacks or other traumatic events, have degenerative conditions of the brain and nervous system such as Parkinson's or Alzheimer's disease, are intellectually or physically disabled, have sensory impairments, in need of psychiatric assistance or are terminally ill. In many situations such therapy can bring a sense of purpose to people's existence. It enables them to maintain their involvement with others around them, and to recognise and relate to their environment. Guided Imagery and Music is also provided in the hospital. This is a music-centred transformation therapy which uses specifically programmed classical music to stimulate and sustain a dynamic unfolding of inner experiences, in support of physical, psychological and spiritual wholeness.

In the 1980s and 1990s a number of new programmes and services have been introduced to meet the increasing needs of the community, like the community psychiatric nurse programme. However, the hospital building in its present form is no longer adequate to meet the needs of the future. Accordingly, forward planning is in operation.

Yeats Country

The contribution of Ireland to the Australian province was recognised in a very practical way in 1951 with their decision to open a nursing home in Ballymote in Sligo. One of the curious features of modern history is that right up to the 1950s so many Irishwomen were ready, willing and able to leave Ireland to enter a convent in Australia, America or Africa. A noteworthy feature of the Australian province today is that so many of these Irish women also have blood sisters in the Congregation.

The nursing home in Ballymote for many years provided general and maternity nursing care for people in the area. With changing patterns of health care, and changing needs, the sisters turned their attention exclusively to the care of elderly people.

When the original building became unsuitable for use as a nursing facility in the 1980s, discussions were held with the

North Western Health Board about the health care needs of Ballymote and its environs. These discussions resulted in an agreement that the Health Board would build a new twenty-bed nursing home for elderly people which would be run by the sisters. This was seen as a significant step in collaboration between the sisters and the local statutory health care authorities.

In the early 1990s the addition of a day-care facility for elderly people from the area extended the ministry of the nursing home in a significant way.

Another welcome development has been the building of a number of small houses for elderly or dependent people, by the St Vincent de Paul Society, on the site adjacent to the nursing home.

Jesus expressed his mission thus: 'I have come that you may have life and have it to the full.' In keeping with the Congregation's commitment to care for the whole person, the sisters in Ballymote, as in all of the Congregation's hospitals and residential homes, devote considerable energy and resources to pastoral care. The objective is to help people have a right relationship with self, others and God. More precisely it is to provide professional and sympathetic support and help, to relieve unwarranted stress and anxiety and to help people to overcome hardships and disability in the quest for true health and a good quality of life. In addition to running the nursing home, the sisters in Ballymote are very involved in the local community, visiting people in their homes and responding to pastoral needs in whatever way they can.

New horizons

In 1954 the sisters moved into new territory, literally and metaphorically, moving to a new country and a new apostolate. At the request of the Archbishop of Wellington, New Zealand, the sisters went to take up residence in Lower Hutt and open a home for unmarried mothers, where they could receive prenatal care and training for the experience ahead of them. The girls were kept in the home until the time came for them to go into hospital to have their babies. During their stay in the home, the girls were engaged in keeping their house in order, learning to cook and developing various skills and hobbies. In most cases the young women gave up their babies for adoption.

The New Zealand venture had always been considered as an interim project, until another Congregation could be found whose apostolate was more in the realm of caring for unmarried mothers. Eventually the Good Shepherd nuns agreed to take over and the St John of God's relinquished the foundation to their administration. They returned to Subiaco in 1965 where the sisters were badly needed for other projects in the province.

All creatures great and small

In 1974 the sisters took over from the Missionary Sisters of the Sacred Heart in the hospital in Geelong at the request of Monsignor Murray who was concerned that the Catholic ethos in the hospital be maintained when the Missionary Sisters pulled out. The St John of God sisters leased the hospital initially but purchased it three years later, changing the name from Holy Cross to John of God.

The hospital is located in the centre of the city, and cares for approximately 8,500 patients every year, delivering more than 1,000 babies over the same period. The hospital was re-built and extended during 1988 and 1992 respectively – and upgraded to an A grade hospital which means it can conduct cardiac surgery. New facilities included four operating theatres with the very latest equipment, new pathology, X-ray, paediatric and gynaecology sections, and an upgrading of all wards which included ensuites and overhead television. The crowning glory is the maternity wing – new mums are pampered in post-natal facilities including a spa, a lounge with a bay view and training videos. The five new spacious delivery suites featured modern labour beds which could be automatically adjusted to any position, to support upright and squatting positions for giving birth. The maternity section also included an intensive care nursery with equipment for premature and sick babies. At the time of writing, the hospital has 106 beds but a one hundred per cent occupancy is a regular occurrence. For this reason it is planned to extend the hospital over the next few years.

State of the art

Appropriately the $65 million St John of God hospital in

Murdoch, West Australia, was opened in 1994 on St John of God day. The history of this state-of-the-art facility goes back much further. In September 1989 the health department had called for submissions for a hospital to serve the southern metropolitan region of Perth. At almost the same time as the tender for Murdoch Hospital went out, the Sisters of St Joseph, whose only Australian hospital previously was St Joseph's private hospital in Bicton, sought to become a part of the St John of God Health Care System in 1989, rather than abandon their mission in health care. The result was a unique collaboration with the two Congregations joining forces to make a submission, proposing a 200-bed hospital. Their joint proposal was successful. The 200-bed licences would come from the closure and relocation of licences from St John of God hospital, Rivervale, and St Joseph's private hospital, Bicton, and in addition securing licences from St Anne's Mercy Hospital, Mt Lawley.

The result is the most innovative health-care complex in Western Australia. It occupies a twelve-hectare site south of the Swan River and sets the standard for modern medical care, combining high-tech medical facilities with home-style patient comforts. The hospital complex includes a three-level medical centre containing medical specialists' consulting rooms, an emergency department operational 24 hours a day, seven days a week, diagnostic facilities including fully-equipped radiology, pathology and nuclear medicine, physiotherapy departments and outpatient care facilities. However, the focus is not on technology but on providing holistic care for each person.

To this end, as in all St John of God hospitals, a sister has been appointed as a 'hospitality sister'. Hospitality, one of the St John of God Health Care System's core values, is integrated in all aspects of care, but these sisters have a special responsibility to represent the origins of care on which the Health Care System is built. These sisters make patients feel welcome, assist with admittance procedures and help allay any fears which patients may have. They also help the pastoral care teams by providing the names of those in need of continuing support. With fewer sisters working closely with patients, the role of sisters welcoming the public helps reinforce the St John of God spirit of the Health Care System.

1994 also saw the sisters involved in another venture in the newly built city of Joondalup in Western Australia. This is a purpose-made city, like Milton Keynes in England. The sisters are in charge of the Medical Centre.

However, the story of the sisters in Australia is not simply a catalogue of new foundations.

Reunited at last

Vatican II was a catalyst in the history of the Congregation in Australia. As we saw in the previous chapter, Antonio O'Brien's decision to take some of the young sisters with her and start a mission in the Kimberley provoked a split and led to the formation of a second John of God province in Australia. Because the sisters were still struggling to establish themselves in Australia, and because they were already overstretched in their apostolate before the call came to help the Aboriginals and, most importantly, because Antonio left for the north-west in defiance of the expressed wishes of the other sisters, her decision caused a lot of resentment. The split left a long legacy of bitterness between the sisters which, at its crudest, degenerated into something of a 'them and us' division.

Over the years, a number of efforts were made to bring the provinces together involving sisters from both provinces, the Generalate in Ireland, and leading church figures in Australia and Rome. The saga generated a tidal wave of correspondence some of which is included below to give a flavour of the discussion:

Letter to Bishop Abraham Brownrigg

February 28th, 1918 Subiaco:

My lord bishop ... You have probably heard that ten years ago M.M. Antonio thought of founding a house in Beagle Bay for blacks and other coloured races. Her projects met with strong opposition from the Community here, in spite of which opposition she left here for Beagle Bay in 1907 accompanied by two novices, without the consent of the then superior of the community; of course with the approbation of the Right Rev Dr Gibney. The circumstances under which they left, the work they have been engaged in since, the distance Beagle Bay is from Perth, the journey taking ten days, the infrequent boat services and the severe climatic conditions, with other enclosed reasons, have decided us to accept amalgamation only if Beagle Bay is a separate province. I am sure there will not be any difficulty about that as their work is altogether different to ours.

This decision has been arrived at only after mature consideration as to what is best for the Institute and I think if any of the members of the Institute in Ireland were here and knew all the circumstances, their decision would be the same. It is thought that you in Ireland have not had the opportunity of knowing how we are circumstanced, which impels me to write this.

Beagle Bay is the only stumbling block. Apart from that we are in favour of amalgamation and consider it will promote God's glory and the good of the Institute. At the same time we fear that if we were in the same province it would mean endless misery and unhappiness for the Sisters.

I am enclosing objections put forward by the Community. Hoping that your Lordship's health is satisfactory. Seeking a remembrance in your prayers.

    I remain, my dear lord Bishop, yours respectfully in J.C.

    Sr M. Aloysius Keating
    Superioress

Report for Provincial Chapter: 20th September, 1946

Work of the Kimberley Province

The Beagle Bay and Lombadina Missions were the only missions where the sisters were allowed to remain during the war years. The Government had offered the sisters to go to Perth when all the other white women were evacuated. At first the children were also allowed to go with the sisters but it was found that this was not allowed by the law regarding leprosy, which forbids blacks and half-castes to travel south.

The nuns refused to go without the children and were allowed to remain at their own risk. When the Broome school children were evacuated to Beagle Bay the nuns kept the school going in a bush shelter. Classes were even formed in typewriting for the senior girls.

At the Leprosarium the sisters were ordered to leave the lepers and go South on the plane. They refused to do so and went into the bush with the lepers. They took the Blessed Sacrament with them and, after a night's vigil, it was given to the sisters by the Superior next morning. No priest had visited the Leprosarium for months. The sisters remained for some time in the same bush shelter as the lepers but were eventually allowed to return to the Leprosarium. It is a great consolation to the sisters that not a single leper has died without baptism in the ten years the sisters have been in charge. A large number of lepers have been cured since the sisters went to Derby.

St Mary's Cathedral, Perth 22nd August, 1956
from the Archbishop of Perth, Archbishop Redmond Prendiville

My dear Mother General,

Please pardon me for approaching you on a subject that is causing much concern amongst a very large number of your sisters. I refer to the proposal to amalgamate the Broome Province with Subiaco. Even though I gave you my candid opinion, it was only a personal and private one. The sisters, especially the senior ones, are far more competent to judge the over-all position than I am. And it is causing unwholesome concern amongst them – a concern that might easily lead to an unfavourable reaction should the amalgamating take place. Please believe me, my dear Mother General, when I say that I am not trying to interfere in the domestic arrangements of the Sisters of St John of God. It is only because I hold them in such very high esteem, (and because I am afraid of the reaction) that I make bold to speak on their behalf.

Could the matter be deferred? ... In God's good time the problem will solve itself. Amalgamation would, no doubt, have advantages as far as Broome is concerned, but it probably would have disastrous consequences amongst the members of the Southern Province – which, may God avert!

It is not that the sisters are not mission-minded, or anxious to undertake a work of charity; it is because they feel that they are already over-loaded – numerically and financially.

Reading between the lines, there does appear to have been an attitude to the Aboriginals which was at best patronising, at worst prejudiced on the part of some of the sisters. This should not be too surprising given that they would have had no contact with Aboriginals. There also seems to have been a residue of bitterness to Antonio and those who followed in her wake amongst some of the sisters in the south which seems disproportionate for her 'crimes'. Finally in 1965, in the spirit of Vatican II, the sisters decided to put past enmities behind them and both provinces were amalgamated.

Responding to the 'signs of the times'.

After World War II, health care entered a rapidly changing era with breathtaking advances in technology which themselves raised a proliferation of important ethical questions. With the Second Vatican Council, the Church, too, went through great changes in its self-understanding. This change was particularly obvious in the religious Congregations. One of the most significant changes was the realisation that all baptised people are called to Christian ministry, that the works of the Church such as health care, must not be confined to the responsibility of religious women and men. Religious life itself was seen to be called to renewal and reassessment.

The decline in religious vocations and the increasing complexity of medical care and medical administration have forced Catholic health-care services, like their secular counterparts, to re-examine their role. One result of all these changes has been a much greater lay presence in the staffing and administration of the Church's hospitals, hospices and hostels. Although the decline in vocations to the religious life has been partly responsible for the expanded lay involvement in Catholic health care in Australia, it is not just a short-term solution to a staffing problem. Rather it reflects a desire to move away from the 'control model' of the past and into partnership between religious and lay staff. Moreover, in the light of the increased complexity of financial administration, a 'skilling-up' has been required in all areas of health care.

The St John of God Health Care System is the sisters' corporate response to those changes and insights. In 1983 the Provincial council began to investigate the most appropriate way of responding to these changing times. Extensive investigations of other Congregations' corporate responses drew the Congregation's attention to the Mercy Health Services System in the USA. A similar system, adapted to suit Australian conditions, was chosen by the Congregation. It was formally incorporated in Western Australia in July 1989. Other religious Congregations have adopted different means of making the transition – the Charity Sisters, for example, have a decentralised council linking 17 incorporated health-care facilities round the country.

The St John of God Health Care System, in fidelity to the Christian Gospel, is a mechanism designed to 'seek to promote fullness of life' for people, through the provision of holistic health care services. The mission is the central focus of each St John of God hospital, and is carefully woven through all system-wide activities. Seeking new and better ways of caring for the sick is matched with a concern to be faithful to the rich traditions of the Congregation. In this respect, the director of mission in each hospital has a key role. Her role is to ensure that there is ongoing fidelity to mission and to the desired culture at all levels of the system. The Congregation has stated its mission in the following way:

> Our vision is a system of health care services that is visibly and consistently hospitable, compassionate, respectful, just and excellent; a health care system that is highly competent, professional and viable. Through these services we will give health care where the human person is central and which involves a harmonious balance of the physical, psychological, social, spiritual and intellectual dimensions of being human. Through the system we will seek to give expression to the Gospel values which have emerged from the traditions of the participating religious Congregations.

> The mission of St John of God Health Care System is authorised by the Catholic Church in Australia. Our health care system shares in the healing mission of Jesus Christ given to the whole Church. Our particular mission is to promote fullness

of life through the provision of holistic health care services which cover and balance the physical, psychological, intellectual, social and spiritual dimensions of being human.

Two qualities are particularly evident in the decision to form the Health Care System, courage and a commitment to justice. Firstly, great courage was required not to take other options, like selling up or walking away or allowing disintegration. It was a bold move designed to take the Institute into the next century which would bring many challenges and make a lot of demands, human and financial, on the sisters in question. Secondly, the concern for justice evident in the formation of the system saw great efforts on the sisters' part to ensure responsible and managed movement by the Congregation to a preferred future for the hospitals, rather than succumb to a future imposed by external forces. The system was specifically designed to facilitate the appropriate formation, development and education of their staff for the future, so that the hospitals will continue to function within the ethical and pastoral framework of the Gospel.

In many respects, the Health Care System is a visible sign of an emerging Church in which lay people assume more responsibility for ministry. The Catholic identity and the ethos of Catholic health care are not determined only by the presence of religious.

From near and far

In nineteenth-century Australia, as in nineteenth-century Ireland, many women responded generously and heroically to the call of a people in often desperate need. Australian women and others joined Congregations established in Australia for Australian conditions, like the 'Brown Josephites', and imported varieties like the Sisters of St John of God.

From earliest times, Australian women who joined the John of God Sisters came to Western Australia to do their Novitiate training there, either in Subiaco in Perth or in Broome in the Kimberley region in the North. Many would have travelled two thousand miles and more. Some of the sisters came from the goldfields in Coolgardie and Kalgoorlie – a four hundred mile journey across waterless country, in the early days, to Perth.

During the same period, sisters arrived by boat and plane,

year after year, from different counties in Ireland. The numbers arriving from Ireland and Australia steadily increased until the early sixties of this century, when the membership numbers reached an all-time high. It seems that it did not occur to anyone that the situation would ever change.

But, as in other countries in the western world, the numbers of people joining religious sisters' Congregations dropped dramatically in Australia from the late sixties on. The steady stream of people arriving from Ireland to the novitiate in Subiaco suddenly dried up, and the Australian province could no longer depend on supplementary numbers of Irish sisters to shore up the number of Australian entrants. The reduced number of sisters meant that established ministries could no longer be maintained in the accustomed manner: the dearth of Irish vocations was keenly felt in the province.

The willingness of so many Irish women to enter religious life, at a time of expanding educational opportunities for women in Ireland, has puzzled many historians. In his book, *The Irish Missionary Movement*, (1990) Edmund M. Hogan contends that the exceptional impulse of sacrificial duty, apparent in the leaders of the 1916 Irish rebellion, carried over to subsequent generations and flowered most dramatically in Irish missionaries.

Whatever the reasons, Irish sisters came in relatively large numbers to the Saint John of God province in Australia. These factors raise intriguing questions. Why did the Congregation not succeed in attracting vocations to Australia on the same scale as other Irish orders, like the Sisters of Charity, did? Was there a complacency on the part of the Congregation that there would always be a constant supply of sisters from Ireland which caused them to be blasé about seeking vocations in Australia? Were the sisters too preoccupied with the problems of the present to be adequately planning for the future?

On a human level, leaving Ireland for Australia would have been a very traumatic experience for those sisters, particularly because at the time they would not have expected to return to the country of their birth. Indeed, speaking to the sisters serving in Australia today, one learns that they spent nineteen years and more before they returned to Ireland. Even if their parents died they were not allowed home. In the more enlightened regime of today, Irish sisters return home on average every five years. Many of these sisters, to encourage them to join the Australian mission, had been fed on a diet of romantic nonsense about Australia which bore no resemblance to the reality. Some aspiring sisters were told, 'If you want something to eat all you have to do is put your hand out the window and you can pick all kinds of exotic fruit off the trees.' They left for the southern hemisphere with homilies ringing in their ears about the need to leave their will behind them if they were to be model, modest and obedient sisters. One sister put this advice to verse:

Long years ago, I left this world,
its joys and its attractions
and turned my back on those I loved,
my home and its affections.
But oh I thought my heart would break,
for my superiors to remind me,
said that to be a perfect nun
I must leave my will behind me.

You see, my dear, she used to say,
there's nothing like subjection
'Twill raise you in a very short time
to the summit of perfection.
Then off I'd go to hide myself
in a place where none could find me,
and think for hours on that poor will
I'd have to leave behind me.
But then I was not such a fool
to yield to such a trifle
so everyday I tried my wilful friend to stifle.

Unlike Lot's wife I looked ahead
to my noble destination
and plough in hand I worked away
with great determination.
The single bit I ne'er relaxed
until today you find me
without the slightest thought at all
of the will I left behind me.

Many of the sisters are now showing the cumulative results of

scarce resources, inadequate diet and demanding work schedules, including seven days a week rosters. However, their contribution has been enormous. George Eliot's comment on
Dorothea Brooke in *Middlemarch* (Penguin, 1994) could apply to
many of the sisters in Australia: 'But the effect of her being on
those around her was incalculably diffusive: for the growing
good of the world is partly dependent on unhistoric acts; and
that things are not so ill with you and me as they might have
been, is half owing to the number who lived faithfully a hidden
life, and rest in unvisited tombs.' These were extraordinary
women who with minimal external help established, maintained and developed these hospitals through the hundred
years up to the present era. Another significant feature of these
sisters' work is that they help fund and maintain the missions in
other areas, as we shall see in the following Chapter on Pakistan.

Pilgrim women

The Christian life is a journey. The journey is the way of holiness, the way towards wholeness, although the contours of this
journey only become clear as the journey is travelled. That uncertain, often frightening – but never taken alone – journey has
been memorably described by the Scottish poet Edwin Muir in
his poem *The Way*:

> Friend, I have lost the way.
> The way leads on
> Is there another way?
> The way is One
> I must retrace the track
> It's lost and gone
> Back, I must travel back!
> None goes there, none
> Then I'll make here my place
> (The road runs on)
> Stand still and set my face
> (The road leaps on)
> Stay here, forever say.
> None stays here, none
> I cannot find the way

The way leads on
Oh places I have past!
That journey's done
And what will come at last?
The road leads on.

Throughout the Old Testament and the letters of Paul and his companions, indeed in the Gospels themselves, account after account occurs of the way in which God has broken into the lives of women and men while they were journeying, utterly transforming their awareness of themselves, their understanding of life, their appreciation of God, and through that experience giving them a broader vision of the character of the people of God. One of the characteristic notes of the Gospels is the invitation issued by Jesus to women and men, 'Follow Me'. This following involves renouncing of the disciple's previous security – the security of the known, and the committing of the disciple to the unknown. The invitation of Jesus to 'Follow Me' was regarded as imperative if the fullness of life was to be embraced.

Discipleship involves moving from one mode of life to another, from one set of values to another, from one way of acting to another, and from a life circumscribed by family and friends to a life in community with women and men of diverse backgrounds and expectations. This journey brings difficulties, trials, temptations, and the yearning for the security of the known and tried. Yet it is only as the pilgrim faces these temptations and leaves behind the security of the known that the way itself becomes clear. To take this journey of God with humanity gives people the possibility of fullness of life. In the encounter with God-with-us, God-for-us, women and men come to a fuller understanding of God, of themselves, of the meaning and purpose of life.

This journey is not just for a disparate group of individuals but for people who are part of a corporate body. The biblical images are images of the community. It is evident that Israel is a people on a journey, a community learning from its covenantal relationship with God, revising and enlarging its understanding as the pilgrim people of God. The Christian life is a communal adventure, a voyage of discovery, a journey, sustained by faith and hope.

In Australia the Sisters of St John of God are making great efforts to take such a journey together. As they co-operate together in trying to clarify their mission, they themselves are learning from each other, and producing insights which are richer and more complete than those arrived at in their separate existences.

The Sisters of Saint John of God have a very good reputation as professionals and are increasingly involved in a greater variety of health ministries: primary health, mental health, holistic health and women's health. The history of the order in Australia is characterised by compassion in dealing with people from birth to death, bringing a faith dimension to people's lives, a willingness to be courageous and break new ground. Today the challenge is to discern within their resources how they can best respond to people's needs while protecting and advancing their staff. If this difficult challenge is to be met, there are certain crunch, even painful, questions to be resolved:

* Why are they there?

* To whom are they sent?

* As we have seen, historically the sisters began their foundations following invitations from various bishops. In the future, will new foundations be made on the basis of people's needs?

* Vatican II brought new theological emphases, notably the importance it attached to the individual. How can the Congregation most fully reap the fruits of this spiritual revolution?

* What is the place for the Catholic hospital in Australia, particularly in an era where there is a plurality of opinions on sensitive ethical questions like abortion?

* What are they to do in Australia with multi-million dollar hospitals?

* In the health care area there is always the danger for a religious order of unthinkingly becoming servants of the middle class and of imperceptibly getting out of the reach of the poor. While the sisters currently treat some people who are unable to pay – is this an adequate response to the needs of the poor?

* What kind of religious life and ministry can they have independent of the health care business?

* What should be handed over? To whom? When? How?

* To what extent should there be collaboration with other orders?

* How much pooling of resources should there be?

* What should the relationship be between the Australian and Irish provinces? Do they continue as two separate provinces? How much interplay is contemplated between the two provinces?

* There is a strong desire to retain the hospitality which has been the hallmark of the order. The question is: how can they continue to be with people in their struggles and to be in the mess of the human situation when so much of their resources, both in terms of personnel and finance, are tied up in institutions?

* It is noteworthy that it was women who began the mission to the Aboriginal hospitals. How can the sisters, as a group of women, be a force for leadership in society and the church in Australia?

* As we have seen most, if not all, of the sisters' foundations were made at the request of the local bishop. What is to be their relationship with the institutional Church in the next century?

* Given that the number of active sisters is shrinking every year, and that there is only a handful of sisters under fifty in the province, what future does the Congregation have in Australia?

* How can the Congregation best respond to the extraordinary opportunities that are presented, by the system's organisational structures and such a vast number of caring and committed staff, in such areas as the development of workplace conditions and environments that are models of fidelity to the Church's social teachings, the potential for effective influence on national health policies, the quality of national health care or ethical health and medical practice in the country, or the capacity really to empower the laity for positions of leadership within the Church?

The Australian sisters are already facing up to some of these questions and are responding to new needs. One of the most tangible results of this self-examination is their mission to Pakistan.

CHAPTER SIX

Finding Life in the Margins

Straight from the heart
From the moment you enter the baggage area of Lahore Airport you are confronted by intense poverty. To see this on television is akin to watching *Cagney and Lacey* or the *Magic Roundabout.* You say to yourself, 'This can't really happen.' But when the stark reality is but feet away from you, it is frightening in the extreme. Over the next ten days the experience would make a much deeper impression than I realised at the time.

The agonising tyranny of the plight of the majority struck me most forcefully on a visit to the slums only ten minutes from the paradisal world of the leafy suburbs which are home to the wealthy élite. It is a highly stratified, paternalistic society without even a notion of *noblesse oblige.* It seems that the lot of the poor is to live frugally on the crumbs from the wealthy élite's tables. The badly faded memory of two lines I had learned in school from a poem by Yeats came to me as I saw the living conditions in which poor people existed:

> For the world's more full of weeping
> than you can understand.

A rich and rare land
Pakistan was formed in 1947 by the division of India, following the establishment of a movement for a separate Muslim homeland inspired by the poet and philosopher Allama Iqbal in the 1930s. Although comparatively new as a political state, Pakistan's roots stretch much further back than colonial India, as far back as the vibrant Harappa culture of the fourth millenium BCE with its Buddhist, Greek, Hindu and Muslim elements. One commentator has written:

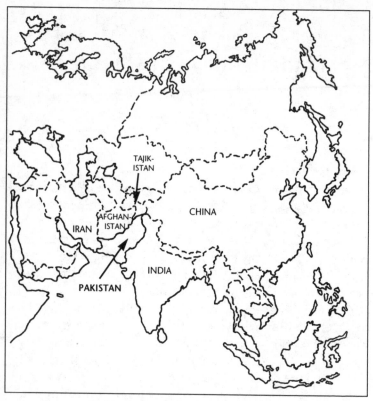

Pakistan in relation to its neighbours

Pakistan is a country of extremes. It has the highest mountains and the deepest seas. It has the most fertile plains and the biggest deserts. There are landscapes of moonlike barrenness from which come the juiciest fruits. It holds ever increasing masses of hungry people, as well as those who are – or have become – extremely rich, the greatest materialists next to the most pious, mystical souls in plenty. It can show a face of immense tolerance and, the next moment, the grimace of deadly hate.

Although it does not appear so on the surface, in many respects Pakistan is a relatively wealthy developing country. It has large agricultural and mineral resources, fairly well-developed industries, strong intellectual resources, and a high degree of technological sophistication. Given this wealth and natural resources,

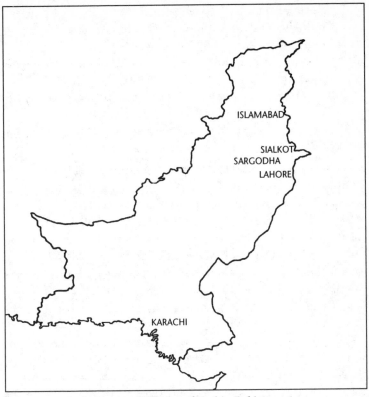

Sisters of St John of God in Pakistan
Sialkot (T.B.Hospital and village clinic)
Sargodha (Maternity and village clinic)
Lahore (Formation centre)

it is nothing less than a tragedy that the vast majority of the Pakistani people live in poverty, illiteracy, uncertainty about their future and with little participation in the democratic and the decision-making processes. The main problems facing the country include:

　　* An import-based economy which does not let the local industry thrive.

　　* Lack of a local industrial infrastructure.

　　* Deteriorating economic conditions, chronic un- and under-employment.

　　* Growing indebtedness, both nationally and individually.

* Widespread ethnic/sectarian strife.
* Complete disintegration of law and order.
* Deteriorating educational situation.
* Alienation from political processes, local and educational bureaucratic and institutional structures.
* Acceptance of corruption as the only *de facto* principle of operation.
* Widespread hopelessness about the possibility of achieving lasting and significant social improvement.

There are many scenes of spectacular beauty, notably the snow-capped Himalayan mountains. One of the most fascinating aspects of life in Pakistan is the importance of ritual. The devout Muslim is bound to pray five times a day, observe the strict fast of Ramadan, refrain from eating pork or drinking alcohol, and one day in his life should make the pilgrimage to Mecca, known as the 'Haj'. Animals are invariably slaughtered by cutting the jugular vein and uttering the words *Allah-u-Akbar*, 'God is greatest'. Meat that is not treated this way may be refused by strict Muslims.

Women must keep their heads covered with the *dupatta*, the fine, mostly beautiful veil. People flock on pilgrimages to the burial places of saintly persons over which elaborate mausoleums have been built. Local people convey their love of the saint and God by using different colours for the mosque design, and for the shrine or shrine cover, with mirror pieces and other embellishments. Worshippers flock in their thousands to pray there and whisper their secret wishes to the saint. Every saint has an annual commemoration called *Urs*. Believers often travel barefoot to these old shrines through deserts and heat, suffering from hunger and thirst. Such spiritual fervour is an outward sign of a deep inner faith. New-born babies are protected from evil spirits by uttering holy verses from the Koran into their ears. Islam is their shield against adversity.

The name *Islam* is derived from the word *salam*, meaning peace, but it has a secondary connotation, surrender. The key tenet of the Islamic faith is the phrase *La ilaha illa Ilah*, 'There is no God but Allah'. Islam is more than a system of rules. It is a way of life. The call to prayer is heard five times daily from loud-speakers from the mosques in towns and villages throughout the country. In the fields, farmers stop their tractors and spread their mats on the ground, facing Mecca.

Their two great religious festivals are the *Eids*. On the first of these, the young of a family receive a new set of clothes and presents of money. Beggars are not turned away, companies normally give a bonus to their employees, and servants get a generous gift of money. They are normally given a couple of days off. The first, the Small Eid, celebrates the end of Ramadan, the fasting month. It is impatiently awaited by one and all. After 28 days of fasting, everybody is ready to greet friend and stranger alike, *Eid Mubarak*, 'Congratulations on Eid', and the celebrations get under way. Ten weeks after the 'Small Eid' comes the 'Big Eid', a day of prayer and sacrifice. Each family slaughters a male goat, sheep or calf.

God is definitely a real presence. Culturally Pakistan is a very rich country, having abounded in mystic teachers, preachers, poets and singers through the centuries. Some of the traditional Sindhi or Punjabi mystics have produced sublime verses which compare with the very best in the world's religious literature. The topic of the love for God features prominently in the poetry and folktales which are recited and sung by almost everybody.

Pakistan has a range of racial groups which are amazingly diverse in complexion, physique and culture. Each tribe retains its distinct culture and traditions. Hospitality is a shared characteristic among all the people. The country is a fascinating mix of the old and the new. In some areas the turbans, footwear and musical instruments have scarcely changed over the centuries. Some people appear to be almost contemptuous of time, refusing to be seduced by the attraction of the habits of the western world despite the so-called march of progress. The new world is evident in the jeans young people wear, the pop music they listen to and watch on television, and the diet of American programmes shown on television.

The cry of the poor

The largest diocese in Pakistan is Lahore, with a population of more than 162,000 Catholics. Ninety miles north of Lahore city is Sialkot. It has a hospital called Bethania. It was established in 1964 by Capuchin Father Ligouri, a Belgian missionary, who became very ill. He promised that if he recovered he would spend his life bringing medical attention to the poorest of the poor. He recovered fully and founded and administered Bethania with a particular mission to develop curative and preventive medicine and treatment for tuberculosis patients. Although it is a small hospital its influence is great. In 1979, for example, about 10,000 out-patients were seen at Bethania.

As in-patients are normally very poor, the fees are kept low. The hospital, the only one of its kind in its area, relies on support from the bishop, who receives help from the Propagation of the Faith and the German relief agency, *Misereor*. All the Pakistani government could offer was anti-TB drugs. In 1980 Bishop Armando Trindade of Lahore appealed to the Sisters of St John of God's Australian Province to send some sisters to take charge of Bethania. The Congregation had received an eye-witness account of the situation in Pakistan from Rev Patrick Ahern, Perth director of the Pontifical Mission Aid Societies. The request came at a time when the Congregation was going through a period of intense soul-searching and actively seeking new ways of bringing a healing presence to the materially poor. A new mission in Pakistan seemed to be a most effective way to respond to the signs of the times.

Four sisters, Felicity Scales, Mary Walsh, Angela Cox and Michelle McHale left for Pakistan in October 1980. Before they left, Fr Ahern informed them:

> You are following the wonderful tradition of your order. Just as the sisters went to fight typhoid in Kalgoorlie during the days of the gold rush, so you are going to fight tuberculosis among the people of North Pakistan.

The sisters prepared for their mission by spending two months in language school to learn Punjabi, which is the language spoken by the poorer people among whom they are working.

First impressions

It is fascinating to read the sisters' early impressions of their mission in Pakistan. After ten weeks, they shared their thoughts with their colleagues in a letter on 17 December 1980:

> Our first impressions of the country were somewhat stunning,

as we encountered the countless people and observed the great poverty everywhere. This was even evident at Karachi and Lahore airports. Our own first experience of poverty was felt when we could not communicate with the people and became suddenly dependent on the goodness of people here.

On our journey from Lahore to Sialkot, there was certainly no monotony. Colourful buses, crowded with people hanging out of doors, horns blaring and travelling at reckless speed. These are challenged by the transport buses, equally decorative and having the same chaotic traffic rules! There are also cars, motor bikes, plus rickshaws which are a three-wheeler, covered-in conveyance. We've already had the opportunity and thrill of travelling through Lahore city in one of them, and glad of same after traipsing up and down the bustling bazaar carrying parcels ... Now to get back to our journey, we must mention the stately camels with their burdens, horse-drawn and oxen-drawn carts – really ancient, and of course the tongas which indeed somewhat resemble the old Irish traps, having a colourful cover and the horse's harness decorated with ribbons and pompons between the ears – Get the picture! Goats, hens, geese, buffaloes and bicycles are also part of the scene. We haven't mentioned the countless people wearing their colourful cultural dress – the shalwar chemise ... The people carry everything on their heads very elegantly indeed ... Along the roadside there are countless stalls selling all kinds of food and drinks, no alcohol of course ...

Soon we were nearing Sialkot and turning off from the main road for Bethania Hospital. Incidentally the hospital is situated about four miles from Sialkot, in a suburb called Pakka-Gharra. It is not of course like the suburbs of the western world. Indeed we are more or less surrounded by agricultural land and it is nice to see the labourers work in the fields from early morning. They have to work hard with primitive farm implements. Sialkot itself is situated approximately two hundred miles from the Afghanistan border, forty miles from Kashmir and fourteen miles from India, so we are close to these countries.

The road leading to the hospital was certainly something of a new experience for us. Between the potholes and the local drainage system, odours that were strange to our noses, food and tea for sale, pots, pans and billy cans, children running in all directions somewhat bewildered by these white ladies appearing, staring in amazement as we drove past in the ambulance ...

As we entered eventually through the hospital gates, shots were fired and an overwhelming sea of faces and colour awaited us. The shouts still ring in our ears, so we were indeed overcome with deep emotion and wondered what we had come to. Staff from the hospital, people from the local colony and local village were there to greet us, together with religious from the Sialkot areas. We were greeted with speeches, prayers, floral garlands and their national foods. My oh my, how they tasted to our Western palates. After ten weeks here, we feel that our palates and gastro-intestinal tracts have adjusted quite well to the local foods. The common dishes are curry, rice and chappatis, somewhat like unleavened bread made with wheaten flour and cooked on a flat hot plate.

The hospital is very different. The patients supply their own bedding. It is quite a picture to see the patients come to the hospital with all the necessary gear for cooking and bedding, all carried on their heads, often a bed comes too, for the relatives ...

The hospital is divided into a T.B. Section and a general ward section. The T.B. area has a capacity for one hundred and twenty beds, with wards for both male and female patients. The general ward can accommodate forty patients and the children's ward twenty three children, which includes those who are sick, malnourished or orphaned. There is a large out-patient attendance each day, and three doctors are busy with consultations. Friday is for T.B. patients only as it is the Islamic holy day and the only day that working people are free to attend for check-ups and repeat of medicines. Sunday of course is our holy day and O.P.D. is closed, except for emergencies. We have two laboratories, an X-Ray Dept, dis-

pensary and Labour Room. The labour room is really anti-
quated.

The diseases and conditions here are many and varied. The
tropical diseases of malaria, typhoid, helminthic diseases, infectious hepatitis, advanced T.B. and tetanus are all part of
daily life. A unit of blood here costs 500 rupees. This is equivalent to 50 Australian dollars and rarely can anyone afford
this. The average wage here for professionals is 500 rupees
per month and the cost of living is disgustingly high in ratio
to the basic wage. Of course it is only the lucky ones who get
employment, at least full time that is. Blood is so expensive to
buy as people do not like to give blood. Really few can afford
to give any or have not suffered from some infectious disease. Due to the unpredictable electricity supply, blood
banks are almost impossible to run in this country.

One of the lay helpers here from Belgium visits varying areas
attending to vaccinations, an important area in preventative
medicine. One of the doctors goes out to varying villages a
few times a week. There is a great need to organise this more
effectively. Our long term goal is to get out into the villages.
Development is needed from the grass roots, commencing
with hygiene, drainage, nutrition and health education. We
have been invited to a specific area to do this work. So much
finance and the preparation of a team, plus a mobile unit is
necessary. One of the doctors here is very keen, so please
God this plan will eventuate. Its all going to take much time
and planning.

Our number one priority at present is to learn the language
and this takes time. You should hear us trying to get our
tongues around some of the vocabulary – you would indeed
laugh. We do laugh at ourselves often. In the hospital
grounds each day there is a school held for one hundred and
forty children from the local colony, both Muslim and
Christian.

Presently we are living in four staff rooms. Our convent is
being built near the local colony, so we won't be lonely. There
is no hot water here, but we have managed to get immersion
heaters, a coil of wire which effectively heats a bucket of

water. We can manage to wash ourselves, clothes and floor with same. We have become experts in hot water economy now. We have Mass each day here at the hospital and can pray together in a little room, so we are close to you all at these times as we pray with the universal Church. Despite the many inevitable difficulties we encounter here, we are very happy and indeed feel carried along by prayer. We cannot help but be grateful to God for his boundless goodness to us in life and especially received from our communities since Vatican II. The approach is to implement the Church's attitude to developing worlds. These attitudes are unfortunately foreign, as yet, to many older missionaries here, so in this area too we have to battle for what is justice, sometimes not understood by the local community. However, we do not fear as already we see the Lord's hand at work in many areas.

Wish you were here?

On a human level the sisters faced a number of problems: the oppressive heat, adjusting to very different food (it is said with some justification: 'The most important thing for a missionary is a good stomach'), dirt and flies, constant noise, chaotic traffic, the sisters' poor grasp of the local language, an inferior social status as women in a patriarchal society with a very clearly-defined social hierarchy, and a sense of isolation fuelled by the inability at the time to make international phone calls to either Australia or Ireland. It is also eye-opening to learn of the type of professional problems they had to confront. For example, in 1981 as the hospital had only one doctor, the sisters at different times served as both nurses and doctors. Triplets were born in a local village in a one-room mud house. Initially all apparently were doing well until their six-year-old brother was drowned in a nearby pond. The mother was so traumatised that she could no longer cope with the triplets and they were neglected. A sister went out to collect them and took them to Bethania.

In correspondence to their colleagues in Australia that same year, the sisters gave a further insight into the problems of the people in Pakistan:

Somebody wrote recently and said that they would visit us

when the place was clean and free from flies, so before she thinks of packing, we wish to say that it will take many a long day before this is possible in Pakistan. With a population of 105 million people, the highest illiteracy rate in the world, and the majority of the people living in rural areas, development from grass roots level will be a slow process. With the passage of time our love of dust and flies hasn't increased; however with our understanding of the culture and its many hardships, we can cope with the reality better than initially. We have to work at educating the people to want hygiene, otherwise we are wasting our efforts. Recently one of our nurses was giving a lecture in the ward on basic hygiene and one of the patients, when she had finished, said, 'Nurse, God made the flies too, so they must be good'. Very naturally they throw all fruit skins etc. on the floor, despite the fact that we have made many rubbish bins available to them. So a full time supervisor is needed to keep the place clean and this is financially impossible. However, we are often consoled by the fact that we have the cleanest hospital in the district, God help the rest.

Given the scale of material disadvantage, it is not surprising that the sisters concentrated their energies in advancing primary health care. Accordingly, in 1982, the sisters reported:

A new venture undertaken by the hospital this year has been the opening of an under-five clinic. This clinic involves the checking of the growth and development of children who are vaccinated, and the mothers are trained in hygiene and nutrition. The following statistics released by the government of Pakistan this year show only too clearly how necessary this work is. There are more than 34.1 million children in the country, of whom some 14 million are under five years of age. Over 4% suffer from severe malnutrition and 72% of all children's deaths occur in those under two years of age during the weaning period. Other common causes of deaths in children are diarrhoea, tetanus, measles, diphtheria, pertussis, poliomyelitis, and respiratory infections, including T.B. Most of these diseases are, as you know, preventable. In time we envisage that this basic type of clinic will be in action in many surrounding villages, with the hospital team supervising.

Historically, many missionaries have been guilty of Christian imperialism – of 'imposing' their faith-view. In Pakistan the sisters have used their time to 'recharge' their spirituality by learning from the local people. The sisters wrote in 1982:

> During our two years here, we have been enriched in many ways by the people. Their life style gives to the Bible an intimate reality. Ninety per cent of the population, which is over 84 million, are involved in agriculture, largely without modern farm equipment. The grain crops are cut with a hook and collected by hand. The threshing is carried out by hand, as is also the winnowing. The good shepherd here is usually shepherding his goats, or driving the donkeys laden with bricks or sand. The camels are a familiar sight along our roads bearing their burden. The refugees from Afghanistan usually use the camels for transporting themselves and their possessions. The common beast of burden is the buffalo, seen drawing the cart filled with hay or sugar cane. Most of the land is owned by a minority of landlords, so the majority of people are employed as farm labourers without any of the rights of even tenant farmers. Because of illiteracy and poverty, they are indeed the voiceless people. Ninety-five per cent of women and eighty-four per cent of men are illiterate in Pakistan. The result of this is plain to be seen in society – with a primitive life style, poverty, sickness and suffering. Realising all this, we are continually planning and developing new ways by which we can in some small way do our part to bring to these people better living conditions, the poor Christ amongst us.

The sisters had to change their methods of communicating with patients because they have to tell them stories to explain why they might need treatment for up to a year. They require to be coaxed with stories that their illness need to go to sleep and finally die. Without that it is difficult to explain why there is need to stay for treatment. They have a fatalistic understanding of death, without the anguished soul-searching of 'why me?' which characterises the modern western world – attributing it to the will of Allah. This attitude has echoes of the old Irish approach to death – 'It's God's holy will.' In Pakistan patients need to be persuaded that they no longer have to accept illness or deformity. Once that is achieved they are keen to co-operate.

The sisters have much to offer the Pakistani nurses. An Australian journalist who visited the Bethania Hospital observed:

> I was amazed at what they could do with so little. We have so much technology that makes such little difference in patient care. In Pakistan, they have got almost nothing – nothing to perform a lot of real medicine and make a real difference to patient care … Nursing was considered a poor occupation for women, because it involved contact with males outside the traditional codes. As a result, nurses did not have the caring aspect stressed as much as in Australia. Often they might dress a patient or give an injection without ever talking or comforting him. The Sisters of St John of God have changed a lot of that. By seeing the sisters' example, and being reinforced, they are making better efforts in their patient care.

The hospital is a microcosm of human existence. All life and death is here – at once a morgue for thwarted dreams and disappointed ambitions and a carnival for joyous exuberance. The fact that the patients' families reside with them while they are in hospital can give an almost jovial atmosphere to the proceedings.

A new seed is planted

Two years after taking the reins in Sialkot, the bishop of neighbouring Rawalpindi diocese invited the sisters to take over the maternity hospital in Sargodha. It was being vacated by German missionaries who could not get a renewal of their visas, whereas Australians were able to enter because of the Commonwealth connection. The circumstances of the changeover of sisters were not adequately explained to the staff in advance and this posed difficult problems for the Sisters of Saint John of God initially. The jockeying for position among some staff members had all the hallmarks of a power struggle. However, the sisters countered the suspicions of the staff and the community in the most effective way possible by proving their dedication to all concerned. Their work had immediate impact. One sister gave 24,000 vaccinations a month and taught local nurses to do the

work. The local community responded favourably to them because they were seen to be doing things and because they went
to villages where religious had not been seen before. Their priority was to build up good relationships with the local people.

Another problem was that the staff had not been trained to
take responsibility. This created a lot of stressful situations for
the sisters, for example, they might be involved in an emergency
operation and discover that there was no oxygen. It required a
major cultural shift before the lay staff would use their own
initiative. A more difficult problem to deal with is that corruption is endemic in all areas of Pakistani life. In hospital care the
problem is a widespread one, from petty theft to bribery in order
to secure preferential treatment. Eradicating this festering sore is
an ongoing battle for the sisters. There were also problems coming to terms with the vastly different culture of the predominantly Muslim patients. For example, Muslims feel it is much
more important to tend to a person when they are sick than to
attend their funeral. Consequently funerals have a lower priority
than in the Western world.

Today the sisters work as part of a team of nursing and para-
medical staff who go out into the villages to bring primary
health care to the local people through immunisation clinics,
training people to recognise symptoms, and promoting health
education, while hopefully improving living standards. In cases
where the patient problems are complicated, they are referred to
the hospital. Team members also visit the schools for health education, and within the villages they try to contact the midwives
to train them properly. There is a distressingly high mortality
rate for mothers and infants due to lack of adequate techniques
and poor hygiene. Yet what is most striking is the smiles of the
children. Poverty and happiness are clearly not mutually exclusive.

The hospital is for women, with a focus on obstetrics and gynaecology. In Pakistan the hospitals remain Church property
but the schools run by other Congregations of sisters have been
nationalised. A hospital operated by women for women is essential in Pakistan since women are not allowed to attend a male
doctor and likewise men do not go to women doctors. A noteworthy feature of the sisters' ministry is that they provide a

truly Christian service for the Pakistani people because the private hospitals are out of the reach of the poor, and the general hospitals are run on the system whereby you have to provide your own hospital and operation equipment. Moreover, the hygiene there is not good and the poor are unable to afford the government hospitals. The sisters run their hospitals on systems which discourage bribery and operate according to Christian standards of compassion and justice, with high standards of hygiene.

Only two per cent of the Pakistani population are Christian, of which one per cent are Catholic. The sisters offer an important witness as their healing ministry transcends sectarian boundaries and everybody can see the face of Christ in these people.

The average life-span is only fifty because, among other factors, there is no village sanitation, with the resultant effect of disease. No one, other than the extremely affluent, has the luxury of running water in their houses. The remainder have to make do with the village wells. In Pakistan there is no social welfare so the family and extended family are essential as bread winners to each other. For Christians there are additional problems. They are disadvantaged in seeking work and having limited promotional possibilities. In hospitals Christians are given only the lowly tasks and cannot expect advancement. The sisters put a lot of emphasis on staff development because they hope that the Pakistanis they train will be able to run their own hospitals.

Infections and diseases prevalent in Pakistan include cholera and typhoid. There is much malnutrition and chest infection and many women die of diseases related to child-bearing. The problems are exacerbated because the patients tend to go to hospitals as a last resort, having spent all their money doing the rounds of the 'pirs', the local healing men who do traditional healing, and the quacks and unqualified medics who 'advise' the sick.

The quality of life of the majority leaves much to be desired with the average mud brick house being of two rooms only with a flat roof for sleeping on top. Their family size is, on average, six surviving children, with an accompanying high mortality rate. Marriages, whether Christian or Muslim, are all arranged. Life is difficult for a Muslim woman if she is divorced, which the hus-

band can do by merely saying three times, 'I divorce you'. She
then has to go back to her own family for survival or, if they are
dead, hopefully another family will take her in. Muslim men can
have two or three wives simultaneously.

Marriage practices in Asia differ dramatically from those of
the Western world. For example, in May 1994 several hundred
children aged under seven were married in the northern Indian
state of Rajasthan in defiance of a law banning child marriage.
Hundreds of boys and girls walked in traditional style around
the fire to become husband and wife. The marriages in the State
were performed on the day of a local Hindu festival, despite a
campaign by the authorities to stop this age-old practice. The
authorities' efforts to clamp down on this practice have proved
unsuccessful because many children, belonging to poor families,
are married clandestinely without any marriage processions or
fanfare. The custom dates back centuries to the time when the
Mughals from central Asia conquered much of India. The
Muslim invaders pillaged and plundered but would not touch a
girl if she was married. Today, the custom is still considered as a
way of protecting a girl's purity. But the main impetus is economic. Poor families often want to be free of their children, and
having many weddings at the same time cuts down on the costs.

In Pakistan the problem is the polar opposite. Families go all
out to make their offspring's wedding a grand affair and frequently acquire enormous debts in the process, which cripple
them financially for years. More positively the marriage ceremony
brings many blessings – joy, colour, dance, socialising and meeting friends, the uniting of two families and an opportunity for
people to escape their poverty if only for a short time. A feature of
Pakistani life is the strength that is derived from the joint family
system because the Pakistani seldom marries outside the family.
It requires a major cultural adjustment for westerners to see, for
example, a grown up woman address a small schoolboy in the
formal manner of calling relatives, with the appellation 'uncle'.

Another problem is that many families, prompted by a desire
to keep their money within the family, favour intermarriage. As
might be expected, this causes many of the children born out of
these unions to be severely disabled. In the absence of a welfare
state, the only way for disabled people to eke out an existence is

by begging. As beggars, loneliness is their roll call. There is nothing in life but to endure and carry on. Each new day breaks on the world with its own pain and misery. It is like living life in a revolving door. They suffer from both emotional and material deprivation.

Most of those with a mental illness are locked up and hidden away. The process of institutionalisation is itself a form of psychological internment, a malignant force which reduces people to human vegetables, incapable of independent thought. The primary objective is docility – the inmates are no longer a 'menace' to society. Like condemned prisoners serving out their sentences, they are compelled to bathe communally, just another humiliation in a long catalogue of degradation. The erosion of personal dignity and privacy, the dead emotions and listless eyes are unavoidable side-effects of a concerted effort to keep the system flowing smoothly. Nobody in authority seems to question or even notice the perversion in the situation where the system becomes more important than the people it is designed to serve.

Among the services the sisters provide in conjunction with other religious is to ensure that patients, who live in appalling conditions, receive one good meal a week. So they provide them with meat, vegetables, curry and fruit which otherwise they would not get.

An unforeseen occurrence

As the new mission in Sargodha was beginning, the sisters were taken aback when a young Pakistani nurse, Josephine Ayub, presented herself as a candidate for the Congregation. The possibility of establishing a novitiate had never been considered nor had the mission to Pakistan been thought of as an avenue for vocations, but after a period of soul-searching it was decided to go ahead with the project. A house was bought in Lahore in 1985 because there are other religious orders there and inter-Congregational programmes were available. Within a few years, ten young women were in training. The number of vocations is quite high, considering the small number of Catholics.

The sisters' mission is a participation in the mission of Jesus who came to set people free. One sign of that is that there has not

St John of God Sisters in Lahore
Left to right: Srs Josephine Ayub, Zenat Barket, Rehanna Inayat,
Rubina Siaej Bhatti, Agnes Morris, Mussaret Sardar.
Missing from the group is Sr Victorine Ghulam.

been the cultural and Christian imperialism that has characterised some missions abroad. All the sisters wear the Pakistani
version of the SJG habit which is the *shalwar* (pants), a *chemise*
(top) and a *dupatta* (head-covering) if they go out, which however
does not necessarily cover their face as is required for Muslim
women. The Pakistani sisters receive a general academic education. There is a big emphasis on education for community development as the masses are crying out for better conditions.

Pakistani sisters are beginning to work among their own
people, making them aware of their own self worth, quality and
dignity. In many respects, to take the option for the poor in
Pakistan is to take the option for women. One of the most striking things about the sisters is that in Pakistani society they are
women with power. It is a burden which falls lightly on their
shoulders because they use it to empower others. St Benedict
distinguished between *servitium Dei* (serving God) and *cultus
Dei* (worshipping God) but in Aquinas we find that service,
worship and mission coincide. That Thomistic vision is plainly
visible in the St John of God apostolate in Pakistan. However, it

has to be said that the sisters can only work in this way because they are financed and receive great prayer support from their colleagues in Australia. The sisters get no financial help from the government.

Today some of the Pakistani young sisters are being trained as religious formators. A gardening metaphor seems appropriate. The sisters from Australia and Ireland have their roots deep in the soil. Their role is to prepare the Pakistani sisters, through the development and channelling of their own giftedness, to respond to the needs of the people. The local sisters are mere saplings, fresh and green, which have the promise to grow to great heights. The variety in the garden is as pronounced as the deep bond of unity. The day is quickly coming when the Pakistanis will have flowered sufficiently to be fully independent. To watch and listen to the young Pakistani sisters at worship is a very uplifting experience, particularly as they sing their songs of praise in their own language. It is a visible sign of the rich cross-fertilisation that can take place between east and west. The Congregation is also considering taking on lay associates.

Although formation is the sisters' primary apostolate in Lahore, they are also active in other ministries such as Muslim-Christian dialogue and involving the laity in the life of the Church. For example, they work with the catechists who serve a role comparable to deacons in western society. They instruct the faithful, perform marriages, bury the dead, prepare children for the sacraments, conduct liturgy when the priest cannot come, and provide a link between the priest and the people. In many respects, working with people at the margins has brought the sisters back to their roots.

Back to foundations

As early as 1919, Dom Cuthbert Butler suggested that monasticism emerged in a series of cycles. Raymond Hostie, in his *Life and Death of Religious Orders* (1972), claims that there is a natural life-span for a religious order but that for it to survive and develop after that, it must be renewed. His studies indicate that the average life-time of religious institutes is two to three centuries. Of one hundred and five Congregations founded before 1600, little more than twenty are still in existence today. The crucial element

which he identifies in this process is what he terms 'the creative fer-
ment', the way in which religious rediscover the essential charism
in their order and, at the same time, see its contemporary urgency
and relevance, which compel them to revive it.

Gerry Arbuckle, in his book *Out of Chaos* (1985), takes a similar
line and observes that religious life has to face up to the chaos
and find and encourage 'refounding persons' or 'intrapreneurs'
if it is to survive. His basic thesis is that religious Congregations
today are in chaos. They are not sure about the meaning, contemporary relevance or mission of religious life and, on the
practical level, they find it difficult to cope with often rapidly
declining numbers, few or no vocations, and the rising average
ages of membership. He claims that the experience of chaos can
be the catalyst for highly creative action. For chaos to be a source
of creativity there must be people who not only see how change
can be achieved but also proceed to initiate such change. In the
process they invite others to join them. As far as religious Congregations are concerned, there can be no refounding except
through the leadership of refounding persons. He stresses the
need for religious to respond to current pastoral needs, with the
equally vital and fundamentally historical task of clarifying the
original charism of the founder, in its specific historical and geographical context, and being creatively faithful to it in a new
context.

Although Hostie and Arbuckle have important insights to
offer, their contention that religious life can only be renewed by
such 'refounding' remains open to question. However, in the
case of the sisters of Saint John of God, such a refounding seems
to have occurred in Pakistan.

No longer strangers but friends

While all the sisters experienced culture shock in visiting the
country for the first time, with some effort they have adapted to
what Pakistan has to offer. They have quickly learned some
essential lessons about the etiquette and customs which prevent
them causing offence. They experience great pleasure because
they have striven to understand the Pakistani's approach to life.

The sisters continue to be spellbound by the tapestry of
bright and dazzling oriental colours. For all the poverty they see

around them, the sisters know and love the country. Their efforts to understand it have reaped a handsome dividend and with the passing of time they have been drawn into the atmosphere of friendship and warmth. To the stranger experiencing severe culture shock, it is baffling to hear the sisters continually speak of the beautiful aspects of the country, people and culture. While they are certainly not blind to the problems around them, the difficulties do not cloud the reasons why they are there as a community of religious women – to receive faith and life and give it in return. They have been greatly encouraged by some important social advances in recent years. In their own hospitals they have seen positive developments, for example, in Sargodha the situation in relation to female and male doctors has changed with the result that both a male and female doctor practise.

The sisters have found the Pakistanis to be an amazingly friendly people and very courteous. Although the Pakistanis are in the main a reserved race, it is very interesting to visit a minority Christian community at their healing Masses. All the people sway, sing and dance almost as if they were attending a pop concert. It is, in a very real sense, a celebration. Such celebrations serve to rekindle the sisters' faith. The sisters from Ireland and Australia who have come to Pakistan have been transformed by their exposure to the poor. As their ministeries have unfolded, their initial culture shock has yielded to a much richer understanding of Pakistani life and customs.

Although the sisters are meeting huge needs in Pakistan, they are nonetheless continuously reflecting on their mission. Their chief concerns are reflected in their Vision Statement of September 1994:

As disciples of Jesus, we desire to be prophetic witnesses of healing in Pakistan, enabling people to develop to their full potential.

Currently our particular foci relate to women, health care, ecological issues and the education and animation of people.

We want to live a simple lifestyle based on Gospel values. The focus of our mission is, and will continue to be, the materially poor and the promotion of local leadership.

The challenge for the sisters is how to strike the optimum balance between idealism and pragmatism.

From the outside looking in

The impression of visiting the sisters in Pakistan is of a shaft of light illuminating the monstrous barbarism of poverty and injustice – noble natures standing with the people they serve and love. Preserving that cherished image remains important for those who see it at first hand. Their testimony of faith strikes not so much a note of hope as a symphony. For all the problems of the country, the sisters' work points to a better future – to a time when, in the words of Seamus Heaney, 'hope and history rhyme'.

CHAPTER SEVEN

Ripples in the Pool

As we have seen in previous chapters, throughout the early part of the twentieth century the sisters were increasingly drawn into different countries and regions. During the 1920s serious problems of organisation presented themselves. The Sisters of St John of God had begun as a diocesan institute in Wexford but, over the next fifty years, as they spread to many other dioceses, there were five distinct centres of authority. There was the motherhouse in Wexford, with eight communities in the diocese of Ferns, in addition to having responsibility for two of the four Kildare foundations and the sisters in Newry, in the diocese of Dromore. The superior in Kilkenny was in charge of the four branch communities in Ossory and the remaining two foundations in Kildare. The two Waterford houses represented another jurisdiction. In Australia, as we saw in a previous chapter, all the foundations were under the superior of Subiaco, Perth, with the exception of the north-western missions, subject to the superior at Broome.

The danger was that the different branches of the Institute might drift away from one another, not simply as jurisdictional units, but more fundamentally in the whole tone of their religious life. Ultimately they might dissolve into a loose federation of increasingly different diocesan Congregations. Although they had a common written rule, that in itself was an insufficient guarantee of a shared life. Their apostolate, expressing itself explicitly in works of active charity, was open to modification by the decisions which had to be taken regularly as to what new works would be undertaken. In the sisters' two main apostolates, nursing and teaching, great changes were under way as a result of technical, social and political developments. The way chosen to preserve a single Institute and shared religious life was by centralised government and direction.

Discussion of a scheme of general amalgamation commenced in 1914, and it was decided to formulate a new Code of Rules and Constitutions. In 1919 these were considered by representatives of the houses of Wexford, Kilkenny and Waterford, and in October 1923 application was made to the Holy See for approval. This was granted on January 7 1924, and on the following 5 August, the first general Chapter opened in Wexford. The immediate result of this chapter was the amalgamation of all the houses in Ireland and the houses subject to Subiaco, Perth, under a Superior General. A central novitiate for Ireland was established at Wexford on 16 October. The fifth centre, Broome, joined in 1929. At the second general chapter in 1930 there was the first formal appointment of provincial superiors and assistants in each of the four provinces: St Patrick's province, Ireland; St Mary's, England, where foundations had begun in 1925; St Thérèse's, Australia; and St Francis Xavier's, Northwest Australia. In 1938 this process was complete with the granting of final approval from the Holy See to the Congregation of the Sisters of St John of God as a Pontifical Institute.

Officers and gentlemen

After the amalgamation the Congregation continued to flourish. One new development in Ireland was Aut Even Hospital. The name is an anglicised version of the Irish 'Áit Aoibhinn', a beautiful place. A hospital in Kilkenny was born during the first world war when a local noble woman, Lady Dysart, conceived the idea of paying tribute to the fortitude of the Irish officers engaged in that war, showing how much she appreciated them for offering their lives for the cause. The hospital, with nurses' home and doctor's residence nearby, was situated on its own grounds, twenty acres in extent and overlooking the river Nore. It was purpose-built, and could accommodate thirty patients. When the government bestowed pensions on these officers in compensation for their services, they retired to their homes. Then Lady Dysart admitted private patients. The hospital flourished up to the time of her death in 1932, when it had to be sold.

The local bishop had long been searching for a suitable site for the Sisters of Saint John of God to establish a hospital in Kilkenny. When Lady Dysart's hospital became available, the sisters purchased it, and it was opened on 21 November 1933. The increasing number of patients, and the demands of modernisation, were responsible for several alterations and extensions being added, for example, St Teresa's wing, St Joseph's wing and an attractive 18 bed maternity wing (1966). During the following years the sisters saw that the existing building was unable to cope with the demands of modern medicine. In 1982 a new hospital was opened. It was designed to be a top class medical facility for Kilkenny and its environs.

In 1944 the house and lands of a small Georgian mansion, Ely House, Wexford, became vacant on the death of its owner, Major General Beauchamp Doran. During World War I, this building and lands were taken over, under the Defence of the Realm Act, by the British Admiralty. Early in 1918, the property was loaned to the US as a site for a seaplane base. When the property came on the market, it was purchased by the sisters, whose motherhouse is on the other side of the river Slaney in Wexford town. Shortly after acquiring Ely House, it was opened as a private hospital by the sisters. In a short time it was found that extra beds were needed. A new wing was added in 1948 to accommodate twenty-nine patients. A resident chaplain was provided to cater for the spiritual needs of the patients. Structural deterioration of the building, medical progress and technological design demanded that a completely 'new Ely' be erected. An expensive and impressive hospital was opened in 1975 which maintains the traditional homely friendly spirit in the most modern setting.

Parkton House in Enniscorthy, Co Wexford, was purchased by the sisters as a private nursing home for £5,846 in 1947. The following year it was decided to admit maternity patients and the first delivery was twins. The building could accommodate approximately fourteen patients when the sisters took over and this number increased during the following years. Its homely personal atmosphere made it particularly suitable for geriatric patients. The passage of time took its toll on the building and in the 1990s the decision was made to close it, as it was no longer suitable for such a purpose. A shortage of sisters was another important contributory factor to the closure.

The Sisters of St John of God in Ireland

In the shadow of the troubles

The sisters consistently strove to improve their earlier foundations. In Daisy Hill in Newry, Co Down in Northern Ireland, a
further building was erected by the local authority in 1935 to
treat infectious diseases. The introduction of antibiotics in the
1940s eliminated plagues such as scarlatina and diphtheria, free-
ing sisters for other medical cases. In 1946 the hospital came
under the Northern Ireland Hospital Authority. After 1969 the
'Troubles' cast a major shadow over Newry and Northern
Ireland in general. Daisy Hill Hospital regularly treated victims
injured in the hostilities. British army and RUC (Royal Ulster
Constabulary) personnel could only be treated in the hospital
for short periods because of the security risk.

The Sisters of St John of God extended their involvement in Newry and answered the need for a private nursing home when, in 1945 they bought, on lease, a decaying seventeenth century mansion. The building, Courtenay Hill, was originally intended as a home for sisters working in Daisy Hill but the needs of the local community dictated otherwise and a nursing home was provided. Many repairs and renovations were necessary. In the early days the sisters had very little comfort. They had to sleep in the attic and use tea chests for tables. The first operation was performed on an improvised theatre table, the kitchen table. When the necessary repairs were completed, patients flocked in to receive physical and spiritual healing from sisters. The first patients were admitted early in 1946. The number of admissions for that year was 180. By 1949, the admissions had increased to 1,949.

A beautiful new hospital, ideally situated by mountain and river, catering for medical, surgical and maternity patients, was opened in 1967 thanks to a marathon fund-raising venture. The number of beds increased from 22 to 47 but the improvements in the amenities were almost as important. From the beginning, the hospital has pursued a continuous up-dating and development process, keeping in line with and constantly improving services on a par with the best hospitals in the country. The development of the health services in the area put additional demands on the resources of the Northern Ireland Hospital authorities, and the sisters in Courtenay Hill were asked to provide maternity beds in 1973.

In 1979 a house was purchased at the bottom of Courtenay Hill for a convent for the sisters. An adjoining house was purchased in 1980 and both were converted into one. In 1980 an extension was added to the house. Up to then the sisters had lived in the hospital.

In the mid 1980s, at the request of the provincial council, the sisters in the hospital conducted a survey of the health care needs of the community. It was decided to open a hospice facility in the hospital. Courtenay Hill had been known locally as the 'palace on the hill'. In converting the building to a hospice the élitist image changed because the hospice served rich and poor, Catholic and Protestant, side by side. Both Catholics and

Protestants are very active in fund-raising for the hospice and it has played a significant role in improving ecumenical relations in the locality. Changing health care needs in the locality caused the maternity unit in the hospital to be closed down in 1992. The almost new incubator was passed on to the Albanian football team – the team were visiting Newry at the time, to play the Northern Ireland soccer team – for presentation to a hospital in their homeland.

Looking south

In Waterford too the sisters tried to respond to changing needs. They continued to serve in the Fever Hospital until its closure in 1960. Successful courses of immunisation, and skilful scientific treatment over a period of years, succeeded in eliminating fever diseases. By 1960 the number of fever cases admitted to the Fever Hospital was so small that the Waterford Health Authority considered it uneconomic to continue maintenance of the hospital, so it was arranged that fever patients in future were to be sent to New Ross Fever Hospital and the Waterford Fever Hospital was officially closed on 31 December 1960. This was symptomatic of a trend to merge smaller, older hospitals and institutions into one.

In 1969 it was decided, and the decision was sanctioned by the High Court in Dublin, to amalgamate the Holy Ghost Hospital and the Fanning Institution – another old people's home in Waterford City. The patients from the Fanning Institution were transferred to the Holy Ghost Hospital. A proposed scheme of modernisation of the hospital proved uneconomic owing to the deteriorated condition of the existing building, so it was agreed to build a completely new home for the aged in the field at the back of the existing Holy Ghost Hospital.

For many years the sisters had sought ways of extending their involvement in the Waterford area. They sought to open a nursing home, in or near the city, with a view to giving the senior figures of the community, who had spent a good number of years in private nursing, an opportunity to enjoy community life, while at the same time exercising their calling as nursing sisters. It was not to be until 1926 that their dream was realised with the opening of Maypark private nursing home.

The Maypark project was part of a wider pattern, the provision of private nursing homes in close association with general hospitals. This was to meet the growing social needs for general institutional care and hospitalisation.

In Maypark, down through the years, additions and reconstructions were made to accommodate the increasing demand for beds in the hospital. In 1970 the local bishop requested that additional accommodation be made available for his retiring priests. Accordingly, an entire new wing, consisting of private rooms equipped with modern amenities, was constructed. The new wing was connected with the old house by a sun-parlour where convalescing patients could sit and enjoy the sun and beautiful view. A regular visitor was popular singer Val Doonican who frequently called in to see his mother who was a patient there. In 1991 it was decided to close the hospital.

Beyond the stereotype

As we noted in Chapter Three, the sisters were involved in the workhouse in Thomastown from an early stage of their history. In 1957, the whole institution took on a new dimension – it was to cater for the elderly only. From then on, the county home was known as St Columba's Hospital. Since then many changes have taken place in the hospital. The building has been reconstructed in parts, modernised, and all wards up-graded. A new scheme, a Day-Care Centre, was started in September, 1979, catering for up to sixty people who attend five days a week with the emphasis on rehabilitation and diversionary activities. In the early days the workhouse was nicknamed 'the place of last resort' and 'place of shame', but the Day Centre has a waiting list of patients to attend there for proper care and attention.

New partners

Lack of numbers forced the sisters to hand over the running of the school at Owning to the local community in 1985. The sisters sold their house and property at far less than the market value to enable a Sue Ryder foundation to be developed. Across the world, the Sue Ryder Homes care for over 70,000 patients in fifteen countries. Sue Ryder was born into a large farm-owning family from Yorkshire. The course of her life was strongly influenced by the example of her mother's voluntary work. A veteran of the highly secret Special Operations Executive, which coordinated the activities of resistance groups in German-occupied Europe, she herself served in the Polish section, and emerged from the war burning with a sense of injustice, determined to give her life to the service of others. A convert to Roman Catholicism, she met Group Captain Leonard Cheshire who founded the Cheshire Homes, and they eventually married. Both channelled their energies into relief work among the millions of sick, homeless and destitute people all over the world. The Sue Ryder foundation is a living memorial, in the sense that it serves an active progressive purpose – the relief of suffering, physical and psychological, whatever its cause, and wherever the opportunity to abate it may be found. Its motto is:

> For the cause that lacks assistance,
> For the wrong that needs resistance,
> For the future in the distance,
> And the good that I can do.

Three sisters are currently working in the homes, where people are provided with 'sheltered living'. One main meal a day is cooked for them and the frail ones get special attention.

The Owning experience was not a unique one for the Congregation. In the aftermath of Vatican II, the community in Kilmore was also affected by a decline of numbers. Currently two sisters are teaching in the school. The convent was sold and now serves as a nursing home. The sisters live in a new bungalow and are involved in parish work.

Education for living

As was the case with their health care mininstry, in education too the sisters established new foundations and extensions. There were no facilities for secondary education for girls in Edenderry, for example, nor indeed for a radius of about fifteen miles, until 1939 when facilities were provided for thirty-five girls to prepare for public examinations. A further extension was added in 1954. By 1962, ninety girls were being provided with secondary education, making extensions imperative. Accordingly, the original buildings were reconstructed and added to in 1964-5. With

BoyleExtra
Loyalty Rewards – Every bet counts!

SELECTION	MEETING	TIME
5 turn, Trap 1	12:16 Oakford	

You can place any type of bet on this slip.
Simply indicate your chosen

1. Stake
2. Selection
3. Time & Meeting

Remember you can pick up your winnings in any BoyleSports shop nationwide.
For your nearest BoyleSports shop call free.

1800 44 00 00

BOYLE EXTRA

Get rewarded for your loyalty! Simply:

- Open or use an existing online BoyleSports Account.
- Record your account number on every bet slip you place in-store.
- Receive points for every €5 staked per individual bet in-store, online, on mobile or via fon-a-bet.
- Earn 1 ticket to our prize draws with every 200 points accumulated
- Free bets, once in a lifetime prizes, enhanced prices, exclusive promotions, invites to events and much more up for grabs every month!

T&Cs Apply - Ask staff for more details

POINTS CALCULATION
*Points calculated on a €5 minimum stake

BET TYPE	5/1 or greater	2/1 or greater	EVS or greater	Less than EVS
Accumulator & Multi-bet	12pts	9pts	6pts	3pts
Double & Treble	9pts	6pts	4pts	2pts
Single	6pts	4pts	2pts	1pt

BoyleSports   boylesports.com   1800 44 00 00

Boyle

Loyalty Rewards - Every bet c

Account #

SELECTION:

letter be

Baby bob 1984

4765858

MEETING:

TIME:

TOTAL STAKE €

HOW TO PLA

BS001 122015

the introduction of free transport and free post-primary education, the number of pupils seeking secondary education increased dramatically, so it was decided in 1968 to change to a full secondary school. By the late 1980s, lack of numbers forced the sisters to withdraw from teaching there, while continuing to teach in the primary school.

The sisters engaged in many other activities down through the century. Music was one of these apostolates, teaching instrumental music to children, training the parish choir and acting as organist. Prayer ministry was also significant. There was a large Sodality of the Children of Mary which in turn gave away to CLC (Christian Life Community) groups.

In Waterford, classroom extensions were added to the sisters' school in 1932 and 1957, with a new block being completed in 1964. Secondary education was provided there from 1943 up to the introduction of the free education scheme in the late 1960s. Also attached to the school was a successful commercial class and a much appreciated nursery class. The nursery school was opened in 1972.

As accommodation was limited in the convent in Rathdowney, a new wing containing chapel, community room, and bedrooms was opened in 1931. School conditions were primitive for a long period. Owing to a lack of finance, indoor toilets were not provided until 1972. The school has a great reputation for excellent music teachers, one of whom, Sr Imelda McDonald, had the distinction of accompanying the internationally acclaimed tenor, Count John McCormack. Students of the school have won many national prizes for choral work and drama.

As we read in Chapter Three, the sisters opened a school in The Faythe in Wexford in 1875. In 1946 an extensive new building, incorporating the old school, was opened in The Faythe. There were some teething problems until the school was fully completed – the junior infant room had no desks. The sisters coped with the problem by alternating the junior and senior infant classes every half hour, doing oral work in the room where there were no desks and written work in the room with the desks. From 1947 to 1970 facilities were also provided in the building for education for post-primary pupils. In 1971 the school was again extended.

The Congregation replaced their old school in Kilkenny with
a splendid new building in 1941. A lot of work has been done in
a discreet way through the school for poor children, providing
meals before school, for children from families who could not afford them. As in Rathdowney, a lot of assistance was given to
travellers' children. In 1971 a sixty-thousand pounds extension
of the school was opened.

The sisters in the Kilkenny community were famous for their
magnificent embroidery, crochet work, and Irish lace-making.
From their earliest days on the banks of the Nore, they began an
apostolate, the making of altar breads, which still flourishes.
Initially the demands on sisters in the ministry were relatively
small because in those days people did not receive Holy
Communion as frequently as they do today. This situation
changed dramatically by the late 1920s when the Church's
teaching was changed to encourage frequent, even daily
Communion. Making altar breads was difficult, tedious work –
mixing batter, baking, cutting of wafers, all call for great
patience. Since the early 1960s demands for altar breads intens-
ified rapidly, necessitating the purchase of speedy, electric
machinery. Another apostolate which has been a feature of the
sisters' presence in Kilkenny since 1896 is 'city nursing', caring
for the poor, the sick and the needy.

The poor will always be with you

From the Congregation's earliest days, the care of the sick poor
in their own homes was undertaken by the sisters. Non-profes-
sional social work has always been an integral part of their apostolate. The late Sr Philip Kelly is still a household name in
Wexford because of her work in this ministry. During the 1920s
four sisters worked in the Old Hospital in Baltinglass. They
worked in the Fever Hospital and in the Infirmary. They were
hardly ever seen outside the hospital grounds except on a first
Friday when they came down for 7.30 Mass. Normally they had
Mass in their own convent.

In the years of the depression, towards the end of the Second
World War, the 'penny dinners' were started by the sisters in
Wexford. For thirty years the poverty stricken, especially
hungry children, were fed daily. Improved social benefits and

facilities terminated this service. To mark the completion of one hundred years service to the people of Wexford, a 'meals-on-wheels' unit was erected by the Congregation. Up to two hundred meals are provided per week to old or disabled people who live alone with no one to care for them.

A sister is also involved in St Brigid's Mother's club, Wexford, where mothers are helped to run their homes more efficiently. Talks, demonstrations and practical experiences are provided on religious, economic and domestic issues.

As shown in Chapter Three, the sisters were involved in Enniscorthy in the workhouse, an institution which has had a number of names. Initially it was known as workhouse; then it became the 'county home' and its name was changed again in 1950 to St John's Hospital. During the nineteenth century the workhouse had a reputation for extremely harsh conditions. The sisters were at the cutting edge of the campaign to bring the patient's living environment into the twentieth century. It was a difficult and painful process. One sister, Sr Malachy Kearns, was sacked as matron in 1934. Her crime – she bought enamel mugs and teapots for the patients. Up to then they drank from jars. She also incurred major expense by buying beds for the patients because they were still sleeping on straw. Long before it was fashionable, she was a practitioner of 'advocacy', speaking out for the rights of the poor and complementing her words with appropriate action. Her dismissal from the post was a very traumatic experience.

It was not until the 1960s, with the advent of a much more en-lightened County Council, that conditions improved dramatic-ally. New beds, lockers and wardrobes were provided for all patients. Resident unmarried mothers did all the domestic work in the hospital with no pay. The sisters were given the green light to change that system and to provide uniforms and wages for these women. Overcrowding was a serious problem at the time and the problem was at last given the attention it deserved. In 1960 there were 408 patients and in 1979 the numbers had been reduced to 210. Changes were also made to improve the quality of life for the sisters. Up to the 1960s the sisters had lived in the hospital with patients. A new convent was built for them and a side-chapel was built in St John's House. The sisters worked seven days a week, with seven days per annum for both holidays and a retreat, for a salary of ten shillings a week. In 1960 all the nursing was done by 16 sisters but in 1994 the nursing work was being done by five sisters and 38 other nurses.

Another chapter in the sisters' association with Enniscorthy began in 1971 when St John of God House was acquired by the Health Board from the Loreto Order who had used the premises as a school. It was set up to provide a service for severely handicapped children from Co Wexford and south Co Carlow. The house operates on a five day week, Monday to Friday, and the residents return home for the week-end. As the Health Board requested sisters for the staff, a number of sisters trained with the St John of God Brothers. Sr Florence McGrath was appointed matron but, with her retirement in 1994, the sisters' connection with this ministry has ended.

From the beginning, a sister worked around the town in Rathdowney doing social work, but it was not until 1972 that the sisters' role in this respect was put on a formal basis. One sister who was very highly regarded for her work amongst the people was Sr Paul Newitt. On the day of her funeral, the Brewery closed and the workers with many other townspeople marched with the hearse for some distance out of town. Sr Paul died in 1940. In 1992 an exciting new era for the sisters began when the old convent was sold for use as a community care facility. A new institution, 'Cuan Bhríde', was established which is a complex for old people who live in a cluster of independent little houses. The sisters are involved as a back-up to these residents, providing services like meals-on-wheels and ensuring that their needs are catered for. The sisters working in this project live in the midst of the community in one of the little houses. The teaching sisters moved into the recently built St John of God house – a building the size of a domestic dwelling. Since 1993 a sister has devoted all her professional energies to the provision of remedial education. Not only does she work in the sisters' own school, she also works in this capacity in the Church of Ireland school, thus providing a valuable ecumenical link.

Handmaidens of the Lord?

In 1886 a new apostolate began for the sisters when they were

The Holy Father's visit to the Irish College, Rome, 1980. Included are Srs Leonard Casey, Catherine O'Brien, Anne Marie Ryan and Mairead Kenny.

invited to care for students in St Kieran's College and seminary in Kilkenny, by the local bishop. Their duties included cooking and supervision of domestic arrangements, infirmarian work and general housekeeping. It was not until 1931 that a community of three sisters became resident in the college. The sisters received similar requests down the years.

Although the motivation for inviting the sisters to these colleges and seminaries seems to be largely expediency, the hard-working, reliable, non-unionised labour of the sisters has provided an invaluable service in terms of providing care to the students under their supervision. Moreover, in the context of their seminary work, they were a feminine presence in an otherwise all-male institution.

The long friendly relationship between Ferns and the Irish College was the background to the St John of God Sisters' arrival in Rome in 1923. Today a small group of sisters continue to render unobtrusive service in their management of domestic affairs, which involves the responsible task of training and supervising the Italian staff and caring for the ill students and staff.

Responding to the appeal of the Bishop of Dromore, two sisters commenced duty in St Colman's College, Newry. The Congregation also took up service in the Ferns Diocesan College, St Peter's, in 1930. The reason for this invitation is revealing – the college superior could not replace an excellent housekeeper who retired. In 1935 following an invitation from the Provincial of the Augustinians, two sisters arrived to care for students in Good Counsel College, New Ross, Co Wexford. The following year three sisters began work in Rockwell College, Tipperary and others assumed similar duties in Knockbeg College, Carlow and St Flannan's College, Ennis.

Appreciation of the sisters' work in Ennis led to the donation of a house and site on the college grounds and an invitation to open a private nursing home came from the Bishop of Killaloe. The necessary renovations completed, the hospital opened and flourished, so much so that a very modern hospital with medical, surgical and maternity departments had to be built in Cahercalla, near Ennis, in 1959. Further renovations and extensions were carried out, together with the erection of a new post-Vatican II chapel in 1968. The necessity of a convent for the sisters was apparent for years, but the requested new maternity unit for Co Clare necessitated the provision of ample room for medical and geriatric patients which was ensured through the sisters vacating hospital rooms. A comfortable new convent was built for the sisters in 1978-9.

Beyond chalk and talk

In the field of education, one major development the sisters got involved in was in the rapidly-growing suburbs of north Dublin at the request of Archbishop McQuaid. During the early 1960s, north city Dublin began to be developed on a very large scale and large building schemes were planned to help solve some of Dublin's housing problems. The sisters undertook to provide primary and secondary schools for girls at Kilmore Road, in the new parish of St John Vianney, Ardlea Road. This is part of the northside of Dublin which has been made famous by the books and films of Roddy Doyle. They began their secondary school in a temporary building in September 1967 with thirty-one pupils. Within four years the number had increased to one hundred and ten.

On the first school day, classwork could not be initiated due to the fact that the furniture had not been delivered and the toilets were not working. Classes were suspended for a week. By Christmas the sisters had moved from lodgings to their convent. They were known locally as the 'nuns in the blue boxes' because the prefabs they lived and taught in were blue. In the following July, one hundred and ninety-one pupils were enrolled in the sisters' primary school. Within four years the numbers had risen to five hundred and fifty. Work was quickly started on permanent school buildings and a new primary school building was opened in 1971 and a secondary school building opened in 1975.

Today the sisters live in a purpose-built building. They are involved in parish work, in the secondary school, in the primary school, in a special school for the educationally disadvantaged, and in retreat work.

Two other houses were established in the 60s. Firstly, the House of Studies purchased in Seaview Terrace, Donnybrook, Dublin, in 1967, for sisters attending university or courses in Dublin. Secondly, a holiday and retreat house by the sea at Ballyvalloo, in the parish of Blackwater, Co Wexford. Work was begun there in February 1968 and the building was blessed and opened on 26 July. It was designed as a holiday house for the sisters during the summer, and for the remainder of the year as a retreat-house, for the sisters themselves and for others.

In 1983 the sisters established a small Christian community to enable a small group (normally four) of young women to live a fuller life in today's world. From September to the following June, the group involved in the project live together as a Christian community with two sisters acting as facilitators. Each person finds some temporary work for the year in order to help finance the running of the house. Those who already work in Dublin continue their jobs. The group dynamic is an important context for growth. Each member commits herself to a community night each week. Weekend courses are provided in the areas of personal growth and development, and spirituality. There are also opportunities for personal counselling and spiritual direction. Participants also have a short experience of working in a socially deprived area.

Any woman in Ireland wishing to join the Congregation is

asked to spend a year in this Christian community with young women having similar interests. During this year she is helped to discern and choose the right direction for her way of life. If she chooses religious life there is a novitiate period which lasts two years. This is a time to come to an appreciation of what God is asking of her in her life. An emphasis is laid on an interior life of prayer – a relationship with Jesus – as a basis for her commitment within the Church. At the end of this novitiate period, the sister makes temporary vows for between five and nine years. During this time she devotes a definite period to religious studies and also to professional training. Then she is ready to make her final commitment.

Reweaving Religious Life

In 1949, at the funeral of the first president of the Irish State, Douglas Hyde, a Protestant, members of the government had to sit outside St Patrick's Protestant Cathedral in their state cars during the service. The hierarchy would then not allow a Catholic to enter a Protestant church. In March 1992, Cardinal Cahal Daly not only attended the 800th anniversary celebration of the same cathedral in Dublin, but preached from the pulpit there. Until 1970, the Catholic Church forbade its members to go to Trinity College, Dublin. Now its Provost is himself a Catholic. The 'special position' of the Roman Catholic Church was removed from the Irish Constitution as long ago as 1972, but the changes since then, both in the Church's view of itself and the faithful's view of it, have been striking.

While a 1992 opinion poll in the Irish Republic found that 93% of the population expressed a belief in God, and 75% thought regular church attendance was important, only 56% of those under 25 were among the latter, and almost half the population is under 25. A survey published by the Augustinian Order, in 1992, found that the Catholic Church was perceived as 'having an autocratic and authoritarian style, distant and out of touch with the experience of the people … on divorce, contraception and sexual morality generally'. It was 'narrow-minded, old-fashioned and male-dominated'. Contraception, made legal in 1980 for married couples only, has, since 1992, been available for all. In 1993 the noted psychiatrist Anthony Clare made an interesting observation: 'Irish Catholics seem to have made their own very personal, idiosyncratic arrangements with their own very personal, idiosyncratic God... It is difficult not to feel that Ireland is closer to being a Protestant nation than anyone appears to appreciate.'

Many people have pointed to the election as President in 1990 of Mary Robinson, as a significant shift in Irish society. Perhaps it is more accurate to see her election as a symptom of the major changes in Irish life over the last three decades, the transformation from a society that was predominantly agricultural and rural to one that is now increasingly industrial and urban. Inevitably these changes have impacted on religious beliefs. One way to sum up the change is to note that there is a swing from the experience of authority to the authority of experience.

Mary Jo Leddy, in her book *Reweaving Religious Life: Beyond the Liberal Model* (1989), argues that religious life lies in an in-between moment of its history, with the past lying in shreds and the future unformed. She even refers to it as the 'dark night', a 'threadbare' moment where religious need to discover the places where they can best position themselves for the future. She suggests three places: prayer, on the periphery, far away from the centre of power, and on pilgrimage. Reweaving religious life demands a letting go, on personal, community and Congregational level. This begins not by attempting survival games but by a radical commitment to Christian discipleship.

While all the sisters are busily engaged in the task of finding a lifestyle which is compatible with both the spirit of the times and Gospel values, the Congregation has responded to the changing realities by establishing new structures. In the 90s in Wexford, three small communities of four sisters, have been set up in Mansfield Drive, Farnogue and Parkside. This more intimate environment is a far cry from the pre-Vatican II days when the sisters' rooms were called 'cells'. A similar house has been founded in Dean's Court in Kilkenny, requiring a whole new participative style of leadership with the sisters involved taking more personal responsibility for all aspects of their life, such as budgeting. Equally important as the sisters having personal responsibility in the participative leadership model, is that there is a personal authority to drive it.

This approach is an effort to bring sisters together who share a common vision to be with people. These sisters, in common with all the sisters in the province, share a need to be in touch with reality and with the presence of God in their lives and in the people they serve. The Congregation's charism of hospitality finds new expression in these houses. Neighbours are invited into the sisters' homes for prayer and important events like the renewal of vows.

In Ennis, one of the sisters is involved in 'Rural Resettlement Ireland'. Today most of the Irish population live in urban centres. The decline of rural Ireland is an emotive subject. Emotion aside, creameries, schools and post-offices have fallen victim to the balancing-books syndrome. A lack of jobs has caused the majority of young people to turn their backs on the place of their birth and head for cities like Dublin, Manchester and Boston. For many country people it is difficult to keep up morale. The rural resettlement scheme is one effort to breathe new life into rural Ireland by encouraging and helping people to move from the cities to the country. Inevitably there are major problems for these people in adjusting to this new environment. Accordingly, there is a new ministry to help those who are finding it difficult to adapt.

Up to recently, in Ennis, as in Waterford, the sisters were involved in a new ministry to the travelling community. Historically, because of their nomadic lifestyle, travellers' children have fallen much behind in educational advancement. As a result of a widespread perception that many travellers are criminals, drunkards and ripping off the social welfare system, they are also victims of much discrimination. The sisters involved in this ministry to date have all worked with the Aboriginal community in Australia and have been struck by the similarities of the problems facing both communities. Their experiences 'down under' have been an invaluable preparation for their current ministry. In their first few months working with the travellers in Waterford, the sisters taught in the back of an old car. Sisters are also involved in other ministries like counselling and parish work. Their commitment to the marginalised is also evident in the fact that one of the sisters works on a part-time basis in Waterford in a home for battered wives.

While the new horizons in ministry have brought new life to the Congregation at a time of shrinking numbers, they have also brought painful choices. In Cahercalla the hospital has been sold to the local community. Sisters will continue to work in the hospital but will be freed from administrative roles.

The sisters' lives no longer contain an inherent pattern as they had in the pre-Vatican II days. For much of their history, the sisters have been so preoccupied with the demands of their apostolate that they have been unable adequately to attend to their own spiritual and personal needs. Now they live a life to be created as it unfolds, with all the fear and exhilaration such heady freedom brings.

CHAPTER EIGHT

Crossing the Channel

> Every beginning is a promise.
> (*Brendan Kennelly*)

Chance encounters have played a major influence in the history of the Sisters of St John of God, as we have already seen. The Congregation's mission to England was the fruit of such an occurrence. In August 1924, Canon (later bishop) Lee, Vicar of the Diocese of Clifton in Bristol, an Irishman, paid a visit to the Bishop of Ferns, Bishop Codd. The bishop's housekeeper was ill at the time and was being nursed by a sister of St John of God, Calasanctius Carpenter. When the canon arrived at the palace he was greeted by Sr Calasanctius. In conversation with the bishop, Canon Lee inquired to which Congregation Sr Calasanctius belonged and the nature of their apostolate. Hearing of their ministry the canon remarked, 'This Congregation would suit one of our parishes in Bristol, St Joseph's, Fishponds, where sisters are badly needed.' Shortly after, Canon Lee visited the Mother General of the Sisters of St John of God, and sought and received a promise that sisters would be sent to Bristol. After a discussion with his bishop, Canon Lee sent the following communication to the sisters:

Dear Mother General,

The bishop is very pleased that you will send sisters to open a new house in Fishponds, Bristol, next July. His Lordship wishes me to tell you that we shall open a new church there on 19 March, Feast of St Joseph, and he would be very glad if you manage to be here for that day. You would be able to see for yourself how things are, and we could discuss the question of a house for the sisters. In fact, there are so many things

162

Sr Jude Doran surrounded by Bristol school-children.

to be considered that a visit will only satisfy. The Sisters of the Good Shepherd here will be only too pleased to give you hospitality.

I hope you see your way to visit Bristol for 19 March.

Sincerely wishing that all under your care are well, and with all good wishes.

Yours sincerely,

Sgd. W Lee.

The sisters accepted the invitation and during their visit arrangements were made to open a house at St Joseph's, Fishponds, on the feast of Blessed Oliver Plunkett, 11 July, 1925. A house, No. 354 Lodge Causeway, was purchased and three sisters, Mother M Angela Delaney, M Ita Kissane and M Josepha Quilter, left Wexford for Bristol. The sisters faced a minor problem at the outset when they went to the solicitor's office to claim the key of their newly-purchased house. They were informed that the key was not in the solicitor's office but in Trowbridge (coincidentally the bishop later made an appeal to the Mother General for sisters for Trowbridge). While waiting for the key of the house, they visited the house adjoining and were welcomed in. The

The Sisters of St John of God in Britain

lady of the house, whose father was Irish and a lapsed Catholic, was the first to volunteer to send her eldest daughter to what was to be the Sisters of St John of God school. Subsequently the mother and all her children became converts to Catholicism.

Having secured the key, the sisters were then faced with the task of buying some basic furniture for the house. They left an umbrella in the hall to show that they had taken possession. Both the Sisters of Mercy and the Good Shepherd Sisters provided them with practical assistance as they settled in.

In September of that year, the sisters set about implementing their plans to open a private school in St Joseph's Hall, the former parish church. The hall served a dual function – by day it was a school, and by night and weekend it catered for parish functions. Initially about twenty Catholic children enrolled. 'Non-Catholic' parents in the area were attracted to the school and in this way it would make a significant, if indirect, contribution to ecumenism at local level. Pupil numbers grew significantly even though facilities were poor; classes were divided by removable blackboards. The parishioners, like the sisters, were poor: the fee in school, for those who could afford it, was one pound per term for people who were Catholics and two pounds for those who were not. The sisters were also very involved in parish ministry. As the demands grew, further reinforcements from Ireland were required as was the purchase of a second house which adjoined their first residence.

The outbreak of war in 1939 impacted on the sisters on many levels. The first casualty was their plan for a new school (planned as a response to the increase in the school population) which had to be put on hold. More serious was the threat to people, as German bombers regularly flew over the vicinity. It was an emotionally taxing time for all concerned, with sirens rumbling constantly.

Emergency dashes to the simple school shelters were regular events for the sisters and their pupils, providing parents with the opportunity to send their children to a 'safe area'.

Two sisters began a new ministry for the Sisters of Saint John of God by taking on 'war duty', taking charge of an air raid precaution station from 8 a.m. to 8 p.m.. This took priority over attending morning Mass. Two other sisters took on a different task, 'fire watching' on Lodge Causeway and the neighbourhood. During an air raid they walked up and down the Causeway to be ready to put down sand bags on buildings catching fire from incendiary bombs. Gas masks were worn during air raids. The threat of death was very real, particularly when bomber planes passed directly overhead, forcing sisters to spend hours in the shelters until they got the all clear.

Apart from reciting the rosary, they sang songs and hymns in the shelters and told stories to keep up morale. To maintain peoples' spirits in the local community they organised social events in the parish, for example catering for dances and socials for members of the forces as they returned for short vacations with their families. They also did catering for holidays for Catholic girls from Bristol, taking groups to a boarding school in Somerset for a holiday at the seaside.

After the war, Bristol changed profoundly with suburbs and new housing estates springing up all over the place. With an increase in the Catholic population, the bishop decided to found two other parishes from St Joseph's: St John Fisher, Frenchay, and St Augustine's, Downend, but there was a time lag until new schools were built there, placing new demands on the sisters in St Joseph's. When the new school was opened in 1951 that pressure was taken off them. The sisters were very involved in extra apostolic activities – instructing of converts, holding Sunday school classes in neighbouring parishes, and preparing children for the sacraments.

As well as by teaching, the sisters sought to be faithful to the charism of their founder by visiting the sick in their homes and in hospital. They attempted to turn their schools into 'faith communities', nurturing links with parents of school children by home visitation as well as visiting the poor, the lonely and the elderly. They were, in a sense, pioneers of youth ministry through their work with Children of Mary Sodalities and Legion of Mary involvement. Their education apostolate extended with the establishment of Kingswood in late 1960s and Downend in the 1970s. One sister later became active in the Catholic Deaf Organisation. Increasingly sisters started to prepare for new ministries like social work, by taking degree courses in the relevant areas.

The original desire, which we have already noted, of Visitation Clancy for her sisters to be like 'ripples in a pond', was very evidently fulfilled in Fishponds. The sisters gave instruction to converts and lapsed Catholics. One such convert was a

Miss Goddhard, who became a Mercy nun and volunteered to nurse the lepers in Africa. She wrote home to her friends to say that it was while she was praying in the oratory at Fishponds that she 'developed a vocation for religious life'.

The convent was rebuilt and officially opened in 1967. In 1985, due to falling numbers of sisters and cost of maintenance, this convent was sold and became a house for psychiatric patients. The sisters moved to a house at 28 Chester Park Road. This change reflected the spirit of Vatican II, particularly its document on religious life, *Perfectae Caritatis.*

Perfectae Caritatis called for a new integration of prayer and apostolate for active Congregations and the emergence of what was termed 'apostolic spirituality'. The energy and vitality of their spirituality would often derive from their discovery of God in the midst of active life. Increasingly the formalities and rigidity of monastic prayer forms and schedules were broken and other people's cares and burdens began to be the more dominant factor in prayer forms and in the structure of daily living. The traditional ordered pattern of convent life was seriously disrupted, if not shattered.

After the Council, the sisters' pastoral work in Bristol was designed to respond to new needs such as the problems of one-parent families as well as continuing traditional apostolates like hospital visitation. They were also at the frontiers of new parish initiatives such as the Rite of Christian Initiation of Adults (R.C.I.A.). Like many others in ministry, they strove to grapple with the problem of those who had ceased to practice, having been alienated from their faith on the erroneous assumption that in rejecting an over-institutionalised religion they were in turn being rejected by, or rejecting, Christ.

As we saw in Chapter Two, in the nineteenth century, centralisation came to be regarded as the only guarantee of orthodoxy in the Catholic Church. Freedom was considered suspect. In the latter part of the twentieth century, many Catholics are turning their backs on the rigidities which are part and parcel of their Church's tradition. While many are certain they cannot accept the old ways they are much less sure what they want to put in its place. In this time of transition, the challenge facing those in ministry is to help steer those who have lost their way in the fog.

The decline in the number of active sisters forced the sisters reluctantly to end their mission in Bristol in 1994. This decision followed three meetings involving all the sisters in England and Wales. Since Vatican II, consultation has become a feature of the Congregation. All sisters are involved in setting goals for the community each year and in the evaluation process at the end of each term. A hierarchical leadership structure has given way to a horizontal one. While this was difficult for sisters accustomed to the traditional ways initially, for example the novelty of sharing one's feelings and innermost thoughts in a frank way in the newly introduced community meetings, it was ultimately a liberating experience for all concerned. The sharing deepened as mutual trust developed. It was only then that the sisters in England and Wales felt a sense of real interdependence and wanted to share with each other. There had always been a tradition that if a sister in England or Wales died, some sisters from each house would come to sympathise, but after the Council the contacts between the communities increased dramatically. This was particularly the case between Trowbridge, Bristol and Cardiff because of their geographical proximity.

A new departure

In 1926, following a steady stream of requests from Canon Lee, the Congregation provided sisters for a school in Trowbridge in Wiltshire. The decision was made only after a period of intense soul-searching, because there were so many competing demands for sisters. Two sisters, Mother Aidan Devereux and Sr Rita Kinsella, left Wexford for Trowbridge on 17 December 1926. They began with eleven pupils, four of them Catholics. School numbers increased quickly, making the construction of a modern school an absolute necessity. As the majority of students were unable to pay fees, the school was not self-supporting making some State aid essential. However, it was not until February 1950 that this was forthcoming.

The closure of the Polish camp at Keevil, in the U.K., the following year, meant that over 150 families had to be housed in the area. Many of these children came to Trowbridge, with a consequent increase in pupil numbers to 253. As pupil numbers continued to soar, further extension to the school building was necessary. In 1961 the sisters were obliged to rent two class-rooms in a school from another tradition to cope with rising numbers. A complete new block was constructed in 1967, which was added to in the 1980s and in 1992.

The new school had created a domino effect. It meant more sisters were required on the teaching staff. This in turn put a strain on living space in the small house which had served as the sisters' convent. A new convent was opened on 7 May, 1938.

In 1952 the sisters began a secondary education apostolate in response to the needs of the local people. Under the terms of the 1944 Education Act, one of the conditions necessary to obtain State aid for primary schools, was that children over eleven years would be removed. For that reason forty children were transferred to temporary classrooms in the convent until proper accommodation could be provided. Bishop Lee again inter-vened and persuaded the Congregation to purchase 'Dulce Domum', a diocesan property at Wingfield Road. In January 1952 the senior girls at the convent moved to the new building. Over the next six years, the school was adapted and extended to cope with the increasing numbers of pupils. The school was reg-istered as proficient by the local Education Authority and the sisters encouraged to go ahead for recognition. By this time, diocesan plans were in progress for a new parochial secondary school. The sisters were advised by the bishop not to make any further extensions to their school, to prevent a duplication of re-sources. Consequently pupils from other denominations were no longer admitted in 'Dulce Domum' after 1963 and the private school officially closed in July 1966.

St Augustine's R.C. Secondary School opened in January 1967 with approximately 140 pupils, girls and boys, to cater for all the Catholic boys and girls in Trowbridge and the surround-ing area. In 1986 the school became incorporated into the new comprehensive system of secondary education and St Augustine's became known as St Augustine's Comprehensive School and in 1992 it became grant-aided to cater for 500 pupils. Although at-taining high educational standards was the primary educational priority of the sisters who joined the staff, it was by no means their only ministry or concern.

The sisters in Trowbridge gradually became ever more involved in the parish, visiting the sick and elderly in their homes, instructing converts, many of whom made their first contacts through the schools, and giving catechetical instruction to children in outlying parishes where no Catholic school was available. From 1975 onwards the sisters made the convent more open to others in the parish, especially in its prayer life, with the formation of a prayer group and even less traditional approaches to evangelisation, like coffee evenings.

Although the sisters' work in Trowbridge, or in England in general, may not have been as dramatic as their ministry in Pakistan or the Kimberley in Australia, their contribution was immense. Local people found them to be very approachable and human and this enabled them to help a lot of people in emotional, spiritual and material terms. This was much easier for the sisters in the British context than for their colleagues in Ireland because they lived in a local house and not in a big institution. Accordingly, it was easier for the sisters to nurture a homely atmosphere.

The Birmingham Five

In 1931 or early 1932, four sisters, Claver Purcell, Cyril Holland, Maris Stella Fleming and Vogue Keogh, went to Newcastle, Birmingham, in response to the perceived need of the local clergy for a Catholic nursing home in that area. They acquired a Manor House, which was located outside Birmingham city. The house was adapted for nursing services and had accommodation for sixteen patients. A major plus was that the house had a magnificent garden which made an ideal venue for patients seeking recuperation. Later Sister Lelia Crowe joined the staff. Although the sisters and staff provided a high level of care, the location out in the country proved to be uneconomical. Access to the home for doctors and pharmacists was difficult and expensive. Moreover, maintenance and domestic services proved much more expensive than had been envisaged. Consequently, when an invitation was received from the local bishop by the Congregation to establish a foundation in Torquay in the diocese of Plymouth in 1934, it was decided to discontinue the Newcastle mission and transfer staff and equipment to Torquay.

By the sea

Torquay is well known as a holiday resort in South Devon. Although it began as a place for retirement, it has also a large number of residential mansions and villas which were built for elderly people. One such person was a Mrs Hole who, in 1934, contacted the Sisters of St John of God, to whom the Bishop of Plymouth had already applied for help. She was becoming old and infirm and she wanted to continue to live near the church. So it was arranged that the sisters should take over the house and conduct it as a nursing home, Mrs Hole being their first patient. Such was the home's reputation of service to the sick and aged that those requiring rooms far exceeded the accommodation available.

One unexpected positive side-effect of this nursing home was that it helped to remove the prejudice against Catholics which prevailed in the West Country at the time. Contacts established with the townspeople and those non-Catholics who used the nursing home did untold good in this respect.

In 1966 it was decided to secure larger accommodation to meet the growing demand, and eventually the Croft Hall Hotel, a private hotel, was purchased for this purpose. The high numbers of patients was the most fitting tribute to the sisters' work with the old, senile and post-operative patients. Most of the sisters were ministers of the Eucharist, enabling them to distribute Holy Communion to patients who were unable to leave their rooms.

This reaching out to the local community reflected a large-scale concerted effort to foster greater public participation in the life of the Church in the aftermath of Vatican II. An important, albeit indirect, influence on this approach, at least in certain quarters, was a community development programme of the 1960s in the developing world, pioneered by Paolo Freire. His experiences in South America made him acutely aware of the attitudes of the would-be 'helpers' upon those who were seen to be in need of 'help'. Often there was a conviction about the unassailable worth of some intervention and the benefits it would confer. Freire characterises this as 'cultural invasion'. The starting point is the world of the 'helpers' from which they view and enter the world of those they invade. This is in contrast to 'cultural synthesis' where those who come from another world do not do so as invaders. They do not come to teach or transmit or give anything, but rather they come to learn.

When this insight was applied to ecclesiology, the focus was on having lay people define their own faith needs, to find and implement their own responses, calling for a much more challenging, more enriching, approach to ministry. The sisters in Torquay and elsewhere were compelled to grapple with these new approaches and to discern how best to respond to the needs of lay people. Increasingly, the challenge for the Congregation as a whole was how to allocate their limited personnel to optimum effect. Sometimes this led to difficult decisions.

Durham Town

Ushaw College, Durham, was both a diocesan seminary and a junior training college for prospective seminarians. During the early years of World War II, it had become very difficult to get staff for the maintenance and domestic life of the college. The president heard that the St John of God Sisters were doing such work in a number of colleges and travelled to Wexford to seek assistance from the Mother General. Despite the inevitable hardships of travelling during war time, it was decided to send three sisters in September 1942. It was quickly apparent that more sisters would be needed to organise the college's domestic arrangements and two more sisters were sent. Then in January 1943, another sister and nine young Irish girls were recruited to assist in the task. The care of the young girls was in itself a major challenge and responsibility for the sisters.

As new missions continued to open without a corresponding increase in the numbers of sisters, painful decisions had to be taken to withdraw sisters from established apostolates. Durham was one such established centre where sisters were reluctantly withdrawn.

By the Rivers of the Taff we sat and wept

In 1948, when the Ursulines of Jesus and Mary were unable to replace one of their sisters who was headmistress of St Mary's Junior school, Canton, Cardiff, Archbishop McGrath of Cardiff invited the Sisters of St John of God to the archdiocese. The archbishop's sister, Sr Dominic, was a member of the Sisters of St John of God for many years. Initially four sisters arrived in 34

Talbot Street, which was the house occupied by the Ursuline Sisters, and were settled in before the school term beginning in September 1948. One sister was appointed headmistress of St Mary's junior school and another as her deputy. A third was superior with responsibility for St Mary's Sacristy and a fourth took charge of catering in the convent and laundering for sacristy and community. The Benedictine monks from Ampleforth served the parish. Among their number was Basil Hume, who after serving as Abbot of Ampleforth, went on to become Archbishop of Westminster and Cardinal.

Both junior and infant schools maintained high standards in academic achievements. The primary educational objective was to ensure that there was a high percentage of passes in the eleven plus examinations which at the time was the dream of every parent for their children as it was a passport to grammar school and, by extension, to a good career.

Although the sisters had no training in this area, at one stage a family they knew well asked them to lay out a corpse. It was a symbol of the high esteem they were held in by the local community. In keeping with the spirit of the Congregation, the sisters involved themselves in parish visitation particularly in two areas: giving instruction to converts, which has always been an integral part of the sisters' ministry in Cardiff, particularly in cases of a mixed marriage, and journeying with families who had gone through the trauma of bereavement. In the autumn of 1960, the sisters were to experience a trauma of their own.

That season saw extraordinarily high levels of rainfall with the result that the river Taff, unable to hold all the water, overflowed into Sophia Gardens, on to Cathedral Road and into the cellar and first floor of the convent. Cardiff took on the appearance of Venice as boats went up and down Cathedral Road and many people had to be evacuated but the sisters stayed until the waters subsided. It took many months for the building to dry out and fungus in the cellar became a major concern. The convent was flooded again in December 1980. A policeman came to the door with a flood warning and within an hour the cellar and first floor were once again covered with mud and water. It was Easter before everything had returned to normal.

Adjusting to flooding was one thing, but a more persistent

challenge facing the sisters was to adequately respond in their ministry to the changing social and ecclesial context. Edward Schillebeeckx, in his *Ministry - A Case for Change* (1981), argues against change for its own sake. Instead he claims that change in the ministry, and in the Church congregation as a whole, is of value only insofar as it is governed by the principle of apostolicity. It should be rooted in, and thoroughly informed by, the Spirit of Christ. The sisters sought out new horizons where they could be apostolic forces of empowerment, helping the laity to become more involved in the life of the Church. Accordingly, in the 1980s and 1990s, the sisters are continuing to involve themselves in new areas of ministry such as Confirmation and R.C.I.A. programmes, in addition to prayer groups and justice and peace groups. A St John of God sister was the first religious to join the justice and peace group in Cardiff and occasionally the sisters' house is used by the group as a venue for large meetings. This reflects the sisters' desire to open up to the community.

At the time of writing, a new area of ministry is at an advanced planning stage. The sisters are hoping to start a Christian community for young women, on the lines of the project in Dublin.

The Streets of London

In 1951, the sisters opened a foundation in St Mellitus Parish, Tollington Park, London at the invitation of Dr Mostyn, the parish priest. The Congregation was taking the place of the Notre Dame Sisters who had worked in the school for about sixty years when the area was home to the well-to-do. In the aftermath of World War II, all that was to change. Many people who had evacuated from London did not return, and the old houses were turned into flats which provided homes for many emigrant families, mostly Irish. The Notre Dame Sisters were forced to evacuate. When they returned, their old pupils had by and large departed. The new residents could not afford the fees which the sisters had been accustomed to and they were forced to close down both their school and convent.

The parish priest purchased both. At the time, the priests of the parish were chaplains to the Royal Northern Hospital where some Sisters of St John of God were training. After consultation

with the sisters, he headed for the Generalate in Wexford looking for sisters to staff the school. His plea for help elicited a
favourable response. The sisters found that their ministry included fund-raising, as the school of necessity had to be run on a
semi-private basis. Parents were asked to contribute two
shillings and six pence per week for its up-keep and many people who were not directly involved with the school supported a
weekly house-to-house collection. The staff, including the sisters, were paid from parochial funds.

Although the high educational standards resulted in a big
increase in pupil numbers, from 90 in 1951 to 480 in 1957, the
school building itself left a lot to be desired. Under the terms of
the 1944 Education Act, 'all private schools had to be registered
as fit places of accommodation for educational purposes'. A full
inspection of the school was carried out by inspectors in 1958.
They issued an ultimatum that the buildings had to be brought
up to standard. There was no alternative but to get a new building. Following lengthy negotiations with the diocese and the
Ministry of Education, permission was granted.

The solution to one problem created another. Where would
the new school be situated? The site of the old convent and
school was the obvious one but the local council had other de-
signs on that site. They were unable to carry out their plans because a place of semi-public worship could not be closed without the permission of the ecclesiastical superiors, who were the
Trustees of the buildings concerned. So the site was saved from
being requisitioned for council developments. Soon the new
school was under construction, though the sisters, like the teachers and pupils, were to experience a lot of discomfort in the
cramped conditions until the process was complete.

There remained the problem of living accommodation, particularly as the sisters had spent nine years living in a boarding
school lacking any modern amenities and even a decent roof.
One sister instructed a visitor, 'Take an umbrella to bed with
you, you may need it during the night!' In September 1959, a
local house at 81 Wray Crescent was bought for conversion into
a convent. The garden of that house had a big crater, the legacy
of a bomb during the war.

Although the new school was ready for occupation in September 1961, it emerged that it could only cater for 280 pupils and not the 480 the Congregation had expected. An error of judgement on the part of the diocesan authorities was the reason for this disappointment. It had assumed that the better part of the old building could still be used for a further few years until an extension could be added. The Ministry of Education were totally opposed to this notion. The resulting tension meant that an official opening could not take place. This resulted in the sisters taking up further apostolic work. A number of parents were forced to send their children to other schools so the sisters provided religious education for these students at the week-end.

One positive result of the new school was that it was maintained by the local authority and this released the sisters from cleaning duties and thereby afforded them the opportunity to take up new areas of ministry such as helping parents and visiting the sick. One sister took up full-time parish ministry. As the years progressed and new sisters arrived, the teaching ministry was extended to two other schools, St Aloysius College, Highgate, and Eden Grove School, Holloway.

In the 1980s, the majority of sisters reached retirement age and in 1990 the final sister retired, ending a long association with the local school. In keeping with the spirit of the age, the sisters were happy to hand on the school to a dedicated staff who continue to maintain the education standards and ethos of the school.

As one door closed for the sisters another opened. The sisters immersed themselves in 'active retirement services', ranging from parish work, chaplaincy to a local hospital, feeding the homeless who regularly come to the door, and visiting the elderly.

From the cradle to the grave

In September 1978, following a request from the parish priest for parish sisters to give support to the sick and elderly, three sisters went to begin a new mission in Hartlepool. Another sister was assigned to the nearby St Patrick's parish where she was involved in a diverse range of activities, from helping the elderly to the instruction of the young in their faith. The new emphasis on youth ministry was timely because, as Karl Rahner pointed out, 'It is more important for the Church to win one new man

(*sic*) of tomorrow than to keep the faith of two men of yesterday.'
Two sisters moved to St Cuthbert's parish were they immersed
themselves in parish visitation, catechetical work, serving as
ministers of the Eucharist and praying with the sick and elderly.
A day centre for the elderly was established which provided hot
meals, activities and, above all, company.

The sisters had gone to Hartlepool on a five-year contract.
Although they had done great work the parish was unable to
promise them any guarantees of financial support. Reluctantly
the sisters were forced to withdraw.

Weaving a new pattern?

The Sisters of St John of God in Britain are sensitive to their heritage and tradition and want to live up to that. In a fast changing
world they are striving to understand the new situation. They
want to listen to the Spirit of God. They desire to let go, to be
flexible. In their intermingling of faith and life, they want to be
attentive to where God is today. They are searching for a way to
live that is authentic and which offers an alternative to an indiv-
idualistic way of life which is increasingly prevalent in the modern world. In responding to the needs of society they are striving
to witness to Christ in their time and to reveal his love to the
struggling world. Moreover, they are pained by the injustice in
the world and have begun to discern the specific shape of
women's potential contribution to this situation.

In the England of the 1990s, there are perhaps three possible
responses for the Sisters of St John of God as a religious Congregation. They might be prophets announcing the better age to
come. Alternatively they could be preservers, making sure that
in the flux of life the validity of past insights would not be lost.
However, by their actions the sisters seem to favour a third approach, to share the drama of the age and work for the advancement of society, the Church and the common good through their
ministry. It is noteworthy that between 1984 and 1986 two communities, Cardiff and Trowbridge, moved into smaller houses,
yet continued the same apostolate, pointing to their commitment
to be inserted in the reality of the people they serve.

The Dominican prayer-poet Paul Murray, in his Office of the
Dead, asks 'What use our ritual?', and asserts:

We who are neither living nor dead
must weave and interweave the Dead
into our lives, and the Living
the new and the live thread –
weave and weave a new pattern.

As they head into the third millennium, the Sisters of St John of God in England and Wales are trying to boldly weave such a new pattern. In other parts of the globe the sisters are also trying to respond to a similar challenge.

The Chair of Peter

As we saw in the previous chapter, towards the end of 1921 the sisters were invited by the Right Rev Monsignor O'Hagan, Rector of the Irish College, Rome, to look after the infirmary and the domestic arrangements of that world-famed college. The invitation was accepted on condition that a convent should also be opened with accomodation for at least six sisters. In October 1923 a pioneer community was selected with Mother M. Zeno Quilter as superior. At that point the new college at Via SS Quattro was not complete, so the sisters began and continued their work for three years at Via Mazzarino. The Irish College provides a link between Ireland and the chair of Peter and it was there that the sisters came into contact with one of the most colourful characters ever to work in the Vatican.

The Scarlet Pimpernel of the Vatican

The late 1930s was a time when Diderot's maxim 'only one step separates fanaticism from barbarism' was getting a resounding confirmation in the atrocities of Hitler and Mussolini. When the second world war broke out in Italy rations were imposed leaving those in the Irish college in Rome with a shortage of food. Mother Enda Murphy, a native of Johnstown, Kilkenny, got around this problem by heading down to the markets every morning at 5 a.m. to buy meat and other essential food items and smuggle them back into the College. As the war developed and Rome was bombed regularly the lives of the students in the College were at risk. It was decided to send them back to Ireland in 1942. At that point some of the Sisters of Saint John of God were withdrawn because it did not make sense to have a full complement of staff in the College with no students present. The sisters flew from Rome on a Dutch plane and because of the difficult circumstances had to endure a three-week delay in Lisbon.

A skeleton staff was needed to maintain the College until the students returned. Mother Enda volunteered to stay on and formed a remarkable friendship with Monsignor Hugh O'Flaherty, better known as the 'Scarlet Pimpernel of the Vatican', who saved approximately 4,000 Allied prisoners of war from the Germans in Rome in 1943-44. His wartime exploits, in which he frequently risked his life to hide POWs with Roman friends, were chronicled in a book, entitled *The Rome Escape Line*, and a film, *The Scarlet and the Black*, starring Gregory Peck as Monsignor O'Flaherty. He was also the subject of a *This Is Your Life* BBC television programme with Eamonn Andrews in 1963. Born in Lisrobin, Kiskeam, Co Cork, he studied for the South African missions with the Jesuits in Limerick, before moving to Rome, where he was ordained, in 1925, after being awarded doctorates in divinity, canon law and philosophy. He was given a post in the Vatican diplomatic service, serving, with a pronounced Irish accent, in Egypt, Haiti, San Domingo and Czechoslovakia, before returning to Rome in 1938. He cut a dashing picture as he stood on the top steps of the basilica in St Peter's Square, standing according to his biographer, Sam Derry, 'six-foot-two in black soutane, with that utterly Irish rugged face bent over a breviary, glasses glinting on his big nose ... scanning the square for a familiar figure while murmuring Latin in an Irish brogue'.

One story gives a great insight into his remarkable courage and cleverness in outwitting the Nazis. When he was informed that a British soldier faced imminent arrest and execution, he arranged to have him smuggled into Rome under a cartload of cabbages. There the soldier was met by a burly man in black who gazed down from the basilica's left-hand steps and whispered 'Follow me'. The priest led him to a building known as Collegio Teutonico (the German College) which was outside the Vatican, but still on neutral ground. They took refuge in a small bedroom-study, when the priest identified himself, 'Make yourself at home. Me name is O'Flaherty, and I live here.' He thought that a British conspirator should be safe in a place filled with German clergy.

The Irish priest delighted in flirting with danger. Once after he had stored a British general in a secret hideaway, he took the 'guest' to a Papal reception, dressed in Donegal tweeds, and introduced him as an Irish doctor to the German ambassador.

His exploits as the *ex officio* head of the underground British organisation in Rome did not go unnoticed and the German ambassador informed him that Lieut-Col Herbert Kappler, the Gestapo chief in Rome, had identified him as the escape line's leader. He was told that if he ever strayed outside the Vatican he would be arrested. A trap was laid to draw him to attend to an injured POW in a village 30 miles from Rome, but at the last second one of his moles revealed that it had been set up by Kappler. After the war O'Flaherty often visited Kappler in prison, baptising him when he converted to Catholicism. The German wrote about O'Flaherty from his cell, 'To me he became a fatherly figure.'

After his death in 1963 he rightly received a whole series of tributes, including a poem written by Brendan Kennelly, entitled *Hugh O'Flaherty's Tree*, which includes the lines:

There is a tree called freedom and it grows
somewhere in the hearts of men.
Rain falls, ice freezes, wind blows,
the tree shivers, steadies itself again,
steadies itself like Hugh O'Flaherty's hand.

While O'Flaherty was the man who got all the credit for heroically serving the cause of humanity, he could not have done so without the help of a small number of trusty assistants. The group had to be very restricted to minimise the risk of being infiltrated by spies. Mother Enda Murphy was an ideal recruit for the Monsignor. Colleagues describe her as 'a big build of a woman with broad shoulders who liked to read a lot but was not afraid of anybody or anything – and as straight as the Empire State building'. She would never betray a confidence and had a nerve of steel. Like O'Flaherty she had no qualms about putting her own life at risk by carrying messages to and fro between the Monsignor and his chain of command if it meant saving the life of another human being. She was particularly adept at bluffing her way past guards while never being so daring that she might jeopardise the Italians who courted death by harbouring soldiers.

After the war she returned to Ireland to serve in Newry. In her final years, she used much of her energies in fund-raising projects for Courtenay Hill.

The years of the Second Vatican Council, in particular, were a very exciting time for the sisters in Rome because they felt close to the momentous decisions which would reform the church. They continue to have an active involvement in the eternal city and at one point extended their influence right up to the papacy. One of the sisters, Ann Marie Ryan, made soda bread (in culinary terms it is the eighth wonder of the world!) for Pope John Paul II. He was smitten by her cooking after being exposed to it by his first personal secretary Fr John Magee, later Bishop of Cloyne.

CHAPTER NINE

Out of Africa

And then all that has divided us will merge
And then compassion will be wedded to power
And then softness will come to a world
    that is harsh and unkind
And then both men and women will be gentle
And then both women and men will be strong ...
And then all will live in harmony
    with each other and the Earth
And then everywhere will be called Eden once again.
(Judy Chicago in *The Dinner Party*)

In response to an appeal from Pope John XXIII and his predecessor, Pope Pius XII, for further help in the African missions, the Sisters of St John of God decided to establish a foundation in Africa in 1960. The Archbishop of Onitsha, in Nigeria, visited the St John of God Novitiate, Wexford, to formally invite the sisters to his diocese. He spoke of the 'fruitful harvest of souls awaiting them in Nigeria where there was an average of one hundred thousand conversions per year in the Eastern Region'. Six members of the community, three fully trained and experienced teachers and three nurses from different communities, left for Adazi, Nigeria, in the archdiocese of Onitsha, to train local girls as teachers and nurses.

Shortly after their arrival, the sisters wrote of their first impressions of their new home. An abridged version of their letter makes for interesting reading on two levels – as an insight into their mission in Africa but also to the pre-Vatican II approach to, and language of, mission:

> On Saturday, 2nd September under a subtropical sun we
> touched down on terra-firma at Enugu. As we approached

The original group of sisters who went to Nigeria in 1960.

Back, left to right: Srs M. Louise O'Farrell, Albert Kenny, Claver Dowling, Michael Joseph Nolan, Irenaeus Donohoe, Benigna Hickey. They are pictured with Most Rev Charles Heery CSSp, Archbishop of Onitsha, the Superior General, Mother Lelia Crowe (right) and her secretary, Mother Dominic McGrath.

our convent, a guard of honour was formed along the avenue, by the staff and student nurses, teachers and the employees on the compound. What a welcome! Here we found a neat two-storey convent with the St John of God crest over the hall-door, and verily we felt we were in 'Home sweet home.'

It was with a deep sense of satisfaction that we heard of the rich apostolate in the hospital, when we visited it on the following Monday. Here our sisters give themselves with a spirit of love and sacrifice in their treatment of pagans, Protestants and fallen Christians. For many of the people admitted, their term spent in hospital is their first contact with Christianity and Catholicism. Thus, not only their bodies are healed, but hearts are opened to the redeeming love of Christ. Dying pagans are instructed and baptised. Many who are admitted pagans, return to their compounds as Catholics, but often polygamist marriages create obstacles to conversion. In these cases, our sisters hope and pray that their contact with them will bear fruit later on. Many dying Protestant patients have asked to become Catholics and were given conditional baptism and then anointed. Fallen Christians are then instructed. Rev Father is notified and these souls make good confessions, receive the last sacraments and die happily, and with obvious gratitude to God and the sisters who helped them. One of the attractions of patients to the hospital is that the people know that the sisters pray for the individual patient's recovery. Pagans in the maternity wing take their babies to Church for baptism. They will give their children what they cannot have themselves. All babies in danger of death are baptised before, during, or after birth.

One of the most important features of the apostolate is the training of Catholic nurses. Candidates are prepared for general and maternity State Certificates. Side by side with the acquisition of practical and theoretical knowledge of nursing, goes the formation of the nurses themselves, as well as the training in awareness of their duty to make the spiritual needs of patients their first consideration. They are given the example and opportunity to minister to the patient's spiritual and temporal wants, so that when they go to the bush maternity clinics later, and to their own compounds, they are not only efficient nurses, but they are the nucleus of lay African apostles for Africa. Africa of to-day is looking for well-qualified personnel in their hospitals, so that the sisters realise that up-to-date methods are important aids to mission work. They are so organised that nurses get a first class training combined with Christian ethics and a Catholic atmosphere. Our sisters do their utmost to keep their trainees abreast of all medical developments, not indeed in a competitive spirit, but they know that such progress redounds to the honour of the Church, and gives Catholics that force which all of us know is so important in the apostolic field. Above all the sisters set a high standard of culture for their African staff. They give of the best they have got, especially in the love of God and souls.

The mission hospital at Adazi had a large concrete administrative block and a maternity wing with an ante-natal ward, post-natal ward, labour ward and a nurses' sitting room. The children's ward included an up-to-date theatre fitted with all the modern 'gadgets' essential to surgery. There was an out-patients department where about three hundred were treated weekly. The sisters recorded their reaction at the time:

> As we watched the numbers pouring in, we could not help thinking of the teeming millions that await the message of Christ's love, and we felt glad that our sisters are having a share in spreading his saving message. As the doctor and sister and other staff busied themselves in ministering to the bodily needs of these patients, a catechist gave instruction so that their souls were being nourished with knowledge of God at the same time.

The nurses' quarters were to the rear of the compound and here the sisters availed of the golden opportunity of training the student nurses in neatness, cleanliness and 'cultured personal habits'. In their diary the sisters observed:

> A rich apostolate is harvested in the two bush clinics supervised by our sisters. A sister and a lay missionary visit these clinics at arranged regular intervals and give treatment, advice and instruction to a large number of patients. The clinic itself is staffed with nurses who have been trained at Adazi and here they have an excellent chance of putting into practice the Apostolic zeal which they have imbibed from the sisters.

> Above all, the day at the hospital is permeated with prayer. All personnel – sisters, staff, trainees, employees – assemble each morning to offer their day's work to God. At mid-day when the Angelus rings, all lay down tools and silently, in pairs, or in groups, unite in a few minutes' prayer. Again the evening is sanctified by the recitation of the rosary, so one soon realises that Africans are a God-conscious people. Their native religion, though pagan in the extreme, has the belief in a supreme being and in life after death. It is this that makes Christianity understandable and easily accepted.

The Archbishop of Onitsha transferred the care of Loreto Teacher Training College to the sisters. Their apostolate was the training of primary school teachers. They strove to give their students a thorough knowledge of the beliefs and practices of their faith, and to train them how to teach religion so that they would be able to assume their role as efficient Catholic teachers. Much emphasis was placed on the students' training as lay apostles because there were so few Catholic missionaries. Every year students made a three-day retreat. The college also maintained a high standard in secular subjects and satisfied government requirements.

The main difficulty facing the sisters in their work in the hospital was not knowing the language. They had to get young nurses to act as interpreters but were often unsure that the interpretation was the correct one. There were also a lot of cultural clashes. The main problem in the maternity unit came with pregnant women who had allowed their condition to deteriorate alarmingly and only came at night to the hospital as a last resort, having received no help from the tribal healer. One cultural trait which the Irish sisters could easily identify with was the attitude of the native women to bereavement. Their wailing until the middle of night was very similar to the traditional Irish practice of keeners (wailing women) chanting laments at wakes. Superstitions abounded. Sisters were advised to burn their hair after they had it cut lest someone take a lock of it and use it to put a spell on them.

Despite the cultural adjustments, the sisters immersed themselves in an ever expanding ministry. In Onitsha diocese in January 1964 a Girls' Secondary School opened in Awka, and in January 1966 a Girls' Secondary School opened in Agulu. In 1966 the sisters went to work in the community hospital in Axhi in Enugu diocese. For ten years, the sisters worked quietly to cater for peoples' material and spiritual needs in Nigeria but then they were swept up in the unfolding political turmoil.

The killing fields

Nigeria was on the boil throughout the early 60s because of ethnic conflicts. The hope and the optimism that underlay the achievement of Nigerian independence in October 1960, floundered in bloody waste. There were uncanny similarities between the situation in Rwanda in 1994 and Nigeria in the late 1960s. The faults were never all on one side. Things came to a head on January 16, 1966, when the Nigerian government was overthrown in a military coup. Over fifty politicians and army officers were killed. The coup was organised by the Ibo tribe from Eastern Nigeria. Many of those killed, including the Prime Minister, Sir Abubakar Tawaw Balewa, were Hausa Muslims from the North. A backlash was inevitable and the Ibo-led regime was itself overthrown. Over the following sixteen months many Ibos were massacred. By that stage the Ibo people no longer believed their lives and property were safe in Nigeria. On 30 May 1967, they announced the secession of the Eastern region and proclaimed its independence as the Republic of Biafra. Of a total Nigerian population of about 50 million, 12 million lived in the Eastern Region, though many of those were not Ibos. Not surprisingly, the federal government did not respond favourably to this development and attempted to crush the Ibos.

The sisters' lives were frequently threatened in the tit-for-tat killings. At one stage they escaped death by a whisker when their convent in Adazi was hit by a canon. They built their own simple bunkers to protect themselves from assault by Nigerians. The locals warned them when an attack was imminent and helped them to conceal themselves by covering the bunkers with grass. During one attack their convent was seriously vandalised. As a safety measure, they changed to green habits and veils. In 1968 Sr Jane Nolan stared death in the face when she flew on a plane from Lisbon to Port Harcourt taking medical supplies to the beleaguered Nigerians. The plane crashed shortly before it was due to land, it overturned, went on fire and burned to a shell. Miraculously no one was killed. The sisters were at the heart of the relief effort, in their bush clinics, one of which they called 'Harley Street'.

Biafra faced a refugee problem unparalleled in contemporary African history. By June 1969 the four million people remaining in beleaguered Biafra were facing starvation in the wake of the Nigerian government's ban on night flights by the Red Cross. This effectively blocked food and medicines. The Nigerians claimed the Biafran rebels were using night flights by the Red Cross as a cover for the delivery of arms. By November 1969 more than 30,000 people in refugee camps near the Nigerian war zone were facing starvation because of a quarrel between the Nigerian government and the International Red Cross.

A contemporary observer reported: 'It was vandalism run crazy. It was wanton molestation and harassment. Whole families were wiped out. Young girls of nine to eleven were caught and devirgined in the most atrocious style, always resulting in death. Men were caught alive and killed in open squares with sharp knives thrust through their necks like cows or goats on the slaughter tables.'

Biafra settled into edgy, bad tempered isolation. Internally scenes of chaos prevailed. The airlift of relief supplies into Biafra by the Churches and the Red Cross was running at a nightly average of 120 tons – but Nigerian Air Force aircraft threatened the pilots of relief aircraft with a sinister message: 'The second you land you'll be a ball of flames.' Their bomb and rocket attacks led to a dramatic reduction in the number of aid flights. The Biafrans persisted in the struggle, even though by 1969 they had lost 12% of their population, and were starving, many to the point of the death. They were being bombed daily in their towns and in their villages, and carrying on their struggle even though they were faced with an enemy superior by more than ten to one in fire power, because they believed that surrender or military defeat could only mean death.

Eyewitnesses to the final fall of Biafra told harrowing stories of soldiers dying in the trenches from starvation and being driven to cannibalism. The sisters' pastoral work was vital because the survivors turned to them for the impossible, aching to be put in touch with any form of justice that would stop their terror, and help them to cope with their bereavement. The sisters had to become accustomed to the sight of old men, nothing more than skin and bones crawling on all fours, and children with bellies as large as pregnant women, their limbs like matchsticks. Mothers, going without food themselves, had to watch their children starving to death in the most hideous way imaginable. The suffering was not universal. There were areas of plenty, or at least where food supplies were adequate to the local population. But equally there were areas where there was nothing – areas where five grasshoppers or a small pile of white worms sold for five shillings. If starvation can be described as the progressive loss of weight due to insufficient food, then 90% of the people of Biafra were starving.

Never ones to flinch in a desperate situation, the sisters went with some sisters and priests from other congregations, under the aegis of 'Caritas', to provide humanitarian aid and do relief work in the so-called refugee camps. The scale of the suffering and sorrow left the sisters trembling and sick. The immediate impact was awful. People lay in agony, uncontrollable bodies shook and shuddered and the stench of human excrement and vomit stunned the senses. The huddled groups of the living and the dying sat around fires. The helpless masses, herded into sheds, could but sit and wait. Efforts were made to move the dead because decomposition spreads more disease. For many, death was a release. The sisters normally were woken to the agony of another Biafran day, as dawn struggled to extract the first rays of heat, by the sound of babies crying. They tried to bring a modicum of order to a world of mayhem. Progress was evident when young children began to sing, weakly at first, then stronger in a swelling poignant chorus. The song was the first sign of hope. The sisters worked long hours in clinics out in the bush. Their hardship was accentuated by the fierce heat. In addition communications were very poor.

The problems did not end on 14 January, 1970 when the Ibo leadership surrendered to the federal government. Furious controversy erupted in the following days. Western observers reported: 'There was a massacre all the way as the federal troops advanced. The people were separated into three groups, men, women and children. The men were all killed. The women were raped.'

Whether or not the country was previously divisible between ethnic groupings, the effect of the genocide was to confirm a genuine gulf, between those who were the targets of murder and those who did the murdering. It was in the interests of the leaders on both sides to spread their murderous hate. Death stalked the roads and ditches. The bodies were laid out side-by-side by the road. It seemed that the international community was not interested. The little humanitarian aid that was provided was apparently intended for the relief of the troubled consciences of the world's television viewers, rather than for the long-term aid of Biafra.

It was virtually impossible to get messages to the outside

world. From the media reports, the Congregation was acutely
aware that their sisters in Nigeria were in grave danger but had
no way of knowing if they were keeping safe. Then they got a re-
assurance via a telegram.

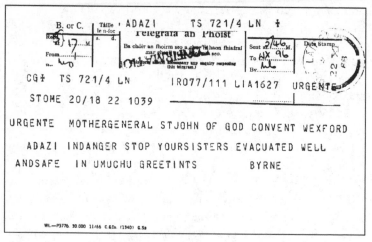

A new twist to the nightmare occurred when the Biafrans were
evacuated to the Portuguese island of Sao Tome. The Nigerian
government wanted to get rid of the missionaries because of
their support for the refugees. They claimed that the foreigners
had illegal passports and used that as a pretext to have them expelled from the country. The sisters had no choice but to obey
this unjust decree, having ministered ten years in Nigeria, then
Biafra. For many of the patients in Adazi hospital, this had been
their first contact with Catholic missionaries. The sisters' sadness
in leaving their adopted 'home' is clear in the following letter to
the motherhouse in Wexford.

Lagos
March 10, 1970

My dear Mother General,

For a long time now I have not been able to make contact
with you and I am sure you are wondering what has become
of us. Well, tomorrow we leave Nigeria, a group of 34 missionaries. Now, no Irish father or sister remains in the East
Central State. All have been expelled. The trial has not been
easy for any of us and now we can only take it from the hand

of God and hope that in some way it will bring a blessing on those poor Ibo people.

Well, mother, to look back over the past couple of months – the war ended as you know on January 12th but since Christmas the tension was something terrible to experience. The Nigerian army was advancing from all sides and closing in on the then very small Biafran area. Refugees, fathers and sisters were running for their lives. We had decided we could not run anywhere as we were as far 'bush' as possible and the shelling was on our very doorstep. The bombers were passing over our house and dropping their bombs on Uga airstrip which was only a few miles from us. As the Federal army advanced into the town, we had fears for the six hundred children in the Kwashionke Sick Bay but their mothers quickly gathered them up and took them away – many of them must have died on the roadside. Now we were left with seventy orphans, thirty old women and the patients in the maternity hospital. The orphans were the happiest of all – they had no idea of what was going on. There was panic on all sides and complete break down of law and order – looting, plundering and all the usual crimes that follow on war. The nurses hid in the fields. They were afraid to stay with us and afraid to go home to their people for fear of being molested on the way.

It was at this stage that Fr Guina got things under control. He organised the men of the town into different groups to guard the complete mission and convent compounds. Over the next twenty four hours there were at least 200 men on duty, all armed with machetes – home made weapons and I would not be too sure if there wasn't a bit of ammunition also. At night we were afraid to go to bed until father returned from his inspection of the troops and assured us that all was well. At this time the missionaries at Aba were being captured and taken under police escort to Port Harcourt. As you know they were tried in a public court and imprisoned – later fined and then deported. Another group from near Ordu met with the same fate. By then we knew there was no hope for the missionaries in the Onitsha area. At first they took away four of our group to Enugu, then to Lagos where they were tried and imprisoned. The women of Lagos, the Christians, went out in protest. During all this time we continued with our usual work until the fatal day came when our entire group of 34 were ordered to report to Enugu police headquarters some 80 miles away – which we did by 9 a.m. The following morning we were met by the chief of police (fortunately for us a Catholic man). He explained to us that he had a painful duty to perform and that we were being charged with 'illegal entry into the country' and 'working without a permit'. (As you know, all that was a fabrication.) We were told we would have to remain in custody for a couple of days. An African monsignor came to our rescue and bailed us out but we were not allowed to leave Enugu and there we had no accommodation at all. The Sisters of the Immaculate Heart (African) very kindly put at our disposal a maternity ward which had not been used since before the war. We had anticipated something like this and had brought some camp beds along with us. After two days we were sent to Lagos by plane under police escort – in an army plane with no seats and many holes in it – by now we had got used to sitting on the floor so no trouble! Next day we were taken in an army bus to Police H.Q. in Lagos. We were told we would be interviewed separately and later put on trial the same as the other groups. But God was good to us, and again he sent us a good friend in the person of Archbishop Aggy (African) who pleaded for us and, after much discussion and string pulling on his part, with the help of the papal legate, they succeeded in having our trial called off. The verdict was immediate deportation and so tomorrow we start on the homeward journey – Rome will be the first stop.

When the war ended we realised that our position in Nigeria was very precarious, so His Grace, Archbishop Arinze decided that three Immaculate Heart Sisters should stand by in case we should have to go. We were happy to see the sisters come on the night before we left. Their Mother General assured us that they would try to keep things going until such time as permission might be given for other sisters to return.

About the re-opening of Adazi convent and hospital – up to recently the military were occupying the compound. Now they have moved out and work has started on re-construct-ion and cleaning the buildings. Some equipment is also being recovered. Awka buildings were damaged and there was much looting there. Angulu college is now a military head-quarters. In Achi, the roofs, doors and windows were re-moved from most of the building to make bunkers for the soldiers as Achi was a war front. However, the convent was not disturbed.

The mission and joint hospitals formerly run by Holy Rosary and St John of God Sisters were held by African sisters until such time as government decided what they were going to do with them. As the sisters' comments at the time reveal, their depar-ture was also very painful for the Biafrans themselves:

At the moment government is not established and there is no money. Biafran currency, which is of no value, is now being collected. Here in Lagos we were told that as soon as this crisis passes, application will be made for re-entry permits for fathers and sisters but they fear this may take some time. It was a terrible heartbreak for the good people of Umuchu to see the sisters and Fr Guina having to leave. They had wel-comed us and given us refuge when we were refugees from Adazi with no place to go. When the news of our going was reported to the people, the whole town and the surrounding villages were alerted and from then on the mission com-pound was full of people; so many different groups with their leaders who came to offer their sympathy and bid us farewell. Fr Guina had done trojan work in the parish all dur-ing this war. His journeys were done on a motor bicycle as petrol was scarce. A car could not travel the bush roads, so all those grateful people turned out in thousands to say farewell. At 4 a.m. they came for Mass in the pitch darkness with the light of only one candle. After Mass the people crowded into the compound to wave us off. I think the sad-dest sight of all was the group of 70 little orphans who just knew we were going away somewhere!

On their way home the sisters and priests who had worked in

Biafra were granted a private audience with Pope Paul VI. He gave the following short address:

> It is a joy to have you with us. It is the Church of Christ that sent you out as missionaries to a great people; it is the Vicar of Christ who receives you back today. In his name we thank you for what you have done to spread his gospel. We thank you for your dedication and self-sacrifice. We thank you for all that you have suffered in the name of Jesus, and for his people.
>
> In you, we greet your brother and sister missionaries throughout the world, those who, as we said on last Mission Sunday, 'have had the supreme courage to give everything, to give themselves', who 'know how to wait without seeing results', who 'die with their work unfinished, tired, alone, sacrificing their remaining nostalgic feelings in the unique invincible love of Christ, alive in his Church'.
>
> We thank you for your faith and bid you place your unending hope in the resurrected Christ.

Whatever happened to the high moral-ground?

By the time the second phase of the sisters' work in Africa began four years later, they were operating with the very different understanding of mission, worked out in the aftermath of the Vatican Council. They were correctly suspicious of truths discovered or formulated without listening to all the voices or attempting to build a consensus, critical of the absence of dialogue or due process, and opposed to any educational structure that shut down participation at any point in information-gathering or decision-making. Historically 'mission' was the private sphere of the clergy and religious, reflected a Eurocentric worldview and suffered from a certain epistemological arrogance. The challenge facing the sisters was to recover the 'listening' character of good missionary activity, to educate in an ongoing conversation, and to find God in the margins and voices previously ignored. The possibility for enrichment in this listening process is enormous. To take one small example, a young woman in the Cameroon who had just had her first baby came to the sisters and said: 'I've touched my baby with life. Now I want to be

touched by life.' Where would anybody find a richer insight into
the theology of baptism?

Meanwhile the rediscovery of 'the law of love' as the corner-
stone of Christianity coincided with new thinking in the social
sciences, uncovering the importance of emotions. Overcoming a
Western analytical bias against emotions, modern missiology
sees the importance of passion for the formation of good missionaries, as a font of action, and as an aid to reasoning.
Conscience formation and decision-making is recovering the
biblical tradition's attention to the 'heart' as a place of discern-
ment, a carrier of identity, and as a source of energy. Missionary
activity is not just a matter of the mind, but also of character and
heart, indeed, of the whole person.

Vatican II gave its imprimatur to the idea of 'an African
Church'. In 1969 Pope Paul VI stated: 'You can, and you must,
have an African Christianity.' Eleven years later Pope John Paul
II went even further: 'Not only is Christianity relevant but
Christ, in his members, is himself African.' While this represents
excellent theory, it is much more problematic to move from a
universal Church to a local Church in practical terms. The distinguished German theologian, Karl Rahner, stated that the
most important new development in Vatican II's ecclesiology
was the stress on the localisation of the Church.[1] There have
been some practical advances in the area of 'inculturation' (the
local church making the gospel present to the local culture). The
so-called 'Zaire Mass' has emerged, which embodies certain
traditional elements, such as reference to ancestors and a partici-
patory way of praying, with dance and gestures. Nonetheless
the continuation of traditional structures has prevented
Catholics in Africa, as in the world at large, from enabling the
people of God as a whole, and especially women, to take part in
decision-making. The sentiments expressed in a letter, written
after the First Vatican Council, by a bishop have often been re-
called in this context: 'We came to Rome as successors of the
Apostles; we left Rome as the Pope's messenger boys.' The
Council's insight about the Church as communion before it is
Church as hierarchically constituted, has not found adequate
expression.

The institutional Churches have not been in the forefront of

Cameroon in relation to its neighbours

the campaign to fight against structures in Africa that oppress women in the same way as they have championed the anti-apartheid cause in South Africa, for example. Pope John Paul II, in his letter on the dignity and vocation of women, *Mulieris Dignitatem*, launched a strong appeal:

> The moment is coming, the moment has come, when woman's vocation is fully realised; the moment when woman takes on in the world an influence, a radiance, a power until now unattainable. That is why at this time, when humanity is undergoing so many changes, women filled with the spirit of the Gospel can do so much to help humanity not to fail.

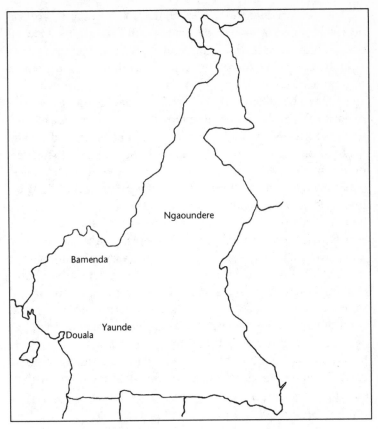

Sisters of St John of God in Cameroon

The sisters tried to give effect to this new understanding of mission when they responded to the 'cry of the poor' in the Cameroon.

Land of Milk and Honey

In 1974 the sisters came to work in Mount Mary Maternity Hospital, Buea, on the side of Mount Cameroon, a scenic spot 2000 feet above sea-level. Buea is a shanty town populated by little houses on stilts on the mountain. Their presence was requested when the Holy Rosary Sisters no longer had sisters to staff Mount Mary Hospital. At the time the country was politically stable. The country itself is very beautiful. The sisters found the Cameroonians a very gracious and gentle people.

Their task was to staff the small mission hospital. There was no resident doctor though the sisters could refer patients to the doctor in the next town. In most cases they also had to act as an ambulance service. As patients had to pay the doctor in advance of treatment because a policy of 'no cash, no service' was pursued, the sisters often had to pay the fee. Emergency cases posed major problems because the sisters were pressed to make decisions which only a qualified doctor should have made. Their greatest agony was not knowing whether or not they were doing the right thing. Often, if a child was seriously ill, the case was first referred by the parents to the tribal doctor for tribal medicine, and only when it had been clearly established that he had no cure to offer did the parents turn to the sisters as a last resort. On the positive side, they were completely free from bureaucracy and this allowed great scope for professional autonomy.

They also worked in a bush clinic once a week, two bone-shaking hours drive in a station-wagon from Buea. Sisters carried out their own water and medicines, often in very hazardous conditions. There were terrible storms at the change of the two seasons, dry and rainy. When the sharp Sirocco winds were blowing dust from the Sahara, travelling was virtually impossible. Malaria was endemic because of mosquitoes. Many people suffered from skin ailments and rashes, as is the norm in tropical regions. Millions of ants populated the territory.

When local sisters were almost ready to take over the maternity unit, the sisters withdrew.

Dire straits

At the invitation of the Holy Rosary Sisters two sisters came from Ireland to Bamenda in 1984 to work on the staff of Our Lady of Lourdes Secondary School. The sisters made a big impact on the liturgy in Bamenda – both in the parish and the school, bringing a whole new vitality to the traditional ceremonies. They also led their pupils to achieve high academic standards. A particular focus was helping disabled children.

Jean de la Fontaine retells a charming story from one of Aesop's fables which highlights the benefits of interdependence for both the strong and the weak:

A rather giddy young mouse emerged from a hole,
suddenly realising that he was between the paws of a lion.
The king of beasts, on this occasion, showed true royalty
by sparing the small creature's life.
This good was not forgotten.
Who could ever have believed that a lion
could be indebted to a mouse?
As the lion left the forests, he found himself caught in a net.
Though he roared loudly he could not tear the mesh apart.
The mouse heard him and returned to gnaw the net
until there was a hole big enough for the lion to escape.

The sisters worked hard to communicate the importance of this insight and nurture a sense of interdependence among their pupils. They placed great emphasis on showing their privileged students how underprivileged children live. This educational exercise had a tremendous impact on the students involved and even when they left the school they continued to send on money to help the sisters assist the poor.

Poverty has escalated in recent years because of a sudden and spectacular downturn in the nation's economic fortunes. The economic crisis was caused by the worldwide recession and in particular because of the collapse in the markets for cotton, cocoa and tea, the main cash crops in Cameroon. As a consequence, salaries were halved, the currency was devalued by 50% and inflation rocketed. Such is the level of uncertainty that every one has taken to cultivating little plots of land. Religious and volunteers found that money sent from home was not as valuable as it should be because of the wildly fluctuating currency in the Cameroon. There were many strikes in essential public services. Part of the government's response to the economic malaise has been to offer many of these services for privatisation to foreign companies. This has led to fears of economic neo-colonialism.

Another consequence of the economic crisis is that few people can afford to pay for health care and hospital treatment. Through their involvement in the St Vincent de Paul group, the sisters began visiting people in their homes. Many were literally dying in terrible pain. Apart from eradicating the symptoms of poverty, the sisters also turned their attention to its causes. They started a Justice and Peace group for adults and involved them in analysing the plight of the poor in their area and considering what practical steps could be taken to alleviate the poverty. The group was never just a talk-shop, but was a force for change. An example of the type of work they did was to help people build their own homes. The Cameroon, like the third world in general, is used as a dumping ground for pornographic videos and literature. The videos are shown illegally in a number of outlets. The Justice and Peace group in Bamenda collated the names and addresses of these venues and passed them on to the appropriate government officials and these outlets were shut down.

The decision in 1994 to leave Bamenda was taken for both principled and pragmatic considerations. Because of the socio-political situation, the sisters found they were teaching mainly the rich. They felt that it would be more in keeping with their charism to work with poorer people. Moreover, there was less need for the sisters because there is now a plentiful supply of young, well-qualified, Nigerian sisters and Cameroonian lay staff. There was also a diocesan educational problem because of the financial situation, that is, the education secretariat was unhappy to be paying the sisters' 'big' salaries. The government policy of retirement at fifty meant one of the two sisters would have had to resign her post.

For all that, it was a difficult decision for the sisters to leave Bamenda because of their commitment to the poor and needy there and a fear of increasing local hardship, their pastoral relationship with the locals, their interest in justice and peace groups and their Vincent de Paul activities, their commitment to the handicapped and blind centre and to the school and the girls.

Bini Dang afforded them the opportunity to move into an 'enabling' ministry as opposed to 'structured' education. Their contacts and friendship with the clergy in Bini Dang was also a major plus factor. Many factors, both positive and negative, had to be considered in making the decision to move to Bini Dang:

This was a French-speaking area. For this reason it is likely to be less attractive for the sisters from Ireland who might consider working on this mission. Sisters also need to learn the basics of the most commonly used local language. There were a multiplicity of languages spoken in the area.

Putting the finishing touches to the sisters' new mud-block house in Bini Dang.

Keeping healthy is a problem because of rampant malaria and mosquitoes and fleas abound.

Life there was harsher physically because it is closer to a desert area.

The climate was hotter.

Roads were generally bad and distances great. It was difficult for sisters not to feel isolated.

While there was food readily available – bread, eggs, maize and red meat – the meat comes from animals slaughtered on the road where it was feasted on by a mass of flies. Moreover, because of the devaluation of the currency, cheese, powdered milk, vegetables and fruit, which need to be imported, had become too expensive for the overwhelming majority of Cameroonians.

The people still lived in the tribal tradition with its associated beliefs.

There was no financial support available from the parish or diocese as they depended for funds almost completely on overseas aid. The Congregation had to finance the building of a simple, mud-block house, the purchase and maintenance of a car, and the upkeep of the sisters.

On the plus side there were distinct advantages of living in Ngaoundere:

It offered the possibility for sisters, who felt a call to work abroad among very needy people, an opportunity for relatively short periods of service. The needs for basic preventive health care education were very urgent, but the needs were so great and varied that any type of experience or skill could well be used, given the willingness of a sister to work in this environment.

It was near an airport.

The political situation in Cameroon was extremely volatile and uncertain and the human rights record was deplorable. However, Ngaoundere has been less involved in the political troubles than Bamenda, as Bamenda is the centre of the opposition party and has suffered immensely, especially in recent years.

Ngaoundere town had a hospital run by Norwegian Protestant missionaries.

There was a relatively good postal service.

In this bush area, where the priority was survival, the native people had a great respect for missionaries.

How the other four-fifths live

Having carefully weighed up the pros and cons, in 1994 the sisters moved from Bamenda to Ngaoundere in the province of Adamawa. This is a French-speaking, predominantly Muslim area. It is generally poorer, more remote and more sparsely populated than Bamenda. Adamawa is, in fact, the most sparsely populated of the provinces of Cameroon. Its population, at the time of writing, is 500,000 with 94,000 living in the town of Ngaoundere. The parish to which the sisters were invited is the University parish of St Thomas More, Bini Dang. An Irish Mill Hill priest, Fr Bernard Fox, is chaplain to the university and Parish Priest of Bini Dang. The parish is 15km from the town of Ngaoundere. It is a huge parish with many outlying satellite communities and a hinterland that is largely unevangelised.

The University of Ngaoundere is located within the parish. This was one of several university centres set up by the State in recent years. In 1993 it acquired university status. Student numbers have risen to almost 2000.

The sisters took a few months listening to the people and finding out what they needed most. They became involved in pastoral care and counselling of university students, especially, but not exclusively, women. The sisters discovered that outside of the university area the pastoral needs were great, especially among women and children, particularly as there was no health care provision. Basically, apart from Ngaoundere town, the people lived in villages, more or less remote – some of them extremely remote and isolated. In the villages, the availability of primary education was very erratic. Up to 90% of the population received no education at all. In the light of the crippling economic crisis, the only hope for the future is to develop self-reliance and self-help among the people. The main focus of the sisters' work is to let the people know that the Gospel really is Good News in their lives here and now.

Barem is a village 75 km from Bini Dang which has a church and a Catholic school. The sisters quickly saw that the women there had obvious unmet needs, such as basic training in health care and hygiene, sewing, craft-work, home-making, personal and faith development. In such a situation, the sisters face many dilemmas. The demand for help is so great that in choosing to save one woman's baby they may have to leave another baby dying.

An advantage for the sisters is that the overall pastoral plan in the diocese is flexible and is dictated by the needs of the community. This was the principal attraction for the sisters because it enabled them to be involved in a 'people of God' model of Church. People are encouraged to apply the Gospel in a very direct way to their own situation and to find hope in the present desperate economic crisis in the strength and inspiration offered by the Good News. Adults were baptised at the end of a three-year preparation period which entailed involvement in the Christian community in every aspect, including justice and environmental concerns at a local level. In this region the Good News and development were intrinsically linked. Since the economic crisis began the death rate has spiralled alarmingly. A lot of these deaths are caused by ignorance. The sisters devote much of their energies to teaching the leaders from each area practical and life-saving skills such as how to treat malaria and how to have a balanced diet. Their teaching methodologies include the use of charts, visual-aids and role-plays.

On a human level, it is very difficult for the sisters in Cameroon because there is so much injustice around them that they can feel powerless. Corruption is rife at all levels in the country. This occasionally poses intense soul-searching for the sisters. For example, in one situation the sisters knew of two twelve-year-old children being kept and assaulted in prison for 36 hours. The only way they would be released was for some one to bribe the prison officers. Since the family were unable to pay, the sisters, having wrestled with their consciences, reluctantly agreed to pay. Despite their repugnance of the corruption the stakes were so high they felt they had to compromise on their principles.

More positively, the sisters' experience in the Cameroon has enriched them in many ways. They have learned to wonder at the simplicity of life, have developed a profound respect for the poor, have discovered what it means to work in faith, and are much more tolerant of other people and other cultures. They can now fully appreciate the truth of the old Celtic prayer, that God is to be found with people, not in places of stone:

> Pilgrim, take care your journey's not in vain
> A hazard without profit, without gain,
> The King you seek you'll find in Rome, 'tis true,
> But only if he travels on the way with you.

Notes:
1. Karl Rahner, *The Shape of the Church to Come*, SPCK, 1977.

CHAPTER TEN

The Winds of Change

What human beings fear most of all is to make a new step, to speak a new word. Change is the law of life, and those who look only to the past or the present are certain to miss the future. (*John F. Kennedy*)

In 1958 the Catholic Church underwent a major shift when an Italian peasant's son became Pope John XXIII. Contrary to popular perception, the Council did not 'fall from heaven'. In fact the ground had been prepared to some extent in previous decades. The smiling pope realised that the Church was standing still in the middle of a changing world. In 1962 he brought the bishops of the Church together to meet him in Rome, the first time this had been done in nearly a century. The Second Vatican Council made many changes in the way the Catholic Church operated.

The winds of change were blowing but not everybody enjoyed the draught. Many of the changes, like replacing the Latin Mass by the vernacular, were immediately obvious. Other changes, like the new emphasis on the individual self, were more subtle and far reaching. The root and branch reform which the Council envisaged caused profound reverberations. The wide-ranging changes in the Church mirrored deep changes in society.

Religious life could not but be affected by the radical developments in society around it, as well as by the changes in the Church. To highlight these fundamental changes it might be profitable to contrast in very broad terms the cultural variables which underpinned the Church before the Second Vatican Council and those which are operative after it. The first such cultural variable is the self-definition of the Catholic Church. In the pre-Vatican II era, the Church was those in authority. Power and teaching were vertically conceived; the basis of teaching was the power of the teacher. In the post-Council situation, the

Church is the communion of the people of God and its basis is the common baptism of all.

Related to this was the Church's approach to ecumenism. Before the Council the ethos of Pius XI's pronouncement of 1927 was dominant, which prevented Catholics from engaging in dialogue with people from other denominations. The Council provided a new ecumenical language and impetus and other Christian denominations were acknowledged to have 'vestiges of the one true Church'.

The influence of the mass media was also crucial. Before the Council, people had little access to information. Hence there was very little criticism of official teaching, and the need for persuasion was minimal. After Vatican II, because of rapid communication, theology is now a publicly debated subject. The scholar is in the marketplace. There is also an awareness of complex issues. Before Vatican II, the Church was, broadly speaking, defensive and cloistered, and theology was studied in isolation from developments in other sciences. After the Council, theology was more in a social and intellectual mainstream, with a consequent exposure to new thought.

The self-understanding of the Church changed with the focus on the model of Church as the people of God. Also changed was the manner of exercising authority. Before the Council, authority was generally centralised in Rome and the diocese, with the presumption always in favour of authority. After the Council, authority became decentralised and open dialogue and consultation were seen to be necessary. The changing educational pattern was also important. Before the council, the clergy were the educated class in the Church. In the current situation, the laity are sometimes more theologically competent than the clergy.

New theological emphases were also important, chief among them a more dynamic understanding of revelation and faith. This replaced the idea of a 'once for all' understanding of revelation, and put the focus on a persistent search for the disclosure of God and of humankind in history. An effort was made to explore the contemporary situation in the light of the Gospels, so as to arrive at a better understanding of the nature of God, and through the fact of the incarnation, the nature of humankind. By persisting in this struggle, we discover God only to lose the divine presence again. As people journey towards the Godhead, they find it always new, always different and yet always the same. Each step of the journey tells something more about this figure, as it recedes continually into the darkness of its own mystery. It is a continual discovery full of new surprises. These new theological insights enabled people to have a critical and adult faith – based on questions as much as on answers.

Deliver us from adolescence

Religious were caught unprepared for the Council. In the pre-Vatican II era, they were formed for religious adolescence. The tendency was that authority always knew what was best for each person and the living of the vows was in a surrogate fashion. The poverty of the individual religious was kept by the bursar, obedience by the superior, celibacy by a confessor.

From their earliest days in the Congregation, young Sisters of Saint John of God were culturally conditioned to think in an 'other-worldly' way. For example, the Rules in the Novitiate, 1946, stated:

Head up, eyes down,
Smiling faces, no frown,
eat well, sleep well,
avoid the parlour,
love the cell.

At that time, the duties of a Sister of St John of God were considered to be:

To kneel and worship, deep and pure
to heal the sick and feed the poor
to speed on angel's wings below
and hover around the couch of woe
to teach, to labour and to pray
to point to Heaven, lead the way.

In their dealings with men young sisters were told: 'Keep control of your eyes. Don't look above the third buttonhole.' One phrase summed it all up: 'If you keep the rule, the rule will keep you.'

It is interesting to read novitiate reports before the Council to see what was considered appropriate for a sister of Saint John of God. Thus in 1957 one novice in Australia got the highest praise: 'She is a model sister – prayerful, obedient, prudent, generous and placid.' Another sister is described slightly less flatteringly: 'She likes to do everything well and is sometimes rather inclined to be self-willed. She is prayerful and unworldly.' Yet another is summed up in the following way: 'As Sister was living an independent life before coming to us, silence and discipline are somewhat difficult, but she is humble and submits to correction.' A complaint about another novice is that she 'is even inclined to be a little forward.'

For the first half of the twentieth century, religious became fossilised in admirable institutions of impeccable pedigree which encased them in a cocoon of continuity, glorified with the term of tradition. After Vatican II, this archaic paternalism was finally consigned to the dust bin allowing for a new understanding of obedience to emerge. The weaker one's personal religious experience the more dependent she or he is on the human mediation of the divine will. True obedience demands reflection and personal responsibility. The Council brought religious face to face with the problems and inadequacies of the old system. What was not so clear was what should be put in its place. Women's Congregations, in particular, were bombarded with advice about how to cope with these changes.

'All changed, changed utterly'

An influential work at this time was Cardinal Suenens' *The Nun in the World* (1962). His book represented a plea for adaptation of the customs and usages in 'active' religious Congregations, so as to better meet contemporary needs. He argued that women have a role, 'for better and worse', which was not theirs before; in his terms, this was 'feminine emancipation'. In the modern world they were wanted, accepted, effective in every sphere of life, but the nun had not kept in line with her sister in the world. The life of the religious devoted to education, care for the sick or social work, had a supernatural and redemptive value, but this is not to say that it is intrinsically apostolic. The term 'apostolic' was used in the 'missionary' sense of making the Gospel message penetrate deeper into all human social activity. Suenens attempted to outline how the spiritual, apostolic and professional aspects of the sister's life might be integrated into a unified whole. Apostolic permeance, personal contact with people, required the forward look, the wider view, the perspective of the foundress translated from her time and period to the present moment. Loving Christ meant 'loving him in his living Church in the here and now'. This involved greater rapport with the world and required that the nun be better informed and *au fait* with current thought. Changes not affecting the essence of religious life were necessary. For example, the central place of prayer in the life of the nun was restated but 'redundant devotions must be mercilessly eliminated'. A re-assessment, and possible pruning of the duties nuns were involved in, was called for. He argued that the concept of enclosure was the chief obstacle to the apostolic advancement of nuns, but separation for an active Congregation is an attitude of mind rather than a matter of walls and grills.

In 1962 nobody batted an eyelid that a man should take it on himself to write a blueprint for nuns. After two millenia of Christianity, Christian women still had apparently to fight for equality despite the fact that the Gospels clearly demonstrate that Christ's sisters were just as fully his disciples as were his brothers. The feminist awakening has had a major impact on religious women. For most of their history they were conditioned to think of themselves as less important than their male counterparts and to accept that fact without much question. After the Council, religious women became increasingly aware of the sin of sexism and of the growing sense of equality between men and women. Sisters have experienced this new consciousness in a deep and pervasive way and have taken what steps they can to facilitate the equality of women in Church and society. This new concern has altered relations between womens' Congregations and the official Church, and also the relations with the local Church, particularly the local clergy. More fundamentally, the new Christian feminist approach is showing itself in religious life by a new valuing of the feminine experience. There is a more experiential approach to the reality of God and a more flexible and plural lifestyle in community, welcoming difference rather than conformity, and a more compassionate rather than rational approach to the apostolate.

Feminism was a significant contributor to the move towards insertion in local society because of its valuing of intimacy and companionship on the common human journey. In the whole field of evangelisation, it has contributed to a shift from a strong emphasis on intellectual conviction and logic to a new expression and appropriation of the mystery of the immanent and transcendent God. The most obvious external manifestation of the sisters' new relationship with the world was their clothing. Sisters had started to modify their dress even before Vatican II, but they had to obtain a special dispensation from the Holy See on each occasion. This led to the ludicrous situation of a Superior General coming before Cardinal Antoniutto of the 'appropriate Pontifical Commission' with the slightly modified habit, modelled by a younger nun, and awaiting for a magisterial 'yes' or 'no' as the will of God. The arrogance of men deciding what women should wear almost defies comprehension. Feminism was only one of the forces for change in women's Congregations.

A breath of fresh air

Although the Council strongly upheld religious life: [The religious state] 'manifests in a special way the transcendence of the kingdom of God and its requirements over all earthly things.' (*Lumen Gentium*, Chapter VI, par 44), it finally buried the idea that clerical or religious life was a superior form. The Council's document on religious life, *Perfectae Caritatis*, called for renewal and adaptation and return to the original inspiration of the founder or foundress. It specified areas such as common life, habit, apostolates, as requiring adjustment in keeping with modern life. Among the Sisters of St John of God, the adapting phase was well under way. Changes in daily living, such as the replacement of religious habits, were rapid and ubiquitous. A symptom of this adapting process was the ever-more sophisticated Chapters which spoke a new language: 'the option for the poor', 'solidarity with people', 'enablement of laity', 'pastoral ministries', etc. There was also a greater effort to release personal gifts which, in turn, allow for a greater variety and plurality in community living and more particularly a new willingness to match personal and Congregational charisms. Older women trained in the monastic life-style had particular difficulty adapting to the new life-style of the religious sister. As the recent television series, *The Brides of Christ*, memorably demonstrated, on a purely human level the scale of the changes posed a lot of problems for sisters.

Working primarily in hospitals, the Sisters of St John of God were the butt of many jokes from their patients about their new dress. One sister who had removed her veil was told by one patient, 'I never thought you had hair.' She responded by asking, 'What did you think I had, feathers?' Another sister faced with a similar situation responded by, in sporting parlance, turning defence into attack, 'Sister can I ask you a personal question?' 'Certainly.' 'Did anyone ever tell you that you were beautiful?' 'Yes. Can I ask you a personal question?' 'You may.' 'Did your bowels move today?' Some sisters tried to get into the spirit of Vatican II, to literally be 'open to the outside world', by learning to drive, which led to moments of high comedy. One elderly superior, who was learning her motoring skills, liked to take a younger sister with her for moral support. The younger women found this a hazardous experience and resorted to all kinds of creative ways to avoid being recruited as co-pilots. Their most common tactic was to hide in the confession box.

The Council awakened a sense of proportion regarding life patterns and customs as against the major task of mission – a love for God's people. A new zeal for the kingdom put preoccupation with rules and regulations into a back seat. Energy was released to respond to the call to justice and love for the poor which found such a ready echo in the hearts of religious women. The seclusion and distance from people, created by large walled convents in the better parts of towns, was felt to be negative and the living situation of religious women became a major question. Since then, the Sisters of Saint John of God, like many Congregations, have deliberately moved residence in a number of areas to re-insert themselves in the midst of people.

Full attendances at community exercises began to wane. A variety of new prayer forms emerged, both at personal and group levels. Communities began to ask about what they did together, why and how they did it and how often they needed to do it to preserve and develop a sense of community. The integration of apostolate and spirituality, perhaps more than any other factor, caused great inner turmoil within Congregations. Often the understanding of these new approaches was uneven and created problems of viewpoint and tensions. It is in the face of this reality that the sisters collectively formulated their response as Christians and as members of a religious community which shares in the mission of Christ – to serve and to save.

The human person is a unity rather than a duality of spirit and body. The process of humanisation is an integral part of spiritual development. A communal model images our relationship with God in the context of a community of faith. The Spirit speaks through all, and we grow in our faith-life with, in, and through others. We are one body. 'Now there are a variety of gifts, but the same spirit and there are varieties of service, but the same Lord; and there are varieties of working but it is the same God who inspires them in everyone.' (1 Cor 12: 4-7) This recognition led to a revolution in the understanding of spirituality – from 'other-worldly' to 'this-worldly', a genuine apostolic spirituality which recognises that sisters work out their salvation by involvement in the human struggle for justice and peace. Spirituality is understood as the experience of consciously striving to integrate one's life in terms, not of isolation and self-absorption, but of self-transcendence toward the ultimate value one perceives.

The Council put a lot of emphasis on freedom and personal autonomy but some sisters experienced this as a mixed blessing. The idea of having to decide for oneself, as Dostoevsky's Grand Inquisitor suggests, can be too great a burden for many people who are unprepared for it. If you have doubts all you need do is to refer to the relevant authority. The Congregation put a very big emphasis on personal development and a leadership policy. Practical changes were introduced to give outward expression to this new understanding. For example, appointments were no longer made by letter but after consultation. There was a determined effort not to repeat the sins of the past and greater attention was paid to the affective. Sisters went on a range of courses. Prayer life changed. A lot of litanies were dropped and individual sisters took more responsibility for their own spiritual sustenance. Outside influences, like the charismatic renewal movement, began to seep through. Outsiders were engaged by the sisters to bring new insights in scripture and this helped open up a new world of personal development. A union among sisters achieved in an external sense was replaced by a union of conviction based on consensus and expressed through free and personal faith.

There was also a much more dynamic understanding of religious vows, an awareness that there is no valid, enduring reason for being celibate in religious life except a passionate love of God. It is only so insofar as we develop the full range of our capacities for loving that we become transparent, more vividly sacramental of God's love. St Augustine recognised this in his famous dictum: 'Thou hast made us for thyself O God, and our hearts cannot rest until they rest in thee.' St John of the Cross put it beautifully:

My beloved is the mountains,
and lonely wooded valleys,
strange islands
and resounding rivers,
The whistling of love-stirring breezes

The tranquil night
at the time of rising dawn,
Silent music,
sounding solitude,
The supper that refreshes, and deepens love.

Back to the centre

Perfectae Caritatis stipulated that each institute would hold a special 'renewal chapter' before 1969, in which the constitutions were to be revised in line with the Council directives. The idea was to formulate a document which would act as the basic charter of the Congregation, containing only the essentials that defined the institute's nature, purpose and structure, leaving all other matters to be dealt with by succeeding chapters. (Most Congregations did not have a province-wide renewal but had a chapter of special delegates.) The Sisters of Saint John of God, on the other hand, made a concerted effort to involve everybody in the consultative process. The importance of this measure for the Congregation was that every sister felt involved, nurturing a sense of ownership of the process.

The Congregation's changing self-understanding was reflected in its evolving Constitution. After the Council the sisters tried to remain faithful to the intentions of the original founders and yet be sensitive to the needs of a rapidly changing world. In 1873 the opening article of the Constitution was:

> The Sisters admitted to this Religious Congregation, besides attending particularly to their own perfection, which is the principal end of all Religious Orders, should also have in view what are the peculiar characteristics of this Congregation, that is, the introduction of religion and salvation into the families of worldlings, rich and poor, above all, in their last moments; the care of the sick, both rich and poor, in hospitals and in their own homes. They can also take charge of schools, and any other works of charity the bishop of the diocese may approve of. (art. 1)

The emphasis in the Congregation's 1930 Constitution was slightly different:

> The general end of the Institute of the Sisters of St John of God is the glory of God and the sanctification of its members, by the practice of three simple vows of Poverty, Chastity, and Obedience, and the observance of the present Constitutions.

> The special object is the perfection and salvation of their neighbour, by the nursing of the sick and the education and training of poor children. (art.1)

By 1977 the opening lines read:

> We, the Sisters of St John of God,
> have been called by the Holy Spirit
> to show forth Christ's compassionate love
> by our ministry of uplifting, healing and enriching
> the lives of his people,
> especially the poor,
> whom, he reminds us, are always with us. (art. 1)

Just six years later, in 1983 the sisters' reflection had extended still further and they reached another stage in their evolving self-understanding:

We, as religious Sisters of St John of God,
in a free response
to the invitation of the Holy Spirit,
come together,
as an evangelical community,
to deepen our baptismal consecration
and enter more fully
into Christ's redemptive death and resurrection.
To enable us
to live out this self-surrender
we take the vows
of celibacy, poverty and obedience
according to the constitutions
of the Sisters of St John of God. (art. 6).

The first seven articles of the 1989 Constitution represent the fullest expression to date of the sisters self-understanding:

The official title of the Congregation is
'The Sisters of St John of God'.
Called into existence by God,
it is an institute of pontifical right
for religious women
devoted to apostolic work.
The members are incorporated
into the Congregation
through their profession of the three vows
of celibate chastity, poverty and obedience.

For the Congregation,
as for the Church itself,
there is but one mission, the mission of Jesus.
Anointed by the Spirit (Lk 4.18; Is 42 and 61),
Jesus was sent by the Father
to set his people free:
to liberate them from oppression,
from everything, within and without,
which prevented them from reaching the full stature of their
personhood.

The Congregation seeks
to continue and make present again

in concrete, specific time and place
this liberating mission of Christ,
and in particular,
to show forth by its ministries,
by the witness of its consecrated members
and by the visibility of its corporate existence,
the compassionate care of Christ for his people.

The particular apostolic concern
of the founders of the Congregation
was the faith-view of the people:
'the introduction of religion and salvation
into the families of worldlings, rich and poor.'

Nurturing this faith-view of life
is the essential apostolic concern
of the Congregation.
In their ministry of holistic health care,
education, catering services,
pastoral and social work,
and in all their activities,
the concern of the members is ultimately
the building up of the kingdom of God.
In working with people,
and in turn being enriched by them,
they discharge their unique role
in the apostolic, social and cultural life of the world in which
they live.

As the Church is missionary by nature,
so too is the Congregation.
However limited in resources,
human and material,
the Congregation holds itself open and responsive
to missionary calls from abroad,
to the needs created by human mobility
and to the Church's call to ecumenical reconciliation.
It also participates in the Church's missionary endeavour
by the prayer, sacrifice, interest and encouragement
of all its members.

Though the mission of Christ is unchanging,

the ways of mediating it in the Congregation
are subject to constant revision.
In order to remain faithful
to the apostolic vision of its founders,
the Congregation constantly seeks to respond
to the changing patterns of society
and the particular demands of time and place,
by reformulating its theology of mission,
adjusting its spirituality accordingly,
and flexibly adapting
its community structures and apostolic procedures.

From the sisters to the sisters

While the Constitutions gave outward expression to the changing philosophy of the sisters, the most important agents for change were the Provincial and Congregational Chapters – effectively 'think-ins' where all sisters were consulted about the direction the Congregation should take. Not all the discoveries made by this consultation were painless. Some of the ideals of the modern institutional Church appeared to be radically different from those articulated by Jesus, notably the excessive emphasis on laws and absolutes. The process led to a sustained critique of the Congregation's role in the Church as a whole. The Congregation offered both diagnosis and prescription in the sisters' comments, for example, 'The desire to hold on to control and power is the most serious sin committed by sisters today.' Sisters went on to outline a new and more expansive approach to the mission of the Church, for example, 'The Sister of Saint John of God must find herself supporting the widow and the orphan, the cause of the old age pensioner, the homeless, the poor and the outcast. She will question as to why some have an unacceptable standard of living. She will want to improve the quality of life for all those she tries to serve.'

The Provincial Chapter of March 1968 offers an early example of this self-examination:

The first and basic principle which the Council lays down is that the renewal of religious life involves two simultaneous processes. First, a continuous return to the source of all

Christian life and to the original inspiration behind a given community. Second, an adjustment of the community to the changed conditions of the times. We need too to bear in mind that renewal will not be effective unless it is appreciated that it is a means to an end, not an end in itself. The Church is renewing herself, bringing herself up to date, so to speak, in order more effectively to carry out her two tasks: that of sanctifying her members and her Apostolic task of bringing all mankind to the knowledge of Christ. Renewal in religious life has the same two objectives in a more particularised way. Sanctification of the Members and the more effective carrying out of the particular work of the apostolate to which the particular Religious Institute is committed. We have set ourselves four principal questions which are closely related and which cover the whole task before us.

1. What are the sources of all Christian life which have special relation to the religious life?

2. What was the original inspiration which brought our Congregation into existence?

3. Are the relevant sources of Christian life adequately expressed in our Constitutions? If not how can they be better expressed?

4. Is our present way of life sufficiently a living expression of the sources and inspiration? Can it be made more so and how?

The purpose of this consultation was to raise questions and to offer distinctions in the spirit of the Gospel. When the sisters did criticise the institutional Church on precise points, their criticism was rarely cynical, never global, but nearly always hitting a very definite point with a definite purpose. The questions were always a pastoral service, an effort to improve the communication of the Congregation and the Church with people in the modern world, while at the same time remaining very deeply concerned for the authenticity and identity of the founding charism. Like a rolling wave, the Congregation began to be involved in this process. The momentum gathered – slowly at first then rising to a crescendo. The sharing of insights and concerns flowed freely between them as if a dam inside them had burst. The range of topics under discussion varied enormously as is evident from the following conclusions from a consultation involving some of the Irish sisters:

Findings of Kilkenny Meeting 28-3-71
Suggestions for discussion at Provincial Chapter
10/- pocket money allowed per Sister per week. All gifts of money to be given up to the Superior.

Travel expenses supplied always irrespective of weekly allowance.

Allowance to sisters going to Hospital.

Six stamps per month and freedom to post own letters.

Trip to Lourdes allowed when financed by Sister's relatives (excluding diversion to holiday resorts.)

Transistors to be allowed.

Tape recorders for communal use only. Cameras considered a luxury, and if used to be financed out of 10/- pocket money.

Discussion and dialogue useful but minority must be willing to submit to majority. Superior has final decisions.

A request for some competent direction on how to run formal discussions successfully.

Present newsletters not satisfactory; news usually outdated.

A request to revert to Baptismal names be made optional.

Meanwhile, their colleagues in Australia were discussing both practical questions and issues of principle. The Provincial Chapter in 1971 reported: 'The question was raised regarding coloured girls entering. The Chapter agreed that these girls should be admitted provided that they were suitable in other ways.'

The document went on to articulate a philosophy of mission:

Policy of The Mission
Christianization and assimilation (*sic*) through various fields of education and a variety of public health areas.

Assimilation: This is in line with Government Policy which maintains that the Australian Aborigines and Part-Aborigines must be guided in all spheres to take their place WITHIN the general Australian-European community.

The above mentioned Policy has and is being pursued through the areas here given.

Education in Primary Schools.

Training in Domestic Science for Senior Girls at Beagle Bay.

Training in Kindergartens.
Education in Infant Health and Child Care.
Nursing in the Public Hospital, Derby.
Nursing in Beagle Bay and Balgo Mission Hospitals.
Specialised nursing in the Leprosarium, Derby.
Nursing the aged and sick Sisters in Broome Convent.
Sisters supervising and cooking for Sisters, staff and children
on the Missions and in the Convents.
Sacristans.
Youth Work.

For many sisters, the extensive discussion was like a painful
surgery which dissected the soul of the Congregation. It was not
for the faint-hearted. In many respects it was a deeply disturbing vision of a future in a society which was fragile and contra-
dictory. As they held up the mirror to the changing society
around them, some sisters could only wince at what they saw in
the reflection. What they were offered was a relentlessly well-
polished looking-glass, positioned at an uncomfortably close
angle to show them where they stood. There were also many re-
assuring findings. The 1976 Chapter reported: 'It is good to read
and observe that all of our houses maintain a spirit of hospitality
which has been a special charism of the Sisters of St John of God.
In this the Sisters share their lives and their many community resources. It is important that each community reaches out to the
wider community, having due regard for the need of individual
and communal privacy.'

While a minority of sisters felt threatened by the new thinking and the changing structures, the majority experienced them
as liberating. The Chapter project in 1982 highlighted the challenge of developing a new approach to mission:

The focus of the Chapter was on mission. The intention was
to have the Sisters come to a deeper awareness of the theological, spiritual and pastoral aspects of mission today. The
key exercise in the whole project was that of individual and
corporate reflection on the lived reality of the St John of God
vocation – 'to be with him and to be sent out'. (Mk 3:14) An
evaluation of the process was done with the facilitators in
May and with all the Sisters in December. All the Sisters re-

ceived copies of relevant documentation as the Chapter Project progressed.

In a provincial Report, 1977-82, the Australian sisters attempted to formulate a strategy which would enable the creativity and energy of their sisters to be deployed more effectively and in a more life-giving way:

> The Sisters of St John of God in the Australian Province are mainly involved in health care and have come to be identified with these works. This has led to a structured life-style where the work determines, dictates and controls the lives of the Sisters.
>
> Today, with the decline in vocations and the ageing communities, it has emerged that the retired Sisters, comprising 60% of the Sisters in the province, will be domiciled in Subiaco.
>
> The Sisters who are actively engaged look towards a life-style which will promote an atmosphere more congenial to human growth and afford the flexibility required for the proper functioning of the integral apostolic (as an alternative to the conventual) life-style.
>
> It is imperative therefore that structures and processes be established which will enable these Sisters to view themselves less as a work force and more as members participating in a mission.

Seven years later, the sisters in the province, during its Chapter in 1989, took a penetrating look at their strengths and weaknesses. Their recommendations provide a revealing insight into the flavour of their discussion:

> As a community of apostolic religious women, we share in the mission of Jesus. This mission is our major concern. The style of our apostolic community, accordingly, is shaped by commitment to that mission, solidarity with all people of good will and a preferential option for the oppressed ... It is recommended that the province:
>
> 1. Develop for use Province-wide, programmes which give expression to Chapter mandates, and which include input from the Sisters in design and implementation.
>
> 2. Provide resources which enable local communities to discern and design programmes to meet their needs.

3. Provide resources enabling individuals to select the most appropriate programmes to meet or discern, developmental and/or professional needs.

4. Establish a provincial policy on formal ongoing formation.

In 1989, the Congregation's Chapter was summed up in the phrase: 'Woman: Religious, Apostle.' The evaluation made it clear that:

More and more sisters in the Provinces have made prodigious efforts to upgrade their academic, theological and professional qualifications. Better educated, able to think, able to stand on their own feet, and better formed affectively and emotionally, these women are already having an impact on the Congregation and the raising of its level of awareness.

A significant number of religious women over the last generations have tended to lose their sense of identity as women. This led to the gradual erosion of the natural emotional and practical energy in women and to the destruction of their vibrancy and creativeness.

The focus says 'apostle', not just 'apostolic'. In doing so it clarifies the identity 'apostle'. Faced with the general eroding of the identity of 'religious woman' many religious settled for other identities – 'professionalism', the '9 to 5 job' mentality, or no clear identity at all.

The post-Vatican II situation brought fears as well as promises. In the aftermath of the Council, the most important question for the Sisters of Saint John of God was: 'Who are we?' As they head towards the third millenium, the most important question facing the sisters is: 'Where do we go from here?'

CHAPTER ELEVEN

Wandering between Two Worlds

Dark and cold we may be
but this is not winter now.
The frozen misery of centuries,
breaks cracks, begins to move
The thunder is the thunder of the floes,
the thaw, the floods, the upstart spring.
Thank God our time is now ...
Affairs are now soul-sized
The enterprise is exploration
into God.
(Christopher Fry, *A Sleep of Prisoners*)

In a sense, the Sisters of St John of God are wandering between two worlds, one dying, the other yet to be born. Like other religious Congregations, they have struggled to adapt to a changing society and a changing Church. Since the dust settled after the reverberations of Vatican II, there have been perhaps four key developments in religious life:

A rediscovery of the prophetic role of religious, a quality of life and ministry which attempts to give renewed heart to the Christian life by a radical commitment to simplicity, sharing and intimacy.

A concerted effort to minister to people where they are, rather than where sisters are, leading to the transition from apostolates based mainly in religious-owned institutions to ones in the field.

The creation of smaller communities, more conducive to deeper dialogue, greater sharing of life and vision and the possibility of exploring in greater depth the search for community in today's world.

The vows are seen more in terms of possibilities than prohibitions. No longer are they understood as personal means to perfection but as an articulation of the ideals to which all people aspire. Celibacy is now understood as growth in living relationships with God and people, transcending the exclusiveness of marital love; poverty is part of the universal desire to share equally and generously the goods of creation; and obedience a deep listening and generous response to the call of life in today's world.

Religious life in its Christian origins was not about a flight from the world but about the *sequela Christi*. The new understanding of religious life reflects very much a return to that foundational myth, a commitment to God incarnate in human history, close to people, healing and nurturing, challenging oppressive systems and structures, reaching out to the helpless and hopeless, praying with people rather than for them.

The self-understanding of the Sisters of St John of God has, since the Second Vatican Council, been the subject of an intense revisionism by its own members, driven by a need to return to the original intentions of its founders. After a period of soul-searching, the sisters have sought to peel back the layers of accretions which have accumulated since 1871 and rediscover the essence of what Visitation Clancy was trying to achieve when she founded the Congregation. Visitation was a woman of foresight who understood the needs of her time, who wanted women to play a full part in the Church and in society, and an individual who provided reason to hope for many people. Her legacy can be seen in the number of sisters and associated lay people who take inspiration from her life. However, the task of interpreting her vision for today and tomorrow is proving a difficult one for her sisters.

On not following the leader

Practically all religious orders are seeking strategies for bringing new creativity out of the experience of declining numbers of vocations and ageing communities. The earliest Christian communities were house-churches, communities aspiring to be equal – where charismatic giftedness was the essential factor. The sisters have attempted to revive this tradition by changing the way they work, to make it more ecclesial, by opening doors to the laity and working with them as authentic partners in the Church's mission. Such an approach calls for courage to free the charisms of lay people and to offer them alternative fields of action. This may bring teething problems in which greater efficiency may have to be sacrificed for more effective witness. While the Sisters of St John of God have commendably invited lay people to share in their charismatic ideals, is the time opportune for the sisters to share more in the charismatic ideals of lay people?

A new model of leadership has emerged which is more circle than pyramid. Where there is a formal leadership, the sisters hope it will be at the heart, rather than from the top. The new understanding of living in a religious community is reflected in the recent adage: 'I am, because we are, we are therefore I am.'

Like many communities and Congregations, the Sisters of Saint John of God have made real efforts to respond to the challenges of the Vatican Council and are experiencing a deepening of their faith and commitment, and discovering a new joy and fulfillment in their vocation. The religious community is a church in miniature, a sacrament of Christ's healing presence among people. Accordingly, there is a move from the convent back to the local community. In many places groups of four and five sisters have moved into 'ordinary houses in ordinary places', closer to the people who need them. This process of moving out of those huge institutions into smaller houses was less than an unqualified success – some worked well but others were disasters, sometimes because of personality clashes.

As this process accelerates, it will lead to a shift away from the sisters' traditional spheres of influence. In the past they were very much associated with institutional ministries like schools and hospitals. In the future they will be increasingly involved in ministering to people in the community. The Congregation was established to meet health care and education needs, particularly of the poor. While this commitment remains, other groups are also responding to these needs today. Accordingly, one of the biggest challenges facing the Congregation is how to deploy its resources, in terms of personnel, property and finance, most effectively, and a challenge for the sisters is to be a witness to Gospel values in a world craving inspiration and guidance.

Pollution is arguably a symptom of a deep underlying spirit-

ual crisis and a metaphor for the human condition. In our rape
of the environment, we are showing our contempt for God's
good creation. When Sartre wrote, in *Les Mouches*, that 'there is
nothing left in heaven, no one will give me orders. For I am a
man, Jupiter and each man must create his own road', God was
relegated to peripheral status.

The crisis of our age is at one level a spiritual crisis, a crisis of
our collective selves. The fate of the soul is the fate of the society;
the soul is the core, the heart, the inner reality of what makes us
human. The conflicts in our society are but symptoms of an
inner torment, of our aberrations on our spiritual journey. If we
are to restore our 'rotten' society, we must begin in the inside.
We all share the guilt for the sins of the past; if we are to be re-
deemed, either on an individual or societal basis, we must be
cleansed at a level beyond the scope of sight and sound. This
poses a major challenge for the sisters to reach out to those who
are seeking meaning in their lives. Thus since the Council, the
sisters have increasingly got involved in a number of faith development initiatives such as youth ministry. Their concern is to
help people at both material and spiritual levels.

As we have seen, both in Australia and Ireland the Congregation responded to people's needs and sisters gave up their lives
in the service of people in need. Are there contemporary paral-
lels to the typhoid epidemic in Australia at the turn of the last
century? Is the AIDS epidemic, for example, a similar pastoral
challenge? In Australia, the Sisters of St John of God in Perth
moved in 1988 to minister to people with HIV and offered a
house to be used as a Catholic AIDS care centre, but the local
council would not consent to the house being used for the purpose. The sisters simply sold the house and bought land in sub-
urban Burswood, where they built a centre with council approval. The Congregation at large has pledged $48,000 annually
to the centre. One sister works full time with people who are at a
critical turning point in their lives and accompanies their loved
ones through the experiences which lie ahead. In this ministry,
the model stems very much from the parable of the Good
Samaritan, with the AIDS crisis centre seen as a place for uncon-
ditional love and care, rather than prejudice or punishment.

The centre is a drop-in facility, where people with the HIV

virus are made to feel welcome. It cares for people with AIDS and helps their families, partners and friends come to terms with the situation and the way it affects their lives. The task is building bridges, bridges between hearts and bodies. The Eucharist is celebrated on set days each week, with a light lunch afterwards. The centre also has a quiet place for prayer and meditation to enable inner peace and healing to happen. There is an outreach programme for those unable to visit the centre. The team goes to homes and hospitals, respite and hospice care centres and to a local prison. Almost as important as the caring is the work to educate people in order to do something about the fear and prejudice still rife in the Church and society at large about AIDS. Ignorance remains the greatest enemy of people with the virus and the sisters are moving to combat this and empower the people with the virus to be as independent as their medical condition allows.

Writing women into history

Pope John II's *Mulieris Dignitatem* (The Dignity of Women), 1988, noted that one of the recommendations of the 1987 Synod of Bishops was for a 'further study of the anthropological and theological bases that are needed in order to solve the problems connected with the meaning and dignity of being a woman or a man'. Unfortunately that challenge has not been adequately taken up. There is a need for a new approach which takes account of the need to build new relationships of mutuality and reciprocity between women and men in the Church.

Many sisters echo the type of sentiments expressed by the Irish President, Mary Robinson, in her inauguration speech in 1990:

As a woman I want women who have felt themselves outside of history to be written back into history, in the words of Eavan Boland, 'finding a voice where they found a vision'.

The intolerable condition of many women around the world has become obvious to all. The economic, political and cultural disadvantages suffered by women are a violation of justice and a serious threat to their lives. For all the talk of women's liberation, the lot of many women has not significantly improved nor have they achieved legal, economic or cultural parity. The sisters are attempting to critically assess how they might most effectively confront the local and national systems oppressing and alienating women.

As we have seen in Chapter Three, a significant motivation of Bishop Furlong in having the Order established was a concern that people's faith was endangered. Today people's faith is threatened by many factors including poverty and family break-up. Many women feel that their faith life is endangered by a patriarchal Church. In the current climate it is not exactly clear what is the role of religious life in the Church. The role of women religious is not to be a stop-gap in the parish to fill the roles the priest cannot accomplish – particularly when this is essentially an unpaid role. As we have already seen the need for sisters in Pakistan, the Cameroon and amongst the Aboriginal community is much more fundamental, to build up people's self-confidence.

Increasingly sisters are aware that the learning and teaching is a two-way process. For example, sisters working in the Kimberley have had their faith greatly enriched by their contact with the 'people of the dream'. Incredibly, Westerners can feel completely at home and at peace in the bush. It invites strangers not only to look at it but to listen to it. A reverence for the soil comes naturally to the Aboriginals and gives them literally a grounded spirituality. It is an ecologically driven faith. They will take eggs from a nest for food, but not all the eggs. They never over-produce or over-stock. The land is entrusted to humankind and they believe that it must be respected as one's mother. In their eyes, the land will always provide and so they find the sermon on the Mount very realistic. In fact they even use images which 'the white man' can understand to communicate this insight. They compare the land to a bank account; people should protect the capital and live off the interest.

This kind of spirituality, which reconnects individuals to their bodies as a temple and to the land as creation, also relinks religion and art to their original friendship. While Aboriginals form only one per cent of all Australians, one in six of recognised artists in Australia is an Aboriginal. Some of their rock paintings are 20,000 years old but the modern Aboriginal artist does not see the need to reject the ancient symbols.

The sisters, in common with many Australians, are fascinated by what the Aboriginals call 'Dreamtime'. This is an inadequate translation of a word which is untranslatable. The 'Dreaming' is all encompassing: it includes, the time of creation by the spirit ancestors who have returned to the sky, and whose power still inhabits sacred sites here below; the eternal cycle; a natural harmony between humankind, flora and fauna and an inner religious experience. It also has echoes of Aquinas's understanding of contemplation as the 'simple enjoyment of the truth'.

The Aboriginal word for meditation is *dadiri*. It holds the sense of a deep quiet listening, a quiet still awareness, a non-questioning presence. In the silence Aboriginal Christians come to realise that what they were listening to was the Word of God resonating equally in creation and in the human soul which is itself part of creation. The indigenous people are not frightened by stillness or silence. Sisters have found exposure to this environment and spirituality very enriching.

From darkness to light?

While the overwhelming majority of sisters welcome the new ministries, they have brought problems of their own. Talking to sisters it is apparent that there is a fear of 'drift'. As Sisters of St John of God become increasingly involved in 'individual ministries' the danger is that they may fall prey to individualism where ultimately everybody does her own thing, sharing only a hazy vision, and communities become little more than boarding houses. More positively, there is a universal sense of being challenged to live a much deeper Christian life, with God at the centre, and a recognition that to be a Sister of St John of God is to answer the call to be their best selves, to be fully human. Out of that they want to journey with all the people of God to enable the kingdom to come. There is a very strong communal desire to be prophets and a sense of being called to reveal God in some way, and a belief that if they fail to do that they fail the world. There is a conviction that if they take the 'God life' seriously, other women may choose to follow them on their pilgrim journey.

The reality of the lack of vocations is highlighted by the following statistics. In 1960 there were 1,330,000 religious women and men in the Catholic Church. In 1978, the total number was

1,104, 129, indicating a decline rate of 17% in less than twenty years. This trend of falling vocations is likely to continue in the years ahead. The original foundation of any religious institute was not chiefly concerned about numbers, but concentrated on being faithful to God's call, responding to a need in the Church and the community. However, as we have noted, the sisters face a rapidly dwindling number of active members.

In the Gospel we find Jesus repeating over and over again the simple advice 'Watch and pray'. This was not merely a readiness for unexpected death. It is far wider than that. It is to be alert to the call of God in one's immediate situation. In discerning how they are to respond most effectively to God's call today, the sisters must confront a whole series of difficult questions including:

* Where are the needs today? Are new ministiries called for to help sexually abused people, for example?

* What is their identity as religious women?

* What does the term 'community' mean when, increasingly, the members do not live under the same roof, work, pray, eat or re-create in physical proximity to one another, and, especially, engage daily in the same kinds of apostolic activities?

* There is a pain for anybody in not knowing where she is going. The changing pattern of religious life, though liberating, in many ways, brings its own pain. It is sometimes difficult for individual sisters to think corporately as John of God sisters. How is the Congregation to maintain it's corporate identity when increasingly sisters are being drawn to new ministries? An urgent priority for the Congregation must be to formulate a common vision of ministry allowing for a unity in diversity of mission.

*How can they best be adult, autonomous but interdependent women? Inevitably this raises questions about the type of leadership structure that is most appropriate.

*How do they prepare people, both sisters and lay people, for leadership?

*Ministers, particularly those who are journeying with many anguished people, need a place where they can share their deep pain and struggles with those who can guide them ever more deeply into the mystery of God's love. How do the sisters continue to handle their human needs as celibate women?

* Who are they for each other?

* How do they support each other?

* Like all Christians the sisters are challenged by the need for conversion from a good life to a better one. What kind of lifestyle allows for a more shared existence between sisters and lay people on the one hand, and for sisters to respond most effectively to the option for the poor, on the other?

* What is the corporate dimension of sharing with the poor?

* How does their shared past prepare the sisters for the present and future?

* What do they want to hand over?

* Throughout their history many of the sisters went to areas where nobody else would go. Today that same courage is needed but for different reasons. Where to, and to whom, are they being called today?

* There is an ethos question. How will a Catholic Congregation with such a commitment to health care deal with the growth of the kingdom of medical ethics, which has been fragmented into three distinct realms, each with its own set of ethical questions? These are: creating a just health care system; the beginning and end of life; and attaining the correct balance between technology and people. Related questions include: What sort of a health care system can best deliver the freedom, excellence, and efficiency which is at the heart of the sisters' traditions while still providing access to basic care for all socio-economic groups?

* What is the future of all the sisters' private hospitals? There are a number of practical difficulties in getting out of private hospitals because of commitments to patients, staff and the local community. Applying the option for the poor principle is not as easy as it might appear on the surface – even assuming that there is a shared understanding of the option for the poor, which there is not.

Deciding what it means to take an the option for the poor, in

practical terms, on a Congregational level, must be a priority
for the sisters.

* The Congregation since Vatican II has devoted considerable
energy to finding out more about Visitation Clancy and
Bishop Furlong, and how they can be true, in a changing
world, to their original charism. One figure who has been
seriously neglected is Saint John of God. Has he anything
else to offer the Congregation today other than his name? He
provided a bridge between rich and poor and enabled the
rich to help the poor and the sick members of society. Could
the sisters perform a similar role today?

Running to stand still

All the old absolutes and certitudes melted away after Vatican
II. The familiar black and white gave way to a breathtaking proliferation of grey. In such circumstances, finding a way forward
is problematic. However, for all the ambiguities, religious Congregations had no option but to tentatively attempt this process,
though as they grapple with their questions, they are often con-
scious of the inadequacy of their answers. For all their failings,
these answers are the best available, and demand action.

As Louis MacNiece perceptively observed in his poem *Entirely*:

And if the world were black and
white entirely
And all the charts were plain
Instead of a mad weir of
tigerish waters
A prism of delight and pain
We might be surer where we wish to go
Or again we might be merely
Bored but in brute reality there is no
Road that is right entirely.

The sisters' motto is: 'The love of Christ urges us on'. The one
thread of unity between the sisters, from Visitation to the
youngest sister in Pakistan, is that they have all been motivated
by the love of Christ. As the old tree of established structures is
dying, it is not easy to discern how to graft anew to the future
vine.

At the moment the sisters are at an in-between time in their history, caught between a rich tradition and an as yet unformed new direction. The only thing that can be said with certainty in an uncertain time is that the love of Christ will continue to inspire the sisters.

Selected Bibliography

Brosnan, Gemma, *The Development of the Sisters of St John of God Foundation in Western Australia*, Perth, 1971.

Clear, Catriona, *Nuns in Ninteenth-Century Ireland*, Gill and Macmillan, Dublin, 1987.

Corish, Patrick, *The Sisters of St John of God 1871-1971*, Wexford, 1971.

___ *The Irish Catholic Experience*, Gill and Macmillan, Dublin, 1985.

Fahey, Tony, 'Nuns in the Catholic Church in Ireland in the Nineteenth Century' in Mary Cullen, ed., *Girls Don't do Honours*, Attic Press, Dublin, 1987.

Fogarty, Phyllis, *History of the Beagle Bay Mission*, Perth, 1963.

Hogan, Edmund M., *The Irish Missionary Movement*, Dublin, Veritas, 1990.

Hoy, Suellen and MacCurtain, Margaret, *From Dublin to New Orleans*, Attic Press, Dublin, 1994.

Jackson, Pauline, 'Women in Nineteenth-Century Irish Emigration' in *International Migration Review*, XVIII, Winter, 1984.

Keenan, Desmond, *The Catholic Church in Nineteenth-Century Ireland*, Gill and Macmillan, Dublin, 1983.

O'Neill, Marie, *From Parnell to De Valera*, Blackwater Press, Dublin, 1991.